OTHER PEOPLE'S MONEY

To my gals

OTHER PEOPLE'S MONEY

ANDREW MAIN

HarperCollins*Publishers*

HarperCollins*Publishers*

First published in Australia in 2003
by HarperCollins*Publishers* Pty Limited
ABN 36 009 913 517
A member of the HarperCollins*Publishers* (Australia) Pty Limited Group
www.harpercollins.com.au

HarperCollins*Publishers*

25 Ryde Road, Pymble, Sydney NSW 2073, Australia
31 View Road, Glenfield, Auckland 10, New Zealand
77–85 Fulham Palace Road, London W6 8JB, United Kingdom
2 Bloor Street East, 20th floor, Toronto, Ontario M4W 1A8, Canada
10 East 53rd Street, New York NY 10022, USA

National Library of Australia Cataloguing-in-Publication data:

Main, Andrew.
    Other people's money.
    ISBN 0 7322 7665 9.
    1. HIH Insurance. 2. Insurance companies – Australia
    3. Insurance – Australia. 4. Business failures – Australia.
    I. Title.
368.005694

Cover photographs: Rodney Adler: Tamara Voninski/ *The Australian Financial Review*;
Ray Williams: Craig Abraham/ *The Age*; Brad Cooper: Peter Rae/ *The Sydney Morning Herald*
Cover design by Louise McGeachie
Internal design by Gayna Murphy, HarperCollins Design Studio
Typeset in 10.5 on 14 Berkeley Book by HarperCollins Design Studio
Printed and bound in Australia by Griffin Press on 79gsm Bulky Paperback

5 4 3 2 1   03 04 05 06

. . . facilis est descensus Averno;
noctes atque dies patet atri janua Ditis;
sed revocare gradum superasque evadere ad auras,
hoc opus, hic labor est.
— VIRGIL, THE AENEID VI, 126

Getting down to Hell is easy: the doorway to
Pluto's land stands open day and night. But
retracing your steps and escaping back up to the
upper air, that's the hard part of the job.

*Even the Romans
understood about
under-reserving
in general insurance.*

CONTENTS

PROLOGUE

WEDNESDAY, 23 SEPTEMBER 1998 started at the ABN Amro office in Sydney much like any other working day at a big investment bank. Early start, the morning meeting at 8.00 a.m. and the call around the Dutch-owned investment bank's major institutional clients.

Michael 'Crow' Crowley had been a stockbroker, as they used to call it, for longer than he liked to remember and had had his share of ups and downs. A long spell at Australian-owned Ord Minnett starting in 1982 was followed by a highly publicised move in 1989 to Baring Securities. Back then, London-based Baring was an international name whereas Ord Minnett was merely a top-ranking local broker. However, the London-based house of Baring, founded long enough ago to get a favourable mention in Gilbert & Sullivan's operetta *Iolanthe* in 1882, blew up in 1995 with Nick Leeson's famous rogue futures trading in Singapore. The Dutch-based ING group bought the wreckage for a few pennies after the London head office let their former scrip clerk trade them into millions of dollars of debt.

But Barings in Australia did not even last that long. Chief executive Peter Meurer was forced to close the doors in January 1992 after just three years' trading because the parent company had made dramatic losses in Japanese warrant trading and could not keep supporting its small but growing Australian outpost. Despite a solid start, the thirty-five staff all had to find jobs elsewhere.

Crowley was offered a post at McIntosh stockbroking, which took over Barings in Australia, but chose instead to move to the English-owned BZW Australia before moving on to ABN Amro. Far from the Gordon Gekko stereotype of a broker who got to the top by gouging every dollar he could from every deal, the big man from Moree in northern New South Wales had and has a reputation around the fund managers and investment bankers of Sydney as a scrupulously honest operator with a gold-plated contact list. He had rubbed shoulders with all kinds of people, having carried the bass drum in the Scots College pipe band and having also driven a cab for a while, and his unmistakable straight back and shining bald head brought greetings from left and right whenever he walked down the street.

He was looking to move to Equity Capital Markets, a part of the business which advises companies on how to raise money, because of that wide network of connections. Not only was he dealing with a long list of regular clients to whom he spoke daily but also with others who had known him for years and who called him if they wanted to do a special trade.

At about 1.00 p.m., while most of his colleagues were out, the phone panel on his desk lit up. 'G'day, Michael, it's Rodney,' said a familiar high, clear voice. There are lots of Michaels and Davids and Peters in the business but, in Sydney at least, Rodney Adler does not need to explain who he is. 'Can you come over to my office? I'd like to have a talk.'

Of all the calls Crowley was looking for that day, this was not top of his list. Crowley knew Rodney liked to talk and wasn't the most willing of listeners. The broker had had his moments with Rodney.

ONE APOCRYPHAL STORY that everyone liked to tell was when back in 1987, before the October share market crash, Young Rodney, as he was then, kicked up a fuss over a small deal in Pioneer Concrete that Crowley had done for FAI.

Because the 28-year-old Adler did not want the market to know that FAI was buying — FAI ended up doing one of its best-ever takeover plays in the stock, in fact, making millions by selling out to Robert Holmes à Court's Bell Group — he asked Crowley to register the stock in a nominee name. This was not illegal. It happened all the time, particularly if big players were looking for a quick trade, but it meant some extra work in the Ord Minnett back office. Instead of registering the stock in FAI's name, which would have set the hares racing, it was to be booked in one of the broker's holding accounts. 'Rodney, instead of charging you the usual rate of 0.3 per cent, what I'd like to do in this case is book the deal at 0.5,' Crowley had said.

Adler had hung up with a noncommittal noise then rang back a few minutes later to say in his most formal of voices, 'Michael, I have to say I'm flabbergasted. From this day forward I wish to inform you that FAI and Ord Minnett have no business relationship.' For a young man who had a reputation as something of a tearaway in Sydney's eastern suburbs, he had a tendency to pomposity. Perhaps he was making up for all that youthful image.

In institutional stockbroking, desperate deeds call for desperate measures. As the story has it, Ord Minnett chairman Gilles Kryger was quickly informed and, like an elevating howitzer being cranked up out of a bunker, his full gravitas was brought to bear. Kryger, who earned an MBA from Harvard before Rodney was born, walked across town with Crowley from the Ord office at 1 York Street, just at the south end of the Harbour Bridge, to FAI's head office in Macquarie Street.

They might have looked like Tweedledum and Tweedledee, with Crowley more than a head taller, but Kryger was known for the glacial gaze he could bring to bear on transgressors. 'Pissholes in the snow' was how dealers and floor operators had described his eyes when he was listening to their explanations of bungled orders and irate clients. As much as his staff held him in awe, he was the best ally Crowley could hope to have.

They called on Larry Adler, Rodney's father and the founder of FAI, and exchanged civilities. Adler senior played himself as a likeable rogue who enjoyed a bit of subtle diplomacy, despite his reputation as a ruthless trader and relentless litigant against anyone who crossed him.

He could turn it on and he did. His major conversation openers by then were chess, his extensive collection of statues in his idiosyncratically decorated office and the blue leather upholstery of his new Rolls-Royce, which he liked people to observe and savour, if not necessarily ride in.

Kryger and Crowley didn't get a ride in the new car but they got a hearing and Larry quickly turned magnanimous. The deal would go through at the higher brokerage rate, and normal business would resume between FAI and Ord Minnett. Larry then banged three times with his fist on the partition beside his desk and seconds later Rodney appeared in the doorway, straightening his tie and making a poor fist of looking as though he had just been walking past. Rodney's father told him what had been decided — no debate — and the two visitors were shown out with more of Larry's central European politeness.

FAST FORWARD TO September 1998. Crowley explained to Rodney Adler that it would be more convenient for Rodney to come over but both men knew what would really happen. In broking, the client sets the rules and in minutes Crowley was making his way up to FAI's Kent Street office, two or three blocks away, as requested, bearing a notebook and a sense of foreboding. He was shown straight to Rodney's office, which FAI had moved to at considerable expense just before Christmas 1997. Rodney was pacing the office and as Crowley could see was all ready to make a speech. Crowley braced himself.

'Michael, the time has come for the Adler family to realise its investment in FAI Insurance,' began Rodney. He told Crowley he had already been in contact with a number of possible buyers including Liberty Mutual in the US, with which FAI had a joint venture in workers' compensation insurance, and closer to home Queensland-based insurer QBE.

Crowley's brain raced: what percentage of FAI did the Adler family own? Was it about 30? ABN Amro was in fact one of the few broking houses that still followed the battle-scarred FAI, whose share price had once given it a market capitalisation of almost $3 billion in 1987 but which was now worth closer to $200 million on a good day. Most brokers give up following stocks that drop below $1 billion but, perhaps out of habit, ABN still kept half an eye on it.

A feeling of unreality came over the big broker. This would be a wonderful piece of business but was this serious? Normally a corporate takeover begins with a bidder identifying itself clearly and offering cash or shares for as much of the biggest shareholder's stake it is allowed. The Takeovers Code in Australia normally limits that to 19.99 per cent but in the case of local insurers taking each other over, as might well happen, the limit was 14.99 per cent without the Treasurer's permission.

So while Rodney ploughed on for a long ten minutes about the end of an era, Michael Crowley was following an altogether more prosaic line. Was it legal to place a big line of stock on the market and just hope someone came along with a bid? What sort of price was Rodney talking about?

As a reflex action Crowley had checked the FAI share price before he left the ABN office and it had jumped during the morning from the previous night's close of 47 cents to a bid price of 55 cents, so something had leaked out.

'I don't know that anybody's going to buy these shares but I'm going to ask you to sell forty-five million shares at 75 cents,' said Rodney.

'Offer thirty-five million at 75 cents and if they sell, ring me and we'll have a look at how the market is,' he said, while Crowley tried to sound entirely calm but produced a series of gurgling noises.

He had done some major business in his time: once, when Robert Holmes à Court's Bell Resources was bidding for BHP, he had bought more than $100 million worth of BHP stock in one day. But this was a much bigger percentage of a smaller company. Not only was this a giant lick of stock for sale; it was, as Rodney was making relentlessly clear, the founder's stake. He asked Crowley to offer the stock 'loudly and clearly' to institutional investors so that they would be aware the stock would be going on the market at 2.10 p.m. Crowley thanked Rodney for the order, made his exit, and got on his mobile phone as soon as he was out of the door.

The first call was to ABN's compliance manager, Michael Hains, to ask if there was any legal problem in transacting this unique piece of business. There wasn't.

The second call was to the head of equities at ABN, Paul Masi, partly to warn what was coming and partly to check further if there were any ethical or political traps in doing the business. There was a silence on the line for a while and then Masi, a stocky man with a flowing mane of dark hair whose job it was to make business happen, also said no.

Crowley entered the dealing room at ABN and walked up to the live loudspeaker linking dealing rooms in Sydney and Melbourne. 'I'm a seller of 35 million FAI at 75 cents,' he declared. All the dealers hit their telephones as fast as possible because Crowley was about to walk over to the operator of the SEATS system, the computerised trading system which links all Australian share traders. There were no immediate buyers reacting to the phone calls, which is hardly surprising. It was like putting a 'for sale' sign on a much loved but battered house and then setting a reserve price more than 20 per cent above the market. So at 2.10 p.m. Crowley told his SEATS operator to put 35 million on to sell at 75. The top bid at that moment was 48 but about 30 seconds after the line was offered, Melbourne broker JB Were jumped in and took the lot. At

2.13 p.m. Crowley called Rodney to say: 'You're done on the 35 million at 75. Can I now have the balance?'

Rodney agreed without asking who the buyer was and the next line of 10 million shares went through in the same way, also at 75 cents. With no other bidders at that price, there were no complications, and Crowley was able to tell his client at 2.17 p.m. that he had sold 45 million FAI shares, which was half the Adler family holding, at the price requested.

JB Were, the legendary Melbourne broking house that until its recent merger with Goldman Sachs was Australia's biggest independent broker, had bought the stock on behalf of HIH Insurance. Crowley could see which broker had bought the stock but not who their client was, although he found out soon enough.

Australia's most unusual takeover had begun.

CHAPTER 1

RAPE AND PILLAGE

THERE IS NEVER a stylish way for an insurance company to go into provisional liquidation, but the last days of HIH Insurance before it collapsed on 15 March 2001 looked more like a closing-down sale in a bargain bazaar during a power cut than a Titanic-style, stiff-upper-lip exit from the corporate scene.

In simple terms, insiders at the stricken Sydney-based insurer or organisations associated with it helped themselves to around $15 million in last-minute cash settlements while the company's policyholders had to put up with a trickle of payouts that was just enough to escape official intervention, but nothing like enough to be fair. Insiders such as Deutsche Bank, which had overseen a number of last-minute asset sales and arranged to keep back $6 million in commission from them. Or lawyers Blake Dawson Waldron, which had had regular legal work from HIH and had a former partner as deputy chairman of HIH, Charles Abbott.

Blakes put in an un-itemised bill for exactly $1 million two days before the company collapsed, and was paid by cheque the day before the end.

Abbott, who had long enjoyed a $500 an hour consultancy with HIH to help new chief executive Randolph Wein turn the company's moribund Hong Kong operation into something new and vigorous, had started sending in invoices to HIH on Sunday, 11 March and by 13 March had sent in three totalling more than $180,000, the last being for only two weeks' work, and including work he had yet to do.

He was so keen to be paid that Bill Howard, the general manager finance at HIH, sent treasury accountant Kirk Perry across the Sydney Harbour Bridge on a train to North Sydney after the banks had closed on 14 March so that he could deposit the cheque at ANZ Bank's North Sydney cheque-processing centre. That only happened after Howard had asked Perry to try to deposit the cheque via Perth, which closes two hours later than Sydney. But to their dismay the Australian cheque-clearing system keeps the same hours across the continent.

The next morning, while HIH was beginning to fall apart in front of employees' eyes, Perry had to send a fax to another bank to ask for a special clearance on the cheque. Abbott was duly paid. Howard had been busy enough, meanwhile, converting his own status from employee to consultant, giving himself an effective payout of $405,000 on 14 March. Howard was supposed to be managing the financial and investment affairs of Australia's second biggest general insurance company, which by that stage had all but ceased to pay out on claims.

Meanwhile, Howard had just spent two weeks driving around in a fern-green convertible BMW that seemed to have been paid for by Brad Cooper, a one-time jeans salesman and motivational speaker who in any conventional company would have been shown the door a long time before.

Not only did chief executive Randolph Wein tick off a payout to Howard of more than $180,000 on the day before the company collapsed, but he also forgave Howard's $225,000 mortgage.

Meanwhile, Cooper had so bamboozled HIH's founder and long-time chief executive Ray Williams that by the time the two came to a parting of the ways in late 2000, HIH had wasted more than $75 million on Cooper's burglar alarm company, Home Security International. And by the time HIH collapsed, Cooper had extracted what lawyers assisting the Royal Commission into HIH calculated to be as much as $11 million on top of that.

Four senior executives had shared about $260,000 worth of 'retention bonuses' paid to them two days before the company collapsed, in case they were thinking of leaving, at the instigation of chief executive Randolph Wein. The decision to leave was taken for them on 15 March when Tony McGrath of KPMG replaced the board and management.

Wein was a Hong Kong-based German lawyer who had been in the top job for just over two months and who got his work permit for Australia two days before the company collapsed. He was paid out

$HK270,000 from his previous posting in Hong Kong as a result of the move, which he later had to say was 'pure coincidence'.

Wein was killed in a motorcycle accident in Hong Kong in October 2002, in circumstances which some people found suspicious. He was a motorcycle fanatic who had already had his face rebuilt after an earlier trip over the handlebars, leaving a deep scar on his jaw. Wein's big BMW motorcycle went under a truck in busy Wanchai, where his office was, and he was killed instantly, but the mystery deepened when the truck 'disappeared'. For all the allegations that flew around the HIH Royal Commission about possible death threats being made against major figures, Wein wasn't a central figure in the drama. And a truck would have to be the most ponderous weapon imaginable to organise an 'accident' in a town where the usual method of despatching expatriates is over the balcony of one of the innumerable high-rise blocks there. It is more likely that it was a genuine accident, even if it has kept the conspiracy theorists busy.

Wein only ran HIH for a matter of weeks, and when he took over HIH it was already a financial wreck. The most questionable element in his role was his proximity to Mr Abbott and whether their collaboration was aimed at making themselves, or HIH shareholders, more prosperous. There was no evidence that they collaborated financially but Abbott was paid more than $800,000 in consultancy fees by HIH between 1996 and the company's collapse in 2001.

The prudential regulator in Australia had been crawling all over HIH, at least since October 2000, not that the public or the shareholders knew. APRA, the Australian Prudential Regulation Authority, was one day away from appointing an inspector to oversee HIH's operations when the doors closed for the last time. APRA's responsibility was to HIH's policyholders while ASIC, the Australian Securities and Investments Commission, was investigating whether HIH had broken the cardinal rule and had been trading while insolvent. ASIC only got involved on 26 February.

It wasn't the last scene in King Lear, since the only people who were in serious pain were the policyholders and shareholders in the wings rather than the players on the stage. It was more like a bear garden, a medieval crowd scene where unfortunate animals found themselves dancing for the benefit of laughing onlookers. In this case the bears were the senior accountants at HIH, who found themselves paying big cheques to half-hysterical creditors who were neither policyholders nor shareholders in the crippled company.

And all the time, officially at least, it was business as usual. The catch was that there was hardly any business left.

Since 1 January HIH had been calling itself a 'virtual' insurance company, having had to sell its main income-earning businesses to the giant Allianz group of Germany two months previously, in a desperate bid to get cash in the door. Unfortunately the cash never got in the door because the $200 million of cash that was supposed to go to HIH ended up being used to shore up HIH's share of the new joint venture with Allianz.

A belated push by Australia's federal government to tighten up on insurers' solvency in 1999 and 2000 meant that HIH's already near-impossible solvency target was about to be raised by an estimated $300 million.

The new solvency rules, which came into being on 1 July 2002, meant that insurers would have to keep more conservative reserves, based on what is called a 70 per cent probability of being sufficient. Until then, the number was an undemanding 50 per cent probability level.

Soft rules, an under-funded and inert insurance regulator in the Australian Prudential Regulation Authority, and a strong lobbying campaign by HIH founder Ray Williams meant that HIH had spent the previous three years successfully staving off a tightening-up of the solvency rules for general insurers in Australia.

At last, APRA was cracking down on the practice of 'aggressive' calculation of insurers' reserves, which had hitherto been kept as low as humanly possible. 'Aggressive' in the insurance world is a polite reference to the 'jam tomorrow' school of reserving. It is also known as the Mr Micawber approach after Charles Dickens' character who was always expecting something to turn up: it meant, in effect, keeping reserves to the bare minimum and thus claiming as much as possible every year as profit.

Williams had resigned in October 2000 after a disastrous scheme of Rodney Adler's called Pacific Eagle Equities, which wasted some $7 million of HIH's money on investments which were either illegal or near worthless. The company spent some $4 million of that sum on HIH shares, which was illegal, and almost as much in buying a pile of Rodney Adler's moribund technology investments at his entry price, even though the technology bubble had burst months before. Both men were subsequently prosecuted by ASIC in a civil action and banned from directing companies, Williams for ten years and Adler for twenty. They have appealed the judgment.

Williams resigned from the top job at HIH in October 2000 in the wake of that affair but, like some Japanese fallen corporate titan whom everyone is too polite to see off the premises, was still there doing what he thought was right and many others found to be interfering. Wein had been appointed in his place after chairing the committee to find Williams' successor. His only possible rival, former FAI Insurance chief executive Rodney Adler, had actually made no bones about wanting to chair or indeed run the company and had launched a spirited media campaign in mid–2000 aimed at securing him Williams' job.

As Adler admitted in evidence, he had leaked Mark Westfield of *The Australian* newspaper a plethora of inside information about the woes of HIH, focusing correctly on shortcomings such as its very shaky reserves. His information was accurate and telling, sounding a timely warning to readers about Australia's second biggest general insurer, but the campaign was a disaster in terms of achieving what Adler wanted.

One reason was that most senior executives and directors at HIH were perfectly aware of where the leaks were coming from and cut Adler out of whatever information 'loop' still remained. The other was that while HIH had got itself in an impressive mess by being under-reserved for years, HIH's decision in late 1998 to buy Adler's company FAI for $300 million had only made a bad situation significantly worse.

APRA, meanwhile, failed to heed Adler's warnings because he was pushing his own barrow, thus confusing the medium with the message. APRA was deeply anti-Adler not only on the basis of its own modest research but also because the relevant minister, Financial Services and Regulation Minister Joe Hockey, had said on 3 November 2000 that appointing Adler to the top job at HIH would not be a good thing. Relations between Adler and the HIH board went from bad to worse after the campaign and a month before HIH collapsed, Adler had been forced from the board.

HIH's chairman, Geoffrey Cohen, whom Adler has since called in evidence a 'café chairman' more interested in a good lunch than serious board matters, presented Adler in February 2001 with a fully prepared requisition for an extraordinary meeting of shareholders to remove him from the board — for leaking boardroom secrets to the press. He had used the Australian Shareholders' Association to requisition an extraordinary meeting and, while it was belated, it was a remarkably effective manoeuvre.

Wein had formally taken over on 15 December, the day of HIH's last and most memorable annual meeting, but had really taken the reins on

1 January, the exact day when the main insurance lines of the business went over to Allianz.

The gallows humour among staff at HIH was that Randolph Wein got the top job because the headhunters had had to find someone with the initials RW to match the monogrammed towels in the executive washroom. That canard was reinforced by the fact that Ray Willing, a former chief executive of NRMA Insurance in Sydney, had also been approached for the top job at HIH but had declined very quickly. Other cynics, who by then were legion, concluded that Wein was appointed because he was the only candidate who had no seizable assets in Australia.

Only in the insurance world do you see the completely illogical spectacle of a company shedding its best businesses to stay afloat. Conventional wisdom among struggling companies is to slash at unproductive and non-core operations to keep costs down and maximise positive cash flow, but in the insurance world the need to conform to solvency regulations sometimes forces insurers to do what is effectively the opposite.

HIH needed cash to pay insurance claims, and in January 2001 had been forced to hold off paying out because of a cash flow crisis. Several policyholders had been presented with cheques in settlement of claims but had been asked to hold off cashing them, one of the clearest signs of financial trouble a company could ever send out.

But at the same time Ray Williams had overseen the biggest spending spree by the executive office of the company that it had ever seen. Despite having a budget of $9 million for the 2000 calendar year, the office had spent $32 million on a huge number of items that might have merited an embarrassed smile in a company that was doing well, but looked like crass waste in a company that was close to insolvency.

There had been $1500 worth of jellybeans, for instance, or thirty-four gold watches, plus four nights' a week accommodation at the Intercontinental Hotel in Sydney for Williams' long-serving personal assistant, Rita Young, for most of the last year. The gold watches were for staff with fifteen years' service, and most indeed got them, but the timing made the gesture look like an obscene waste. On 9 January 2001, the day that staff were told to stop processing claims, jeweller Percy Marks sent HIH an invoice for thirty-eight Baume & Mercier watches at almost $8000 each.

Ms Young was regarded by Ray Williams as his 'right arm'. There wasn't anything funny going on between Williams and Young but in a company that was sinking like a stone, and where policyholders started going seriously unpaid in late 2000, it was inexcusable extravagance.

It is also a fact that HIH's 1999 Christmas staff parties in mainland capitals cost over $1 million, of which more than $700,000 was spent in Sydney. The Sydney party gained its organiser, Lena Malouf, an award at a subsequent conference in New Orleans for the 'best event produced by a corporation or association'. Unfortunately, it was held not long after HIH had declared its first-ever loss, a $21 million negative result for the six months to June 1999.

News of the award produced this impressive 'Lady Bracknell' type exchange at the HIH Royal Commission on 27 September 2002 between QCs Wayne Martin and Bob Stitt, one of HIH's directors, who incidentally did not attend the $900-a-head bash.

Martin: 'The Christmas party won an award. You weren't aware of that, I take it?'

Stitt: 'Award?'

Martin: 'It won an award for ...'

Stitt: 'A Christmas party?'

Martin: 'Yes, for a special function. You weren't aware of that?'

Stitt: 'Well, you just told me.'

Even the travel budget looked pretty foolish. Although Williams had announced when he resigned in October that he was going to concentrate on getting the Allianz deal done, for some reason he undertook a first-class trip to the UK and the US in January 2001. No one ever seemed to know who authorised it because of course no one did. Williams had come too far to enjoy any role at HIH that smacked of subservience and the only man who was going to stop him was the company's chairman, Geoffrey Cohen.

Cohen was a retired senior partner at Arthur Andersen in Melbourne with all the right-sounding antecedents and connections, but he was no admiral pacing the quarterdeck and scowling expertly and wisely through his eyeglass at insurance storms ahead. Like most of the other directors, Cohen knew very little about insurance. The joke goes that when he was appointed chairman in 1992, someone had said 'all those who don't want to be chairman please take one step backwards' and that Cohen was last to react. Rodney Adler said his role was to fly up to Sydney from Melbourne for HIH board meetings, have a nice lunch, and fly home again. One of the senior lawyers close to the Royal Commission joked of Cohen that 'it wasn't that he was asleep at the wheel, he wasn't even in the car'. The official and more digestible term used in counsel's summing-up of the evidence was that he was 'utterly ineffective'.

In that perfect world where companies play by the rules, the chairman's major role is hiring and firing the chief executive. Unfortunately HIH, like a lot of other companies in Australia, had its board, its corporate governance framework, 'retro-fitted' around a chief executive who appears to have regarded the whole thing as an encumbrance.

Ray Williams was the driver of the company's float in 1992 and Geoff Cohen was suggested to him as chairman by Justin Gardener, the company's long-serving external auditor. There were to be a lot of awkward ripples following that appointment, not just because Cohen does not appear to have ever overruled Williams about anything of consequence but also because the appointment put HIH far too close to its auditors.

Back in 1992 when the company floated, no one seemed to raise an objection but such an appointment would be all but illegal now. Most major audit firms now ban former partners from being directors of audit clients, but here was a former Andersen partner not only chairing an audit client for almost ten years, but keeping the use of an office at Andersen for almost that length of time as well.

Meanwhile, in February 2001, Ray Williams was parked in a succession of first-class airline seats visiting the UK and the US at HIH's expense. The purpose of his trip, and no one is yet exactly sure, seemed to be to challenge the growing internal conclusion at HIH that the company was under-reserved. (The view now is that the company had understated its reserves for so long that there was actually more than $1 billion of falsely claimed profits in the company's nine years of existence as a listed company in Australia.)

Williams was well received in London, where he had a number of old friends since he was by then the longest serving board member of CE Heath plc, the original parent of HIH. Indeed he had lent one of the old CE Heath friends, Fred Holland, $400,000 in 1993 without consulting his board, and presented Holland with a $1600 box of Dunhill cigars in 2000 before he had even asked for the money back. Holland had never had any role in the Australian company and although Mr Williams told the Royal Commission in 2002 that the principal of the loan was eventually repaid, the $300,000 of forgone interest most certainly was not. And there was also a lot of doubt about whether the principal was repaid or just quietly written off by some complex accounting process.

But when Williams got to the USA, where HIH had had a major operation in California, he put the cat among the pigeons by announcing that the operation was not under-reserved. He was in the process of closing it down or, as they say in insurance, putting it in run-off, so there was some logic in 'talking it up'.

But his claims merely meant that two other hard-pressed executives from HIH, Peter Thompson and Bill Howard, had to follow him over to the US in February 2001 to investigate his claims. He was wrong — there was no secret hoard of gold to rescue the ailing business, aside from a claimed one million dollars in Hawaii — and meanwhile three first-class airfares and a lot of limousine time had once again been wasted.

The Allianz deal which allowed HIH to claim it was solvent had also signed a death warrant for HIH in taking away its major income stream. Some HIH directors had clung to the optimistic belief that the money received from Allianz would allow HIH to keep trading but in fact the $200 million payment that HIH had hoped to pocket from the Allianz deal had to be put straight back into the joint venture trust that was being established to fund future claims. Despite the fact that Ray Williams was meant to be overseeing the transaction, he does not appear to have noticed, and the board certainly was not told. Only Dominic Fodera, another former Andersen auditor who in this case had jumped ship in 1995 to become HIH's finance director, knew but does not appear to have explained the problem to his board.

What was supposed to happen was that HIH would place $450 million worth of other assets in the trust and use the $200 million to keep going but, because it could not otherwise find $450 million, it had to use the money to top-up the asset pile. As Garth Hackshall, an auditor at Andersen in London, wrote to colleagues in Sydney, the Allianz deal was a 'hospital pass' for HIH.

It turned out that Allianz expected HIH to start to get financial returns from the deal five months after the deal began on 1 January 2001. Unfortunately HIH only lasted until 15 March of that year because while the revenue dried up, the cash drain hits just kept on coming.

How did HIH get itself into a situation in which it was ready to bite its own arm off in order to stay alive? That is because insurance companies can get themselves into an agonising situation called a death spiral, in which the payouts creep ahead of revenue and the only thing they can do to prevent collapse is to chase new business.

The problem about chasing new business, and the Lloyd's market in London knows this better than anyone, is that all the other insurers know when another is in trouble and they leave the desperate insurer to take the risks they do not want. Although it is more true in the wholesale reinsurance market (such as Lloyd's) than in the retail business, exactly the same principle applies. In the same way that a herd of antelope will merely put on an extra spurt of speed when one of them is brought down by a lion, so will insurance companies close ranks and allow the weakest insurer to dominate whatever category, for instance public liability insurance, is in a low point in the cycle and which offers no profit for them. And if they go under, hard luck.

HIH wrote around half the public liability insurance in Australia when it collapsed, which merely reinforced the anguished cries of policyholders who went from having cheap (i.e. underpriced) insurance to no insurance at all.

If HIH had been a prospering insurer with already significant reserves, the chance to pick up new premium income would have been welcome, logical and probably profitable. But HIH had none of those advantages.

By the end of the year 2000 HIH had been hit by a 'triple whammy' of around $1 billion of losses in the UK, $620 million of losses in the US and losses of $650 million calculated by Royal Commission counsel assisting as stemming from the acquisition in late 1998 of Rodney Adler's family company, FAI Insurance. The losses were more than $2.2 billion altogether. The judge later calculated that HIH lost $590 million on FAI, but concluded that overall losses may have been even bigger.

Faced with the prospect of having to lift its reserves — earmark more money for payouts — if it took in any new business, HIH had to virtually give away its best business to ease the pressure.

That left the shell of a company based in Sydney, which no longer had a mix of profitable, 'short-tail' insurance policies or lines and the long-tail business it had started with in the 1970s such as workers' compensation. All the good short-tail business such as house and car insurance disappeared into Allianz.

Allianz management in Australia, headed by the magnificently named Terry Towell, was understandably reluctant to put money into a stricken insurer and be left with what might turn out to be bigger claims liabilities than forecast. On HIH's form, that was justified pessimism. HIH also had a put option to sell the other 49 per cent of the asset to Allianz, for some $80 million, but by early March was in such a chaotic state that no one in management noticed.

A quiet word from one of its kinder advisors saw HIH duly sell the asset for a knockdown price, a much better outcome than if the management had merely sat tight. If they had done that, Allianz would have picked up the second half of HIH's main business for nothing. As it turned out, Allianz has only paid part of the $80 million price.

Auditor KPMG had had a number of staff in HIH's Bridge Street head office in Sydney for about two weeks, without any official announcement of what they were doing. It was, unsurprisingly in retrospect, a review of whether HIH was solvent, and was being managed by Tony McGrath, one of Australia's best known liquidators. There were management consultants from the Boston Consulting Group and accountants from Ernst & Young who had been sent in by Westpac Bank to do a report on similar lines to KPMG's. Westpac was owed around $300 million because it had backed the letters of credit that HIH had used to do business via Lloyd's of London, and because it had been alerted in mid–2000 by Jeff Simpson, HIH's former chief general manager finance, that the company was in far worse financial shape than its declared results suggested.

'It was a feast,' investment manager Bill Howard later told the HIH Royal Commission, which was set up by Australia's federal government in the months following the collapse.

HIH had effectively gone into a self-managed run-off of all its other businesses from which there were only three possible outcomes: the arrival of a 'big brother' investor to take over the shell of the company and revive it with a long awaited injection of capital; the successful payment of all insurance claims when due and a repayment of the surplus to HIH's long-suffering investors; and the collapse of the company.

The second outcome would only happen if everything in the company's financial reports was true and that all the reserve 'case estimates' that had been calculated by consulting actuary David Slee turned out to have been conservative enough. Slee, who had known HIH's original chief executive Ray Williams since the 1960s and had an office in the middle floor of HIH's three-floor office in Melbourne, had been sounding a number of loud warnings in recent months about HIH's financial position but had long ago got the reputation of doing his best to come up with reserve estimates that suited the numbers required of the HIH management.

While that might be understandable in a long-term relationship, particularly when in this case Mr Slee's consulting business by then got 80 per cent of its revenue from HIH, it was not healthy and the warnings came way too late.

They left the company's reserves in dire shape and Mr Slee told the HIH Royal Commission of 2002 that if he had been forced to report any threat to the company's solvency by the new APRA rules that eventually came into force on 1 July 2002, sixteen months after the company collapsed, he would have sounded the alarm in September 1999 because some $600 million of claimed reserves 'simply were not there'. Since the rules did not apply then, no such clarion call went out to the regulator APRA in 1999, and the company complied with all the predictions by collapsing in 2001.

Wayne Martin, QC, an old-style barrister from Perth with a sense of humour slightly drier than the Nullarbor Plain, summed up HIH's problems in a speech he called 'Insurance 101' on 13 January 2003.

Noting that liquidator Tony McGrath of KPMG had estimated HIH's deficiency at $5.3 billion, Martin said that the gap was between how much money HIH had pulled in as premium, and how much it was going to have to find to meet liabilities. Rather than being spirited away, the money 'hasn't gone anywhere because it was never there', he said.

He said HIH had priced its premiums incorrectly on the cheap side because it had persistently underestimated how much it would need to keep back for reserves, a problem which had been disguised by the fact that as its liability shortfall got worse, it had sold more and more policies so that it actually looked as though it was making money. Not only that, but HIH was able to hide trouble by 'the use of financial products and accounting treatments to obscure and in some cases conceal the fundamentally unprofitable nature of the business'. He said those products were 'used to paper over the large cracks which had appeared in the fundamental structural elements of the group, concealing them from the gaze of investors, consumers and the regulators, enabling HIH to trade unprofitably on until the cash simply ran out'.

Which might explain why there were so few acts of selflessness as the creaking and groaning ship HIH sank beneath the waves; there was no modern equivalent of the band playing 'Nearer, My God, to Thee' as the stern climbed out of the water.

A better analogy was of a big fish or whale that ended up carrying so many parasites and sucker fish along with it that the body lost its few reserves of energy — in this case cash — and it writhed painfully out of sight. And quite aside from the sucker fish, the sharks closed in at the end and bit the biggest chunks they could from the carcass. In his 1500-page report delivered on 16 April 2003, Justice Owen described the company as 'shambling into oblivion'.

Considering that HIH Insurance had been known since its listing in 1992 as being 'lean and mean', something catastrophic had happened to its culture. Ray Williams, the man who put it all together and ran the company like a family patriarch, appears to have switched in the late 1990s from being a focused and workaholic autocrat to being a helpless target for every carpetbagging scheme put to him by young men on the make who correctly saw HIH as a piggy bank from which they could take money when they wanted.

The follies included a $250,000 sponsorship of Collingwood Football Club on 8 December 2000, promoting the brand of FAI Insurance. That deal was engineered by Brad Cooper, who exerted a Svengali-like influence on HIH director Rodney Adler, who in turn had the previously autocratic Ray Williams wrapped around his little finger.

It was Shakespeare all over again, with Williams blacking up to play Othello and Adler falling seamlessly into the role of Iago, the smooth plotter who can turn everything around and convince Othello to murder his wife Desdemona. If Adler didn't ask Williams to murder anybody, he certainly helped the silver-haired autocrat to park the knife neatly in his own company.

Cooper had been standing as a candidate for the Collingwood board, on a ticket supporting chairman Eddie McGuire. McGuire, ebullient son of Scottish migrants and a man dubbed 'Eddie Everywhere' for his multiple media and Australian Rules football interests, did what any normal club chairman would do and accepted the sponsorship with thanks.

Australian Football League clubs in Melbourne have long been an absurdly easy source of public credibility for cashed-up entrepreneurs — mining promoter Joseph Gutnick bought years of support in the late 1990s by promising to spend $3 million on the cash-strapped Melbourne Football Club — but the only moral issue Collingwood faced was the awkward timing of being offered money while a club board election was going on.

At least Joseph Gutnick was being logical in what he did: he is Jewish, Melbourne Football Club was predominantly Anglo-Saxon and it was a clear opportunity to raise his public profile in a football-mad city.

But the $250,000 sponsorship offered by HIH in December 2000 was to put the name FAI in front of supporters at a time when FAI's most consistent backer, Rodney Adler, had already sold the company. And the company name was, in his own words to his friend Brad Cooper, 'soiled' by its bad reputation.

If FAI had been regarded as dodgy in its life between 1960 and 1998, it was what Justice Owen called a 'substantial contributing cause and an important circumstance surrounding the collapse of HIH'. The wags had long said that FAI stood for 'Fuck All Insurance' but aside from that, FAI was about to disappear anyway.

As part of the life-saving exercise of selling its more successful insurance businesses to Allianz, HIH was about to dispose of most of FAI and the FAI name would disappear into Allianz.

So HIH was spending a quarter of a million dollars of desperately needed money on sponsoring a subsidiary that was about to be sold. That was clearly an act of financial folly at a time when the claims department of HIH was holding off paying claims for as long as possible, but it was no more ridiculous than the fact that on the same day that it put the money up, HIH was effectively writing off some $85 million that it had put into Cooper's burglar alarm sales company, Home Security International (HSI). Desperate to get away from Cooper's incessant demands for money to help keep HSI afloat, HIH's managers allowed Cooper to pay them $1.25 million for 47 per cent of HSI on 8 December 2000, at a time when there were much bigger issues that they should have been wrestling with.

Williams and then Wein were trying to refinance HIH and simultaneously stave off the demands from creditors. But instead of conducting measured debate with them to buy time and hopefully some stability, HIH's managers appeared to outside eyes to be behaving like a drunken punter who has blown most of his money at the races and is standing on a street corner handing out what is left to anyone who walks past.

Wayne Martin described it as 'a veritable flood of cash pouring out of HIH during the last six months before the appointment of provisional liquidators'.

The 'spotter's fee' affair was the sort of nonsense that could only happen in an organisation that was falling to pieces. On 13 March 2001 Bill Howard, the company's investment manager and chief general manager finance, authorised the payment of a $1.9 million spotter's fee to business partners

Brad Cooper and Ben Tilley for having introduced the Packer family as potential buyers of HIH's property portfolio. HIH had twelve properties with a book value of about $218 million that were being offered at a price of about $136 million — a discount of 38 per cent, or $82 million.

Tilley is an old Cranbrook schoolmate of James Packer in Sydney's eastern suburbs, and a regular card and golf partner of James' father, Kerry. He is close enough to the family to have been offered the Packer yacht *Arctic P* for his wedding in Positano, Italy, in 1998.

Instead of writing a cheque, which would have taken at least a day to clear, Howard took the unusual step of authorising a telegraphic transfer or TT, which is instantaneous. The fee went to Cooper and Tilley's Goodwill Group Pty Ltd, which was genuinely described in its literature as having been founded to foster 'random acts of kindness'.

They got one of those in the spotter's fee despite the fact that the idea of the Packers buying HIH's property assets at a bargain basement price of 'between 58 per cent and 62 per cent of the book value' was effectively a non-starter from the very beginning, because most of the properties were tied up in ways that made them unable to be sold.

Howard was by then the longest serving local executive at the top of HIH, since newly appointed CEO Randolph Wein had just come down from running HIH in Asia. Wein's long-time associate, finance director Jock MacAdie, had just been appointed from Melbourne.

Howard had a specific problem because less than a month previously he had allowed the mercurial Brad Cooper to order him a $118,000 convertible BMW in his preferred colour, fern green, and had been driving around in the car for at least ten days without, according to his later evidence, knowing what the car was worth. During HIH's last three weeks Cooper was able to obtain from Howard, who by then was one of the three executives actually running the company, some $11 million in very questionable financial benefits via the settlement of a number of claims Cooper had made. Cooper maintained in evidence to the Royal Commission that he (Cooper) never paid for the car, since the $118,000 cheque he paid to the dealer was a deposit on a BMW X5 four wheel drive which he had ordered. The dealer made no such distinction.

The top management of HIH was by then in disarray.

Ray Williams should have walked out of the door when he resigned in October 2000 after concluding with chairman Geoff Cohen that he had lost the confidence of the share market. But because no one had told

Williams exactly what his role would be and he had spent a decade motivating his staff and ruling with as much sense of democracy as the Roman Emperor Caligula, he stayed and no one had the nerve to tell him to go. It was to his eventual loss, in fact, since he not only lost the value of all six million of his HIH shares in the company's collapse, but he also lost any chance of collecting any of his statutory entitlements.

Tony McGrath of KPMG was appointed provisional liquidator of the company on Thursday, 15 March 2001 and a report published a short time later estimated that HIH's liabilities might possibly reach $5.3 billion, which made it the biggest corporate failure in Australian history. And it is to history that we must turn if we are to come to some understanding of how this catastrophe occurred.

CHAPTER 2

THE MIGRANT DREAM

LASZLO ADLER LOOKED no different from the mass of refugees coming off
the ship when he arrived in Melbourne on the Norwegian ship
SS Skaugum in December 1949. He was seventeen years old, on the short
side and about as far from the image of the bronzed Aussie as he could be.
But inside he had an ambition to succeed that was almost tangible.

If you believe family is the biggest influence on a person's character
and career choice, he had an impeccable pedigree. His father, Bela, had
walked away from the idea of studying law in order to go into business.
Following a trip to Ecuador shortly after the First World War, during
which he served in the defeated Austro-Hungarian army, he built up a
successful button-manufacturing operation in the late 1920s and 1930s in
Hungary using the otherwise low-value stem of a plant called a stone nut.

He set up a factory inside the walls of the prison at Vac, some thirty
kilometres up the Danube from Budapest, around the time that Laszlo
was born in 1931 and his business prospered throughout the 1930s
despite the global depression that followed the Wall Street Crash of 1929.

For Bela Adler, as for some 400,000 Jews in Hungary, the Second
World War put paid not only to his business but to his life.

Although Hungary spent the earlier years of the war relatively
unscathed by Fascism, and Adler was able to circumvent discriminatory
anti-Jewish laws by using a trusted gentile friend as nominee owner of the
business, all that counted for nothing when the Nazi regime clamped

17

down on Hungary in early 1944. Tired of vacillation by the Hungarian puppet regime and the worrying prospect of a treaty between Hungary and the Western allies in the wake of the German army's retreat from the shattering defeat of Stalingrad, Nazi SS forces under the command of Adolf Eichmann moved in to occupy the country on Sunday, 19 March 1944. With the help of the Arrow Cross movement, the Hungarian pro-Nazi organisation, they had assembled lists of prominent Jews and liberals. Bela Adler was clearly one and possibly both, and within two hours of the first SS units rolling into Budapest, he was arrested. (The Arrow Cross, a pro-Nazi and anti-Semitic party led by Ferenc Szalasi, actually ruled Hungary from 15 October 1944 to January 1945. In its four-month life it oversaw the deportation of 80,000 Jews, mostly women, to concentration camps where they almost all died.)

Although he was briefly held in a transit camp in Budapest and was even subsequently allowed to spend one closely monitored day with his wife Antonia, daughter Tessa and son Laszlo, who were fifteen and thirteen respectively, Bela was deported to an unknown destination. Like so many others at that time, he simply disappeared.

After Hungary was liberated by Russian troops in April 1945 the Adler family pursued whatever inquiries they could and eventually discovered that Bela had first made the long and miserable journey by train to Auschwitz in Poland. He had subsequently been moved again and died on 19 February 1945 in a forced labour camp near Muhldorf am Inn, a town around eighty kilometres east of Munich, where huge numbers of slave labourers had been brought in to build an underground jet fighter factory. It was also known as Dachau 3b since it came under the administration of Dachau camp, one of the Hitler regime's original *Konzentrazionslager*, on the outskirts of Munich.

By one of the cruel twists of war Bela Adler died only two months before the camp was liberated by the US 99th Infantry Division. His family were unable to find out whether he had died from pneumonia or malnutrition or typhus. But, from letters that his wife Antonia received in the chaotic months following the end of the war in May 1945, they did learn that he had met a distant sixteen-year-old cousin in the camp and that he had shared his already inadequate rations with the boy during one of the hardest winters to strike central Europe for many years.

One survivor of the camp who gave testimony to an Israeli Holocaust memorial website stated that working conditions at the underground factory site were particularly bad because the main work was carrying cement in 40-kilogram bags. Many of the slave labourers became what were dryly called Moslems because they sank to their knees while trying to carry the bags and in many cases they died where they lay. Carrying a 40-kilogram bag of cement any distance takes a huge effort by a healthy adult man but the combination of ill health, malnutrition and Bela Adler's age, 59, would have marked him out as a certain victim.

And when his son Laszlo set off across the world in late 1949, a near penniless refugee, he knew all of that.

But aside from the horror of what had happened to his father and of the hand-to-mouth life forced on him by the last year of the war, he had had a better time of it than a lot of his fellow passengers, most of whom were from Russia, Poland, Hungary and Czechoslovakia.

His path had been made easier by his father's reputation and the debts of gratitude owed to the Adlers by many people in Hungary and even Austria. When he made his first attempt to escape from Hungary in 1948 he was caught before being able to cross the border. By that time the communist regime was well established in Hungary — which was why he was trying to get out — and attempts to escape usually resulted in an automatic prison sentence. Fortunately, one of the ministers in the Hungarian government had worked in Bela Adler's factory while he was incarcerated in Vac jail, and an approach by Laszlo's mother Antonia was able to secure Laszlo's release. Clearly Bela Adler had been a benevolent employer, even if his factory had benefited from very cheap labour in the jail.

It took a year before Laszlo tried again and in that time he became more aware than ever that as a middle-class *bourgeois* from a Jewish family he was never going to get the chance, for instance, to study at university. The new communist regime in Hungary practised clear discrimination against Jews, hiding its anti-Semitism behind the convenient idea that the Jews' expertise in the hated private enterprise made them capitalist exploiters of the proletariat.

Laszlo's elder sister Tessa had initially been taken in by the supposed egalitarianism of the communist belief system, but her party membership lasted exactly six weeks before she was denounced and ejected in true party tradition as having come from a highly suspect capitalist background.

Laszlo was never tempted, though he did agree with the communist propaganda about the need for a class war. The only thing was, he planned to fight it from the other side. Accordingly, he was determined to get out of the country and to establish a new life in the West.

It took a year before Laszlo tried again and this time, in the summer of 1949, he was successful. His family still had enough portable assets such as silver to pay a group of people smugglers to get him across the border and thus into Austria. And although Vienna was seething with refugees from communist central Europe, Laszlo more or less fell on his feet there.

His mother Antonia's brother had fled to Vienna before him and was able to help Laszlo financially during the four months when he was in limbo, waiting to see if he could be accepted as a migrant by Canada or Australia.

He had no particular preference except that he wanted to move on, and soon. The weather was already beginning to cool with the onset of autumn. Even though his uncle was helping him, he was living in a cheap hotel. The die was cast when after several interviews with Australian officials in Vienna, he was given a train ticket to Palermo in southern Italy and a berth on the relatively comfortable migrant carrier SS *Skaugum*, leaving in late October 1949.

THE AUSTRALIA THAT greeted Laszlo Adler in 1949 in many respects resembled a miniature Britain spread thinly across a continent almost the size of the US, with a population of just over 10 million, an economy that was based heavily on agricultural exports, and a culture that was thoroughly Anglo-Saxon.

It is easy to smile now about Australia's shortcomings in 1949, but after the horrors and then frustrations of Budapest in the 1940s it offered Larry a lot. But as Peter Denton's biography of Larry Adler, *From Cabbie to Chairman*, published in 1990, pointed out, it took him a while to get established. He first had to take the train to Bonegilla migrant camp, an old army camp on the shores of the Hume Weir near Albury where the huts appeared to have been designed to be as cold as possible in winter and hotter than Hades in the summer.

There may have been method in the authorities' madness because migrants were quick to move on to the next stage, which entailed two years of indentured labour that they had promised in exchange for their passage. They were paid, but not well, and had some choice about what particular type of 'labouring' or 'domestic' work they might take up.

Many of the ex-soldiers and rural workers among the displaced persons opted for the Snowy Mountains scheme, where the pay was better, and indeed many of them stayed on well after their two-year 'hitch'. Towns like Guthega and Cooma still have a heavy leavening of eastern European names, as do the timber towns of the south-west of Western Australia and the sugar towns such as Tully and Innisfail in Queensland.

But Larry had no dreams of the horny-handed life of the pioneer. He was a city boy and he opted for a job as a train cleaner with the South Australian Railways in Adelaide. While others squirrelled away their modest wages, Larry was more focused on learning English. He chose two ways to do it, one more obvious than the other. He listened avidly to the radio and also attended church services regularly on Sundays. He made the unusual choice to do the latter — he was after all Jewish — because he found that sermons tended to be expressed in clear, precise language. So by the time his two years as a train cleaner ended, he was ready for the Big City in more ways than one. (Rodney Adler has noted with pride that his father stuck out the train-cleaning job for the full two years, as his contract required, rather than leaving early as many migrants did.)

Larry Adler's next decade was almost a textbook transition from migrant to man of substance. There were a number of early jobs, not all of them for very long, but work was plentiful both in Adelaide and Sydney. In the 1950s he leased and drove taxis before setting up an electrical retailing business, Radioland, in Sydney. But it was in finance, insurance and investment that he was to make his fortune.

ON 11 MARCH 1956 Larry married Ethel 'Bobby' Kaminer at the Great Synagogue in Sydney's Elizabeth Street. Their first child, Rodney, was born on 19 August 1959, followed by daughters Kathy and Roxanne. Rodney's birth appears to have coincided with Larry Adler's big decision, to start an insurance company.

Denton's book records a conversation which all too probably took place between Larry Adler and partner Joe Barrington, who thought they were about to buy a General Motors franchise. Adler told Barrington he was going to start an insurance company and Barrington said, 'Look, Larry, finance is OK but I'm not an insurance man,' to which Larry made the lapidary reply, 'Neither am I. But we'll learn.'

On 15 November 1960 Fire and All Risks Insurance opened its doors at FAI House, a small office building at 36 King Street which Larry had bought. It is worth noting that FAI started with a mere £7500 of capital, although Larry increased that to £25,077 when he was told the bigger number would be more likely to impress potential clients. He also borrowed £20,000 to pay a mandatory deposit to the Insurance Commissioner, the regulator of all insurance companies in Australia. He was on the right side of the law at that point but he spent the rest of his life battling with the Commissioner over whether FAI was truly solvent.

In essence, insurance companies in Australia at that time were expected to have reserves strong enough to pay out on 15 per cent of all policies at any time. Cash is the most prized reserve but Larry was always going to have a battle on his hands since he saw insurance as the perfect cash cow to finance an investment empire. And he wasn't talking boring stocks with low yields. For him, high-growth and high-risk stocks were his predominant interests.

Bill Thiele, who in 2002 was a senior vice president at General Cologne Reinsurance responsible for South-East Asia and Australia, put it succinctly when he said: 'You don't get many entrepreneurs running insurance companies: most of them are run by boring, conservative people.'

There was no legislation that banned entrepreneurs from running insurers and indeed Larry's logic was entirely reasonable: as long as the company could earn more from its investments than it was paying out in claims, it would be profitable.

That was radical thinking in the Australia of the 1960s. There were already a group of established insurers, almost all British-owned, which made their money insuring shipping cargoes into and out of Australia. They were a cartel, and they knew it, since they charged what they called 'Tariff' rates and had regular conferences to make sure rates were fair and profitable. By modern standards that sounds inexcusable, unless of course you consider that banks still behave in a similar fashion. And there was another important factor in the cartel, which the banks also adhere to now: if any member was looking like going under, the others took over their liabilities and business carried on as before.

Adler's approach has been compared with farting in a cathedral. He wasn't in the cartel and he would charge whatever rates he believed the market would bear. The Trade Practices Act of 1974 turned to law everything that Adler believed in, at least on the premium side, and the insurance cartel was outlawed.

What was less charming was that Adler was not greatly concerned about mixing his personal share trading with his company's trading, particularly at the speculative end of the sharemarket. He floated a cashbox mining company in 1971 called Secmin at 10c a share, but the poor timing of the float saw the shares sag to 2c each. It did not help that Secmin was named after a much bigger cashbox called Minsec which went broke a month after Secmin floated. In an uncanny rehearsal for what his son Rodney did in 2000 in using HIH money and Pacific Eagle Equities to buy his near-worthless technology stocks, Larry Adler kept Secmin alive by selling some of its assets to FAI at inflated prices.

In 1971 Larry Alder incurred the wrath of the NSW Workers' Compensation Commission, which began an inquiry into FAI in September of that year. In March 1975 the commission's registrar applied to cancel FAI's licence but a point in Adler's favour back then was that FAI was able to retain its licence as long as the case was before the courts. The result was that the case stayed before the courts, in one form or another, for more than a decade. Adler was always a determined litigator, especially when FAI's future was at stake.

The main reason for the case was that the commission believed that FAI was financially unsound but, as often happens in these cases, most of the action turned on technicalities. One allegation was that FAI had failed to notify the identity of its holding company, Lader Pty Ltd, in its annual report. Another allegation had to do with the purchase of shares from Adler interests. The case was ultimately decided by Justice Frank McGrath of the Compensation Court of NSW. His judgment of 31 October 1980, was scathing: 'In view of the unsatisfactory nature of the conduct which persisted up to and throughout the hearing it is my view that it would be futile imposing conditions upon the licence in an endeavour to prevent future recurrences of the particular type of conduct ... I consider the conduct to be serious and do not consider suspension appropriate. For these reasons I consider the licence should be terminated.' The hearing also disclosed several disturbing points about FAI's finances in 1973 and 1974. The registrar had alleged that FAI's investments did not comply with the commission's liquidity guidelines. FAI held no Australian or semi-government securities and an excessive proportion of its funds were invested in subsidiaries.

Larry Adler frankly admitted that FAI had never attempted to conform to the guidelines. His investment philosophy differed diametrically from the official view. While he loved the gunpowder end of the share market, the regulator wanted insurers to invest mainly in fixed interest such as government and semi-government bonds, with a secondary layer of blue chip shares for capital growth.

Larry Adler also admitted that FAI's provision for outstanding claims of $10.4 million at June 1978 had been shown by analysis to be underprovided by $3.2 million, which again presaged similar problems on a much bigger scale at FAI and then HIH in the late 1990s.

However, he announced he would appeal to the Privy Council in London. That sounds like an expensive and time-consuming course of action for a Hungarian migrant to Australia but Adler had done his homework: FAI was again able to continue in business pending the appeal. In the end it never had to be heard.

FAI was also threatened by another court case during the 1970s. FAI was badly hit when Cyclone Tracy devastated Darwin at Christmas 1974. FAI's share of the payout was $4.5 million at a time when its total premium income was only $12 million.

As FAI struggled to meet the claims, the Federal Insurance Commissioner alleged that FAI did not have net assets equivalent to at least 15 per cent of its premium income as required by law. FAI claimed its 1976 accounts showed $5.6 million in shareholders' funds, well above the $2.9 million required.

But the commissioner queried several items in FAI's accounts, including $1.7 million in future tax benefits, $1.4 million in paper profits from the acquisition of subsidiaries, and a $300,000 overvaluation of the share portfolio compared to market.

(This was another classic rehearsal for FAI's adventures in the late 1990s. FAI regularly revalued assets upwards where possible, on one occasion selling half of FAI Finance Corp to a company run by Brad Cooper shortly before the end of the December 1997 half. That deal, whose price was never made public, allowed FAI to revalue the remaining half upwards so that the company could report a half year profit. That in turn allowed FAI to retain some $57 million worth of Future Income Tax Benefits (FITB) as an asset in the balance sheet. The only financial conjuring trick that Larry never tried was financial reinsurance, simply because while Larry was tussling with the commissioner, financial reinsurance had yet to be invented.)

JOHN PALMER, A former head of the Canadian prudential regulation authority, was hired in late 2001 by his Australian equivalent, APRA, to review APRA's role in the HIH collapse. His report, which the HIH Royal Commission described as 'impartial and thorough' was hard on APRA but also took an historical line in criticising John Howard's 1978 decision to allow FAI to operate when he was Treasurer in the Fraser government. Following an Administrative Appeals Tribunal hearing, FAI's assets were found to be inadequate but Howard was persuaded to issue a trading licence on the condition that $800,000 was injected into the company.

Palmer said that the FAI companies may have been commercially insolvent at the time, a much direr allegation than mere statutory insolvency, and noted that Adler had had at least one meeting with Howard before the then treasurer exercised his discretion. Palmer believed that FAI should have been permanently shut down at that time.

His report stated: 'I would recommend a full review of these files be made and documented to ensure that there is an accurate record of the circumstances under which the FAI companies were authorised and their condition at the time of the authorisation.'

John Howard has been the Prime Minister of Australia since 1996, and he has never chosen between 1978 and now to explain what particular arrangement he came to with Larry Adler.

THE ABSURDITY OF all those battles is that neither Larry nor Rodney Adler was actually interested in running an insurance company *per se*. Larry Adler's real interest at FAI remained on the investment side. Insurance, for him, was a sort of banking licence whereby people put their money in and occasionally asked for it back.

The flat post-mining boom period of the 1970s gave way to a credit-driven takeover boom in the 1980s and Larry was in every takeover bid worth a mention, usually as a greenmailer.

Unlike blackmail, greenmail is legal. It essentially involves buying shares in companies you believe will be takeover targets and then holding out until you get the price you want from the anxious bidder. Modern corporate law in Australia prevents bidding auctions but there are plenty of ways to buy profitably into a takeover play if you have a parcel of shares big enough to make a difference.

For instance, he bought into Sydney retailer Grace Brothers and sold a 6.5 per cent stake on to the Myer group for a $5 million profit. He then put FAI into Myer and made a further profit of $27 million. After the investment desert of the 1970s, it was a dazzling way to make a living.

His best coup of the 1980s was a $200 million punt on an 18 per cent stake in Pioneer Concrete. Larry was no more a concrete entrepreneur than he was a concert pianist, but he was in the right place at the right time. Robert Holmes à Court, who memorably once used a Western Australian tractor distributor, Wigmores Ltd, to make a bid for BHP, bought the stake as part of a bid and FAI was suddenly $194 million richer. FAI had effectively ceased being an insurance company and had effectively become an investment company. If Larry was breaking a few portfolio rules in having big punts, the genuine financial profits he was making in these deals removed any doubts about FAI's solvency as an insurer. At that time at least.

Larry had gone from being a fringe player to a grand master of the local corporate chess game. And by that time Rodney was coming into his father's business as investment manager, a role he took on in 1985.

Rodney was always going to take to that business like a duck to water. One of his abiding memories, according to accounts of his childhood, was of sitting between his father's feet under the boardroom table while great affairs were being discussed. Other accounts say that Rodney spent a lot of his weekends in his childhood and teenage years inviting friends to the Adler family's eastern suburbs house to play tennis. That was normal enough, but his father was more often than not closeted behind curtains at the far end of the house planning his next business move. It was better than many childhoods, but it probably never offered Rodney a lot of 'man to man' conversations with his father while he was making that gradual transition from teenager to adult.

Rodney's education unarguably had gaps in it, particularly where discipline was concerned. On a number of occasions when he was in trouble at Cranbrook, his father came to the school and made accusations of anti-Semitism. Rodney certainly was in a minority in that regard but his contemporaries have made it clear that he was not in trouble for being Jewish, he was in trouble for being a real pain. As fellow Cranbrookian Adam Shand wrote in the *Australian Financial Review* magazine in late 2002, in 1976 Adler helped to pinch the grade book kept by ancient history teacher Harry 'Fossil' Nicolson, thus preventing teachers from assembling full reports on the pupils. While his partner in crime Darcy Lawler was all for returning the book, Adler consigned it to a stormwater drain that took it out to Sydney Harbour.

Rodney Adler did not undergo any great transformation in his early working life, either.

26

After Larry asked Michael Payne, a co-founder of HIH Insurance with Ray Williams, to give Rodney a job in his London insurance operations in the early 1980s, Rodney lasted precisely a month before the staff mutinied and said to Payne: 'He goes or we go.'

Since there were about eight staff in Payne's booth or 'box' in the big Room at Lloyd's, there was no debate and Rodney went. Payne was left to explain to Larry what had happened.

Asked by Simon White, counsel assisting the HIH Royal Commission, for more details, Payne winced and explained: 'It's getting very personal, but it was mainly his arrogance and his endeavouring to tell people who had been doing the job for most of their lives how they should do it, in his opinion, while knowing absolutely nothing about it himself.'

Larry Adler laughed uproariously when Payne rang him to say why Rodney would not be staying, happily adding 'That's my boy!'

Larry was almost certainly an indulgent father to his son in private, while mother Bobby once noted proudly that 'We never placed any restrictions on Rodney.' Write your own script on the consequences of that attitude.

But in public it was a different matter. Back in the 1980s when corporate presentations relied on a slide projector and a presenter pointing a billiard cue at the screen, Rodney was a natural choice for the projector job and Larry inevitably had his moments as slides went in occasionally upside down, or back to front. It was a situation Rodney was never going to look good in and sure enough it got all round the investment community when Larry once banged the cue with emphasis and burst out: 'RRRodney, how many times do I have to tell you?' at his hapless son. Larry had an endearing habit of rolling his 'R's at the back of his throat, which in the case of this story just served to embellish it.

In fact Rodney achieved a Bachelor of Business degree at the University of New South Wales, a Masters in Economics at Macquarie University and a chartered accountant's qualification at Deloitte's, which later became Deloitte Touche Tohmatsu. Contemporaries and clients remember that it was Rodney who asked the most searching questions during audits, so he was certainly exposed to both the theoretical and practical aspects of commercial life.

But two events in the late 1980s changed Rodney's life for ever. The first was the share market crash of October 1987, which hit the FAI portfolio even harder than the rest of the market. While most major stocks were marked down by about 40 per cent and bounced back gradually thereafter, the smaller stocks were left 'seller, no buyer'. And smaller stocks were where FAI was most heavily exposed.

The second was that Larry died in December 1988, a victim of a heart attack related to a diabetic condition that manifested itself soon after he first arrived in Australia. He was fifty-six. If Larry was ever going to bare his soul fully to his son, he almost certainly missed his chance.

One could argue that Rodney has spent too much of his life as that most dangerous of sociological phenomena, 'The Man Who Can Do No Wrong'. In a tape-recorded interview in 1999 or 2000 Rodney told his then friend Brad Cooper: 'Dad was my greatest support. I bumbled through Uni, I got through my chartered accounting, I got through my masters, and everyone thought that I was a pretty good mediocre person. Dad thought I would be great. Dad marketed me as if I was great,' he added.

That suggests Rodney was aware there was a gap at that stage between the promise and the delivery, but he then told Cooper something much more alarming.

'Do you know what? I rose to meet his aspirations,' he said. And 'If it wasn't for my Dad I wouldn't be where I am today.'

He was absolutely right on the last one, although he may not have noticed the irony when he said it.

Almost everything about Rodney Adler's situation in 2002 and beyond is a consequence of his father's actions, or views, or both. Of all the dire combinations of business circumstances, inheriting a cash-strapped insurance company with a raft of illiquid assets in a difficult financial period would have to be one of the worst. For his many faults, Rodney knew that in 1988 FAI was held together by string and baler twine and he spent the next decade trying in vain to make it look like a serious insurer.

Unfortunately, it was permanently hamstrung by two deals started in 1988, by which Western Australian entrepreneur and America's Cup winner Alan Bond borrowed $500 million, most of the company's core capital, and never paid it back. The interest alone from that $500 million would probably have been enough to keep FAI going as a small to middle sized insurer through the 1990s, instead of which it bled slowly to death via the twin woes of losing money through its core business, underwriting insurance, and losing money on its investment portfolio.

The origins of the deal are lost in the mists of time, and in various people's embarrassment, but it reportedly started out in 1988 as a loan of

$100 million, unsecured. Larry Adler acquired the reputation in the high-borrowing 1980s as being a lender of last resort to entrepreneurs, charging a reputed 25 per cent per annum on loans while most other borrowers were paying less than 15. The story has it that Larry Adler renegotiated the loan to obtain some security and duly got it, but had to lift the loan sum to $500 million. In exchange FAI was given the rights to a number of assets, mostly property, and mostly very complicated.

(There was one mischievous theory that it was Rodney Adler himself who made the first unsecured $100 million loan, but most FAI experts believe that Larry Adler would never have authorised anyone but himself to make a loan of that size. It does, however, leave the mystery of why Larry Adler, a noted wheeler-dealer who knew Alan Bond's reputation as well as anybody, lent Bond the money unsecured in the first place.)

One property asset was the St Moritz Hotel in New York, a well-located pile at the south end of Central Park that spent more than a decade in dire need of renovation before being reopened under new owners as a Ritz-Carlton. Then there was the old Emu Brewery in Perth, which has now been vacant for almost twenty years but is finally being marketed as Mounts Bay Waters, an upmarket residential development that appears to have overcome the problem of proximity to a major Perth freeway.

In the 1990s those property assets came to characterise FAI, which never managed to shake off the image of being too tied down by them and far too active at the shonky end of the sharemarket.

Adler did his best to talk the company up but the more he talked up FAI's new respectability, the more the market found something wrong with it.

On 29 June 1994, for instance, subsidiary FAI Life put on a slew of last-minute orders in the share market just before trading closed for the day, pushing up the prices of at least twenty-nine tiddler shares. Such actions normally take place on 30 June and are called window-dressing, since they allow fund managers to mark the value of their shares at a higher price. But FAI Life's Fund No 2 ruled off on 29 June, for no particular reason. It doesn't seem to have done a lot of good: although the expenditure of $205,000 on shares allowed FAI Life to lift the valuation by a total of $715,000, most of the shares subsequently sunk back to previous levels and the fund came last in the June 1994 surveys.

Pont Securities got an order from FAI Life to buy 12,000 shares in speculative mining-related stock Ausdrill Ltd 'at the close', when the price was $1.20. FAI Life got most of the shares at that price but had to pay $1.25 for the last 2800 shares, leaving the price 5c up on the day and allowing the company to value every Ausdrill share it had at $1.25. But the stock price dropped to $1.15 on 1 July and $1.10 two days after that.

ASX Ltd and the Australian Securities Commission (ASC), as it was then, investigated the trades but no prosecution followed, not least because there were nine different broking houses involved and it could not be proved that the buyers of the shares obtained any benefit.

Rodney Adler was a director of FAI Life and sat on its asset-allocation committee. He was also heavily involved in supporting the share price of Anaconda Nickel Ltd in July and August 1994, along with the new float's underwriter, Far East Capital Ltd (FEC). FAI was an original supporter of the stock, taking 4 million shares, or 13.3 per cent of the issue, while FEC was associated with Andrew 'Twiggy' Forrest, the company's founder. The shares listed at 25c in February but by 7 July had sagged to 14c. FAI and FEC simply waded into the market and, by buying around 67 per cent of the shares on offer in the market for the next six weeks, pushed the price up by 100 per cent to 28c. Both of the supporters risked breaking the 20 per cent shareholding rule after which it is obligatory to make a bid for the stock, which was not the supporters' strategy at all.

Although FAI and FEC were clear and loud in the fact that they were buying shares, they made less noise about the fact that they then in many cases passed the blocks of shares 'to the beneficial owner of the shares' via an off-market transaction. Which means they went off to a warehouse somewhere, most probably offshore. Anaconda Nickel's share price rose to almost $1 in 2000, enabling both FAI and FEC to make good profits in selling.

But when Rodney Adler spoke to *Business Review Weekly* in October 1994, he was full of how his approach had changed. He told reporter Adele Ferguson that the market's negative assessment of FAI was 'entirely unfounded' and that FAI was more attracted to middle-ranking stocks, with only a sprinkling of speculative stocks thrown in.

He said FAI had hired management consultants Booz Allen & Hamilton to review every aspect of FAI's business processes.

'We are one of the most solvent companies in the industry,' he trumpeted.

Ms Ferguson was not entirely captivated. 'Of the listed insurance companies, FAI is the one least favoured by investors,' she wrote, after talking to analysts and fund managers. 'This is based on its high level of gearing, its large exposure to property and its claims paying ratio, which is believed to be higher than the industry average of 78 per cent.'

What she did not know and Rodney Adler clearly did not tell her was that between 1993 and 1995 FAI was statutorily insolvent by what Justice Owen called a 'significant margin'. After significant pressure by the relevant regulator FAI made a capital raising and, for a short time anyway, resumed what looked like solvent trading.

(The general insurance company had a statutory deficiency of $631 million in 1993, reducing that to a $127 million deficiency in 1995 and a marginal surplus in 1996.)

CHAPTER 3

RAY'S WAY

INSURANCE COMPANIES DON'T just appear. Back in the dim dark days, groups of people started 'mutuals', initially at Lloyd's and then in more conventional form such as General Accident in Perth, Scotland, which has always been touted as the world's first general insurance company. CE Heath International Holdings Ltd, as HIH was first known, was something of a bastard child.

It wasn't a mutual and it had been around in various guises in Australia since 1968, but its English parent and vendor, CE Heath plc, only floated it to reduce its own risk. Most companies join the share market lists in Australia for that reason, but most companies are not insurers whose very purpose is to accept and manage risk.

What wasn't writ large in the prospectus in 1992 was that the company was floated in Australia because the parent in the UK, CE Heath plc, didn't actually want to own an insurance company in Australia. At all.

It kept 44 per cent, certainly, but the Australian company's origins were inauspicious all the same. People close to the company back then say that CE Heath plc in the UK was looking to obtain a low-risk profile because it had been merely an insurance broker, and its global tentacles were making the market nervous.

In short order the parent disposed of a reinsurance arm in Bermuda — where such companies are traditionally based for tax reasons — and something over half its Australian business, so that insurance analysts in the UK would stop rating it as a high-risk enterprise. That part of it worked, and the share price of CE Heath plc in the UK started moving up in response.

To be fair to the new company's chief executive Ray Williams, he had all of the best intentions in listing the Australian business. First of all, he had been involved in insurance in Australia and the UK for years but he clearly wanted to grow Heath in Australia and his speciality, workers' compensation, was profitable at that stage. CE Heath had had a varied relationship with its Australian offshoot, having reportedly had to inject about $100 million into it in the mid–1980s, although the company was trading profitably in the lead-up to its Australian float in 1992.

Ray Williams had often said he wanted to build a strong Australian general insurance company and his connections and experience appeared to be a major plus. The company raised $108 million in a float handled by Ord Minnett Ltd and, although $40 million of that went to pay a bank loan and $17.8 million went to pay off intercompany debt, it put the respectable total of $45.2 million at the disposal of management to grow the business. So far so good. It wasn't a huge bankroll by international standards but if the company stuck to its knitting it would grow steadily if carefully managed.

Ray Williams looked the part. Square jawed, silver haired and with a knuckle-popping handshake, he liked to hear it said that he had forgotten more about insurance than most people in Australia would ever learn. He had been in the business since 1957, mostly in the area of workers' compensation in Australia, after joining the Sydney Water Board as a clerk at the age of fifteen. Williams had discovered he was good at establishing a rapport with the many European migrants who worked for the board and who were injured in the course of their work. His loyalty at that stage of his life was clearly with the underdog, and in a statement to the Royal Commission he said he remembered how much more quickly one man recovered from a serious work injury after Williams bought him a bird in a cage. 'By chance, following the purchase of a small bird for one such lonely injured worker, I saw an instant improvement in his demeanour and subsequent recovery,' he said, adding that he then took the same initiative many times over the years thereafter. For a man with a tough exterior, Williams was not averse to being a big softy.

33

He had not had a golden start in life, being brought up in the modest north-western Sydney suburb of Epping, but his low Anglican background set him on a philanthropic course, which he believes he has maintained. There was much evidence at the Royal Commission of how absurdly generous he was to his staff, and how he played favourites, but that was an extension of that earlier view about the benefits of looking after people.

But there was another side to his personality, the insecurity-driven relentless drive to succeed, which meant that when he bought his second Rolls-Royce, he greeted the question of how much it cost with the answer: 'If you need to know what it cost, you shouldn't be buying a Rolls-Royce.'

The two sides of his personality came together most obviously in the area of charitable donations, where Williams not only spent his own money but lavished big amounts of HIH's money on projects of his own choosing, mostly medical research.

In the year 2000 HIH gave more than $5 million to charity — the board only found out afterwards where the money had gone — at a time when the company was beginning to have difficulty paying out on claims. There was nothing controversial about the charities, mostly research organisations such as the Garvan Institute, but there was a growing perception that while it was mostly HIH's money being spent, it was mostly Ray Williams getting the kudos for spending it. He even received an honorary doctorate from Monash University in Melbourne and insisted on being called 'Dr Williams'. While he revelled in his new title, Williams did not permit his staff to include genuine academic qualifications on their business cards!

HIH had put $2.23 million in 2000 alone into Monash University and its Institute of Reproduction in 2000, without any personal contribution from Williams, while the Ray Williams Institute of Endocrinology and Metabolism at the University of New South Wales only ever received donations from HIH and not Williams himself.

He was also awarded an AM, membership of the Order of Australia, in 1998 although he was not quite as obvious in mentioning it as his nemesis, Rodney Adler, was in mentioning his at every opportunity. Adler got his in 1999.

Williams' medal was clearly connected to donations that HIH had made to the Liberal Party, since its citation noted his support for the Free

Enterprise Foundation, a trust entity which funnels money directly to the Liberal Party. HIH was never one of those organisations which made equal donations to both sides of politics.

Back in the 1960s in Sydney Ray Williams was just plain ordinary Ray, but had a lot of drive and ambition, and the ability to make friends at many levels. One of those was English insurance underwriter Michael Payne, who by his own admission was one of the most successful underwriters that Lloyd's had ever had in the area of public liability insurance.

Payne, who was made a director of the company that listed in Australia, had met Williams in 1964 on one of his regular visits and liked him. Together they set up in 1968 MW Payne Liability Agencies in Melbourne, one of the first insurance companies in the world that was supported by Lloyd's but was outside the UK. Payne had convinced the traditionalists in London that even upstarts in the colonies were as good at paying their debts as gentlemen in the City of London, and at the third attempt was able to persuade Lloyd's to issue a document called Lloyd's binding authority, which would allow the company to underwrite workers' compensation insurance in Australia. They borrowed $20,000 from Hugh Stenhouse, a Scottish insurance broker friend of Michael Payne's whose organisation is now part of the Aon group, and they got a business up and going in Queen Steet, Melbourne, that offered workers' comp and public products liability insurance, via a second binding authority.

It was an unusual way to start up an insurance operation in Australia, but it worked. The binding authorities allowed the small company to play in a bigger league, and were in due course replaced by reinsurance out of London via the same Lloyd's underwriters. Indeed Lloyd's was so impressed that several people came out to Australia looking to set up a bigger operation on behalf of Lloyd's, but it didn't happen. There was already a network of insurance brokers in Australia that used Lloyd's and they jacked up at the threat to their margins. Ray Williams put it more politely in his statement to the HIH Royal Commission, stating that 'they held a fairly unique position in the Australian market which they used to their advantage in placing business into London'.

The biggest headache that Payne and Williams had in the 1970s was their own success. State governments in Australia became interested in the 1970s and 1980s in setting up their own workers' compensation schemes. As the States moved towards creating their own schemes they 'lifted the bar' regularly for insurers already participating, and in 1974 CE Heath in the UK put up capital for Payne and Williams' business to allow it to renew a licence to underwrite workers' comp in Victoria. Not surprisingly, it took the Heath name and called itself CE Heath Underwriting and Insurance (Australia) Proprietary Limited.

New South Wales was the first State to bring in its own scheme, in 1977, with John Cain's Labor government in Victoria following in September 1985. South Australia followed not long afterwards and in Williams' words, 70 per cent of the company's business disappeared in the space of nine months.

That is not quite correct. In fact the existing insurers were kept on as managers of the State workers' comp businesses while the States took the risk. While there was a cap on how much the companies could earn, they had all the downside taken out of the equation. It meant there was no room for expansion but it did give the companies a safe earnings base.

So to enlarge the business the company had to diversify into other areas such as professional indemnity and public liability (PI and PL), two areas that were to end up affecting the company's fortunes in different ways. While PI was more of a disaster for companies that got involved in US business, such as FAI Insurance, PL was a category that HIH ended up dominating in Australia, with more than half the market by the time the company collapsed in 2001. Unfortunately, it had underpriced its premiums for so long that it left a huge gap, which is why so many public events in Australia have had to be cancelled since the collapse.

A restructure of the parent company, CE Heath, in 1987 cut off London as a source of capital for the Australian operation and in the late 1980s there were three serious attempts to sell it or have it taken over. The share market crash of October 1987 ruled out one bid by the Battery Group, a Melbourne-based company controlled by cardboard box manufacturer Richard Pratt, and the Belgian group Fortis came close in that year before its board backed away from CE Heath because of what Williams called 'global aversion to the professional indemnity business'.

Professional indemnity is all about accountants and lawyers insuring themselves against being sued for areas such as negligence and incompetence, and in fact the Fortis board was very prescient about the risk. CE Heath was very small in that area in Australia at that time but Rodney Adler's FAI Insurance took on some reinsurance risks from US professional indemnity policies at about that time that ended up being responsible for a 'hole' of more than $125 million in FAI's reserves when HIH took it over in 1998.

In fact FAI even looked at buying CE Heath's Australian operation in 1989, within a year of FAI founder Larry Adler dying and Rodney Adler taking over. The deal didn't happen because the UK company wanted more than Adler wanted to pay, but it may have sown a seed in Ray Williams' mind that led to his ill-considered and ultimately disastrous bid for FAI nine years later. His attitude would not have improved when FAI made another approach in 1993 and Adler volunteered to run the merged company.

The public float of CE Heath in Australia in 1992 was a prize example of Murphy's Law: If Anything Can Go Wrong, It Will.

Williams had to talk down a minor investor revolt that was accidentally caused by Nick Selvaratnam, an insurance analyst at BZW Australia, a broker owned by Barclays in London. A former Deloitte's auditor in Australia and the UK with experience in the arcane world of insurance, he had written a report suggesting that a 'fair' price for CE Heath shares would be between 70c and a dollar. This was before Ord Minnett floated the company and named a price of $1.50 per share.

Selvaratnam, who is the personification of civility, was the first person to be mortified by the obvious clash of views. He had visited CE Heath's senior available executive, finance director Terry Cassidy, with a copy of his twenty-page report before the Ord Minnett float process began and they had a constructive and lively debate, but agreed to differ.

'It was never my intention to say that HIH was going to go bust,' Selvaratnam admits now. 'I saw as many positives as negatives in the company being floated, but it simply turned out that on a risk-reward basis I couldn't get a valuation above a dollar.'

He was all for circulating the report widely but he had been specifically asked by a number of institutional investors to do it, so those eleven 'sponsors' got first look at the report. His bosses, Tim Crammond and Steve Crane at BZW, reminded him of that fact and the report stayed in narrow circulation. This was long before the current share market disclosure regime in which companies may not supply sensitive information to selected analysts but have to disseminate it as widely as possible.

But while Ray Williams was off in London getting a roadshow under way, the initial enthusiasm for the float among potential investors in early

1992 was looking more fragile by the minute. David Williams, the Ord Minnett director responsible for the float, remembers the effect of Selvaratnam's report. 'The issue was originally very keenly sought and was going to walk out of the door at $1.50,' he said. 'But after Nick's report came out, buyer enthusiasm evaporated to a major extent and an overseas roadshow to London did not get much extra support.'

Selvaratnam's report merely highlighted the fact that the company had focused on 'long tail' business, as well as seeking new business at such an aggressive rate that it was hard to assess its profitability. Selvaratnam knew that however good Heath was at workers' compensation insurance, and Ray Williams was the acknowledged master in Australia, it was what is called classic long-tail business. And it was now being taken over by the States.

Most domestic insurance like car and house lasts a year, claim or no claim, but workers' comp claims can take years before they are even made, and even longer before a decision is made on paying out. They are all about bad backs, repetitive strain injury and, worst, asbestos. Leaving the latter aside (and the whole asbestos story is still hanging over the global insurance industry like an incubus), Heath was attracting Selvaratnam's suspicions on a purely financial basis.

He believed that Heath had been building up its business with an eye more to premium income than eventual claims, a claim later backed by Wayne Martin of the HIH Royal Commission.

Heath had bought a small workers' compensation business in California in 1987 and wrote $10 million of business that year, and by 1992 it was taking $100 million in premiums. But Californian claims jumped sharply in 1991 and Heath made an underwriting loss of $11.1 million that year, compared with a loss of $3.29 million the year before, and profits in the three years starting in 1987. Even the HIH prospectus conceded of California that 'slower growth in premium and underwriting surplus is projected due to recent inadequate minimum rate increases and difficult economic conditions'.

This was not the stuff of instant riches.

(HIH actually went well in California for two years and sold out for a good profit, but then went back in 1995 and was taken to the cleaners because the Californian State legislature had changed the rules and put a cap on premiums while allowing doctors more leeway in helping to assess claims.) The effect on the float of Selvaratnam's polite scepticism, which invited a second look at the projected numbers, was dire. For a brief moment it looked as though the float might not get up.

David Williams and his colleague David Ballhausen had to put the proposal to the underwriting committee at Ord Minnett and, once it became clear that CE Heath directors were prepared to put some of their own money up, it was decided that one more push would get the float across the line.

There are now around 5.3 billion reasons (the estimated deficiency in Australian dollars) why it would have been an inspired idea for everyone to 'walk' at that stage, but Ray Williams in particular was not a man to tap the mat. He was 55 years old, he had been in the insurance industry for 40 years and this float was his baby.

He walked into the underwriters' group and announced: 'I'll put another brick on the chimney.' He already had a number of shares but he personally sub-underwrote some 6.3 million shares in the issue for a fee of 3.5 per cent.

Sub-underwriting is a critical role in a float: by doing so, you are saying 'If no one else buys these shares, I will.' No one else did and he found himself asking CE Heath's house investment bank in London, Hambros, for a $10 million loan. Terry Cassidy, a long-term friend of Ray Williams and the head of CE Heath in Australia, also sub-underwrote some stock. Ord Minnett also took some more risk in sub-underwriting some stock.

It was a brave call, since the shares listed at $1.50 but subsequently slumped to $1 and it took another three years before they definitively broke up through their issue price.

Was Ray happy? He made it known that he was mightily displeased with Selvaratnam and had him permanently banned from any contact with HIH, a problem since HIH was at the time one of the fastest growing insurers in Australia.

He told Wayne Martin, QC, counsel assisting the commission, that he did indeed have a blacklist of analysts he 'didn't particularly like'.

'It's well known, your honour, Nick Selvaratnam was one such broker and the background is when we were floating the company, Nick Selvaratnam wrote a report that was not very favourable. He's entitled to do that. What concerned me was that he wrote that report without any reference to the company, without any discussions with the company and he went and published it … and spoke to fund managers and then subsequently tried to come and talk to us to justify what he had written,' he told the commission.

Selvaratnam believes that when Ray Williams found out about the report he 'hit the roof' and that the mild-mannered Terry Cassidy may have decided not to explain to him that Selvaratnam had indeed referred to the company before publication.

Ray Williams has always had a tendency to see clear distinctions and while HIH was alive, he divided the world into two clear camps: those who believed that HIH was headed for global success, and everybody else. If Terry Cassidy had told Ray Williams that he had sat down with a doubting analyst and decided to 'agree to disagree' about HIH's value, he would have removed himself permanently from the optimistic 'stars' camp, to which the only alternative in Ray Williams' eyes was outer darkness.

A few months after he had been banned, Selvaratnam received an invitation from a public relations firm to an analysts' briefing and he thought that the wind had changed. But a few minutes later he got a frantic phone call to explain that there had been an error and could he please un-invite himself. That should have been that, you might have thought, but there was a strange and vindictive sequel when the analyst moved from BZW to Credit Suisse First Boston in 1997, five years later.

On arrival at CSFB he found himself having welcome drinks with all the major players there including Kent Wilson, head of research, and chief executive David Trude. Wilson took him quietly aside and asked, 'What's with you and Ray Williams?' Selvaratnam laughed uneasily, assuming that an out-of-date, five-year-old rumour had just resurfaced.

But Wilson told him that Ray Williams had personally telephoned him just days before and told him that if CSFB hired Nick Selvaratnam, he would withdraw all of HIH's business from CSFB immediately.

Despite the threat, the CSFB executives stood behind their new hiring and in fact CSFB was hired by Swiss group Winterthur Insurance in 1998 to help dispose of a 51 per cent stake in HIH which the Swiss company had optimistically acquired in 1995. There was much contact between HIH staff and the research department at CSFB, where Selvaratnam's colleagues officially took all the phone calls from HIH, and life carried on as though nothing had happened.

In his April 2003 report Justice Owen specifically recommended that the Australian Stock Exchange tighten its listing rules to prohibit blacklisting.

'Discrimination against individuals who do not "toe the line" has the tendency to undermine the integrity of the briefing process,' he wrote.

If Ray Williams can play hardball with analysts, he can play schmooze. Once the company's share price turned around and began climbing, he got many analysts 'onside' and sold the idea of HIH being a fast moving, globally acquisitive and dynamic insurer. It was all of those things, even if the fragile artifice of its rapid expansion concealed a perennial lack of financial reserves.

David Williams, the unrelated namesake who was more responsible than most people for bringing HIH to life as a public company in 1992, paints a picture which suggests the float caused Ray Williams to change the way he operated the company, from 'aggressive' to 'more aggressive'.

'Aggressive provisioning' is the accounting term for excessive optimism on the part of insurers. In insurance there is a simple inverse relationship between profits and provisions for future claims.

'We can see now that they were always aggressive in their provisioning but that after the float it got worse. It's an interesting issue but it may be that competition issues among insurers listed on the share market made them behave in that way,' he said. 'But while people questioned the provisioning, it was all signed off by actuaries and certainly at that stage there was the belief that if something was signed off by an actuary, there's been some science involved.'

Which brings us to another complication. Calculating the reserves that an insurer is going to need in future is the job of the actuary. No one ever expects the actuary to get it exactly right but over time a good actuary should overestimate reserves as often as he or she underestimates them. That means that over the long haul, the company's reserves are adequate and if there is 'claims deterioration' in one year — the claims are more than the allocated reserves — then it must be fixed straightaway by moving funds from profit to reserves. And you would like to think that after such an experience, the actuary would re-examine the future calculations to make sure next year's earmarked reserves were going to be enough. At the simplest level, that equalisation exercise is called the '50 per cent level of probability', on the basis that the good actuary is as likely to be 'over' as 'under'.

Most good insurance companies have long used prudential margins or 'cushions', which would allow them to say there was a 70 per cent level of probability that the reserves were adequate.

HIH did not use them, nor indeed did Rodney Adler's FAI, which it took over in 1998.

In the film *Wall Street*, Michael Douglas' predatory character Gordon Gekko memorably observed that 'lunch is for wimps'. Ray Williams took the same view on prudential margins, arguing that they were an excuse for his claims officers to put their feet up on the desk.

Wayne Martin, QC, got him going on the subject at the Royal Commission. After taking Williams through the effects of HIH's inadequate reserves in the late 1990s, he asked: 'In the context of these disastrous years, did you ever give consideration to introducing a prudential margin?'

Williams was ready for the question. 'I supposed we'd get on to prudential margins at some stage. The greatest smoothing technique of all, prudential margins. I mean, my aim is to find figures that I think are realistic and achievable with the book of business.'

'One of the worst problems with prudential margins is their smoothing capacity, you are not really looking at what the true claims are, you are just building in a figure that next year you can take a bit out of and make out it's all very nice and everything is going well when in fact it isn't,' he said, in one of the longest sentences used by anyone in evidence at the commission, with the probable exception of Rodney Adler.

'I personally want to know what the actual claims are so I can have my people, my claims people, working their insides out to really settle those claims at that level.

'I don't want people putting in prudential margins that allow them to put their feet up on the table and say, "It doesn't matter if we have got to pay another $100 million," he told the commission.

Singling out the claims officers is another part of the jigsaw of what goes on inside Williams' head: that was his way of noting that there are two ways to get future claims right, only one being actuarial prediction. The other is to keep a close eye on policyholders' claims and only pay out when you absolutely have to.

Kevin Troy, a veteran director of Ord Minnett at the time of the float, spotted that in Ray Williams and reportedly noted to him: 'Ray, I wouldn't mind being one of your shareholders but I wouldn't like to be one of your policyholders.'

In fact, as everyone involved now knows, both categories suffered horribly and, while the federal government in Australia took steps after the collapse of HIH to safeguard policyholders by setting up an emergency relief fund, ordinary shareholders were reminded of where ordinary shares rank in the order of preference among creditors of a failed business: stone motherless last.

The federal government has now made it mandatory for insurance companies to maintain prudential margins at the 75 per cent probability level, along with several other measures that make it much harder to run an under-reserved insurer. Unfortunately those measures only came into operation after the collapse of HIH, with much press commentary in July 2002 being based on the stable door and the bolting horse.

It subsequently emerged that Ray Williams had been a major lobbyist against a change in the rules, as deputy chairman of the Insurance Council of Australia (ICA). The ICA is like any industry body, a lobby group of its own, and although the ICA has now fallen emphatically into line with the new rules, it was not ever thus.

Sources inside APRA, the much-maligned insurance regulator, indicate that Williams' campaign delayed by around nine months the introduction of the tighter standards on provisioning. That suggests they could have come into existence in September 2001. In retrospect that still would not have saved HIH, which fell over in March 2001, but it was a reminder that Ray Williams was a man who would do everything in his power to keep his insurance company afloat, even if by any conventional measure it was dying.

Justice Neville Owen's natural politeness and civility are apparent in most of his 1500-page report but there is a clear note of anger in his description of the personal consequences of HIH's collapse for what is already more than 10,000 affected policyholders. Page xiv of his very good introductory essay, 'The Failure of HIH: A Critical Assessment', includes this under the heading 'A Far Reaching Calamity':

A 50-year-old school principal who had contributed a portion of his weekly earnings to an income protection insurance policy developed a brain tumour in 1996. Unable to work, he and his family survived on the monthly cheques that came from HIH under the policy. In February 2001 the monthly cheque was dishonoured on presentation; his policy is now worthless. His spouse was forced to approach Centrelink in an effort to obtain a disability support pension.

About 200 permanently disabled people no longer receive their regular payments from HIH. These people have joined other unsecured creditors and policyholders, and they all face a wait of up to 10 years before receiving what the liquidator has predicted will be a 'very poor' payment.

Retirees who invested their superannuation or life savings in HIH shares to fund their retirement have been left with nothing. A person who owned a small business and was insured with HIH became embroiled in a legal dispute. Just weeks before its liquidation, HIH encouraged him to settle the claim out of court for $90,000. The subsequent collapse of the insurer left the business owner liable for the payout.

Thousands of holders of professional indemnity, public liability, home warranty and travel insurance policies have found themselves uninsured for claims made by or against them. A family whose HIH-insured home was destroyed in a fire was forced to live in the burnt shell of the house after HIH defaulted on their caravan rental payments.

As with most corporate collapses, the employees of HIH were also dealt a bitter blow: one morning in March 2001 about 1000 of them woke to find themselves unemployed; hundreds of others lost their jobs in the ensuing months.

Some of those people will by now have received compensation under the government funded HIH Claims Support Scheme, however that scheme was necessarily limited in scope and operation.

He noted that by the end of February 2003 the federal government had paid out $195 million through the scheme and that 11,400 applications had been made for help, of which 5850 had been approved. By the end of April that had risen to $221.3 million.

'The full cost of the scheme is yet to be determined,' he concluded.

CHAPTER 4

THE LURE OF LLOYD'S

HIH WAS FLOATED in Australia in 1992 under its original name CE Heath, at a time when its backers believed its appearance would coincide with the whole global insurance business heading for a purple patch. History shows that as with most ventures the company made, optimistic guesswork by Ray Williams trumped any amount of advice or careful planning sent his way. Just one example of the miscalculation was that the biggest insurance market in the world, Lloyd's of London, imploded within a year of Heath listing.

Instead of climbing steadily from the $1.50 listing price, CE Heath stock suffered initially from the pre-float exodus of support and then from the slew of bad news from Lloyd's, even though at that stage Heath was not yet involved in the London market.

The share price ended up taking eighteen months to break back up through the $1.50 level, despite Ray Williams' careful squiring of insurance analysts in Australia. Meanwhile, in London, the Lloyd's market blew up and forced the share price down towards $1, mainly because 1993 produced the biggest financial disaster that the UK insurance market had ever known.

In simple terms the market lost a total of £8 billion (over $20 billion Australian) between 1993 and 1998 in the worst five-year period it ever had.

The losses were caused by a combination of asbestos and pollution risks, plus a series of systemic problems inside Lloyd's that meant that instead of risks being spread across as many investors as possible, professional underwriters were off-loading as much risk as they could onto the amateurs who had become the mainstay of the market since the innovations of Cuthbert Eden Heath, or CE Heath, almost a century before.

Some 20,000 individual 'Names' were either ruined or had their personal assets badly reduced by the collapse, which had followed two decades of comfort and prosperity. Although most Names were in the UK, a recruiting drive in the 1970s and 1980s by Lloyd's managing agents in countries like Australia had brought in a number of Names such as former Prime Minister Malcolm Fraser. Fraser, whose family had owned the sheep station 'Nareen' in Victoria's Western Districts for most of a century, was forced to sell it in 1997 for around $3.8 million to Gordon Dickinson, a Western Districts neighbour who also happened to be chief executive of investment bank UBS Warburg . . . and was not a Lloyd's Name.

Fraser, who was Prime Minister of Australia from 1975 to 1983, confessed to *The Australian* newspaper in 1996 that he had had some 'traumatic' experiences at Lloyd's. He was one of 812 Lloyd's Names in Australia in 1992, of whom the worst hit 179 were believed to have an average liability of $405,000 each.

Lloyd's worked then on the basis of having a wide net of prosperous individuals who expected regular annual dividends in exchange for pledging their assets, often rural landholdings. Farm ownership may be many people's dream but it is seldom a big earner, so the 3 per cent or so in annual dividends from Lloyd's used to be a welcome addition to similar levels of return from landholding. Few Names paused to consider that in pledging their assets, they were writing a blank cheque not only for all that they owned but 'unlimited liability' thereafter. In 1993 those Names — 15,000 of them in the UK alone — found that instead of getting a cheque for some 3 per cent of their assets, they were being asked for a cheque for some 20 per cent of them. In the worst hit syndicates, some were being asked for half their assets.

There was also a strong suspicion that Australian Names were brought into Lloyd's late in the 'good' cycle to take up the risks that others closer to the action wanted to avoid. There were four Lloyd's Names in Australia in 1975, 284 in 1984, and 660 in 1991, an exponential growth at the butt end of a twenty-year purple patch. In a painful echo of our casualty rate in the First World War, Australian Names lost more per person than almost any other nationality when Lloyd's melted down in 1993, because they were brought in to take the excessive risks. One apt name for the high-risk syndicates they were parked in was 'dustbin' syndicates.

It was a painful fate for Lloyd's, the byword for honest dealing and an organisation whose motto is '*uberrime fides*' or 'with the utmost good faith'. And by association, for CE Heath plc.

(Cuthbert Eden Heath, born in 1859, was the doyen of the global insurance industry in the late nineteenth century. He invented many of the forms of insurance we know today and was a pioneer in the field of underwriting.)

The near-collapse of Lloyd's in 1993 was as much caused by the greed and laziness on the part of professional underwriters as it was by the ignorance and either bad luck or bad timing on the part of the amateur Names involved.

Asbestos, the sleeping killer that takes fifteen years to manifest its terrible effects on human lungs, was a big part of the problem at Lloyd's. A huge blowout in asbestos compensation claims that started in the 1970s and is still going today took most of Lloyd's by surprise, and served to lay bare the systemic problems at Lloyd's that twenty years of comfortable dividends had buried nicely.

Not only did asbestos have a deadly effect on miners but, being used to lag pipes on ships and to help fireproof buildings, it took a horrible toll among shipbuilding and office construction workers.

Not every investor at Lloyd's was taken by surprise. A number of professional underwriters who joined a Lloyd's group in 1980 called the Asbestos Working Party were alleged to have been among the first to take out reinsurance policies that off-loaded their asbestos risk onto other insurance syndicates at Lloyd's which did not have that information. A 21st-century share market observer would call that a classic insider trade, but Lloyd's still likes to believe that you can overcome inherent conflicts of interest by behaving honourably.

There was another problem besides asbestos that gave Lloyd's a very bad name in the late 1980s and early 1990s: the LMX (London Market Excess) spiral. Because Lloyd's syndicates tended only ever to seek reinsurance with other syndicates, risks on some of the broadest policies started to go round in circles, which was the very opposite of Cuthbert Heath's theory about spreading the risk from the shoulders of the few to the shoulders of the many.

One hurricane in Florida had a damage bill of around $US20 billion but the actual payouts within Lloyd's came to $US60 billion, a situation as complicated as it was unnecessary.

The big financial regulatory shakeup in the early 1990s in the UK which created bodies such as DTI, the Department of Trade and Industry, and FSA, the Financial Services Authority, ended up bypassing Lloyd's thanks to some nimble lobbying. While other industries such as stockbroking and financial planning were forced to increase transparency and eliminate favouritism and conflicts of interest, Lloyd's was able to convince the authorities in the UK, particularly the Conservative government of John Major, that it was a special case. Lloyd's promised self-regulation and was left alone. Given the thrashing the insurance market had just had, it wasn't hard to convince the Tory government that the boat did not need any more rocking, if London was to stay the centre of the world's insurance industry. Most Lloyd's Names were and are dyed-in-the-wool Tories and, pain or not, they were not going to yell as long as they felt something was being done.

The biggest change was that in the reorganisations after the 1993 disaster, Lloyd's admitted corporate investment capital for the very first time, which would in 1998 enable HIH to buy directly into six Lloyd's syndicates. HIH paid £14 million to buy control of the Cotesworth Group. HIH liquidator Tony McGrath noted in early 2003 that he was still concerned at the rise in outstanding claims. His London colleague Richard Wilkinson reported that Cotesworth's liabilities had grown by more than $400 million since the HIH collapse and up to December 2002, because reinsurers were reluctant to pay out.

HIH's messy, ill-considered and ultimately disastrous charge into Lloyd's started in late 1992 when Michael Payne, Ray Willams' oldest friend in London, wrote him a letter not long after the HIH float noting that he had just retired and was looking for something to do, a clear hint that he would love to do something for HIH in the London market. Payne had been running a syndicate at Lloyd's which had not made a loss in twenty years, and at one stage not long before, he had been underwriting about 25 per cent of the public liability insurance written in Australia ... out of London. And here he was now offering to start a London operation for an aggressive Australian-based insurer.

Ray Williams agreed without consulting anyone, and in early 1993 the newly listed company started HIH UK from a small office in Gracechurch Street in the City, under Michael Payne.

What neither insurance veteran knew was that far from climbing out of an earnings hole, the UK insurance market was to have a brief recovery in 1994 and 1995 followed by another 1993-style shocker, by which time HIH was fully committed in the UK market. And almost none of the business that HIH UK was writing was what Payne was good at, which was workers' compensation, public liability and professional indemnity.

The branch in fact made profits for its first three years and then chose to expand at a rate described by HIH internal auditor Greg Waters as 'explosive' from 1996 onwards at exactly the time when insurance premiums were sagging back down again and payouts were rocketing.

It didn't even have an easy start. So instead of easing nicely into a rising UK market while all the locals were still picking themselves up from an earlier shellacking, HIH UK found itself a lot more like a poor relation scrambling for business in a complex market where the last person in is the bunny.

HIH had to chase premium income from a wider and wider variety of policies, which notably included insuring members of the Taiwanese armed forces against personal injury and indemnifying the owners of Real Madrid soccer club against their winning the European Cup in case they had to pay bonuses to players. That is called contingency insurance and is one step up the intellectual food chain from bookmaking.

HIH appears to have lost almost $500,000 when Real Madrid won the European Cup in May 1998, although the company made a small profit when France made the final of the World Cup in Paris.

As with bookies, they were betting against events happening. Evidently the company stood to make £75,000 if France had not made it to the final.

Executive Peter Thompson of HIH was asked by the Royal Commission if HIH should have been dealing in such risks. 'Well, I think it's got very little to do with underwriting, personally,' he replied.

HIH's Contingency and Weather department, which had also been responsible for a disastrous foray into film-financing insurance, was wound up not long afterwards. HIH's dalliance with insuring film producers, which began in 1997, was almost certainly the worst performer of its diverse activities. It spent at least six months in 1997–98 letting HIH UK's own underwriter, Steve Mitchell, insure Hollywood film producers against financial loss without knowing anything about the films being insured.

In simple terms, the insurance was effectively a gamble by insurance companies taking on credit risk that was normally held by bankers and financiers, about ventures whose prospects of success were almost impossible to predict. Premiums per film were about 10 per cent of possible payouts despite the fact that about two out of three films never make any money for their backers.

And while HIH UK was charging headlong into this new Eldorado under the light control of Michael Payne, its South Australian office was pretending to offer the same cover to producers without knowing anything about the films because HIH had been offered a 10 per cent commission by Australian-listed reinsurer ReAc to 'front' for it. Reinsurers have no licence to offer insurance directly so they have to use a conventional insurer in such cases, except that in this case there was more than one problem. One, HIH's internal rules did not allow 'fronting' without the specific permission of the HIH management, and the other was that ReAc went into run-off even before HIH collapsed and may not be able to pay all its claims, which are believed to be more than $65 million. ReAc, the company that used to boast it was the only company listed in Australia that had none of its earnings in Australian dollars, ended up having modest earnings in any currency and was the company that was supposed to be taking all the risk.

One of the most poignant day's evidence to the Royal Commission came on 10 July from Ian Small, a former rural insurance expert with a strong knowledge of horses who now styles himself a primary producer.

Small, who managed HIH's contingencies division in Adelaide, was shown film insurance contracts carrying his signature and admitted very early on that 'I have to say I probably did sign things that I didn't truly understand.' That would not make him unique in HIH, although admitting it might do so.

'I'm an old-fashioned insurer, I don't believe in writing any class of business that you don't have some knowledge of,' he said.

The business was referred to Adelaide by HIH's manager international, George Sturesteps, who like Mr Small has a better knowledge of horseflesh than the movie business. Mr Sturesteps got a bumpy ride from the commission about the fact that he, the first employee Ray Williams ever took on, had broken HIH's house underwriting guidelines.

Just to reinforce the notion that HIH was a benevolent simpleton operating in an alien environment, it turned out in evidence that ICE

Media, the company which assessed how much risk insurers were taking, was owned by Graham Bradstreet, the same man who owned the company that started borrowing the film funds in the first place.

Most of the films were hardly household names. As Justice Neville Owen put it, 'I don't know where I've been for the last few years but I don't think I've heard of any of those films.'

He was not alone. For every *The People vs Larry Flynt* and *The Truman Show*, both of which HIH had some involvement with, there were four or five with names like *Letter From a Killer* that appear to have made a very quick transition from commercial release to video.

The business appears to have originated via the broking arm of CE Heath, the UK company, which in 1995 took HIH into what it called 'gap cover' for a slate of films produced by Mike Medavoy at Phoenix Pictures in the US, including the Flynt title and *The Mirror has Two Faces*. They were the good ones.

More characteristic is a $62 million payout that HIH found itself making to a UK production house called Flashpoint to cover a number of films which made no money. The reason was simple enough — the films were never completed — and the $62 million payout is one of a myriad that HIH is still in legal action trying to recover. Because there are reinsurers involved as well, and reinsurers hate having to pay out when they know there won't be any repeat business in the future, this may all take some time.

Exactly how much HIH blew on film financing is still being worked out, not least because some of the cover lasts for years after the films are made. Backers do not know how much money a film has made or lost until all the video rights and other sequential payments have been worked out.

Simon White, a barrister assisting the commission, said that of the London business alone, HIH had taken on some $US185.5 million worth of risk before the underwriter moved on to another job where his skills might be better appreciated, as his reference put it. And there was still some $A65 million outstanding, he added.

If an insurer is chasing business in a market where premiums are slumping, they have to accept more and more risk. Giving his evidence to the Royal Commission, Michael Payne conceded that the strategy was a disaster. He disputed a claim by Wayne Martin, QC, that the office had lost $500 million in less than ten years, but he was excluding the

Cotesworth business, which may end up losing $1 billion for HIH on its own. He admitted the office suffered from errors he made, plus an international downturn, poor management and internal controls, personality differences and careless underwriting in areas where he lacked expertise. All it lacked was a plague of frogs. HIH UK even had hurricanes and floods aplenty, none of them in London and all seemingly more expensive than the last.

Tom Riddell, an Australian auditor who has become one of the best known liquidators of insurance companies in the UK, was given HIH UK to untangle in 2001 and worked out that between the time the branch started in 1993 and closed down in 1999 by being put into what insurers call run-off, it paid out about 130 per cent of its premiums.

Asked by the HIH Royal Commission which parts of the business had gone badly, he simplified his answer by discovering that only 6 per cent of the business actually went consistently well: the non-marine liability class. Unfortunately it was small beer, with premiums of £16.2 million in six years and payouts over the same period of £11.9 million, a gross gain of £4.4 million.

In insurance, as with most endeavours, success has a thousand fathers and failure is an orphan.

The numbers on the 'bad' business are infinitely woollier, in many cases because there is a long-tail risk that may well still be current, but Mr Riddell produced the best estimate yet seen on exactly how big the hole was that HIH dug for itself in the UK. He said that the UK operation was split in two, one side being the HIH UK operation started by Michael Payne and the other the Cotesworth Lloyd's syndicates that HIH bought into in 1998.

With almost uncanny bad timing, HIH bought into some of Lloyd's most successful syndicates just in time to suffer some of the worst losses ever recorded. Syndicate 535, which in earlier years had had Lloyd's Names clambering over themselves to get a piece of the action, reportedly made Lloyd's biggest-ever loss at that time.

By 1999 HIH had secured more than 65 per cent of it, after incidentally bidding against no less than four HIH directors for capacity on it in 1999. Ray Williams, Michael Payne, Bob Stitt, QC, and chairman Geoffrey Cohen were all Lloyd's Names (and all suffered grievously for it). Payne, who knew a lot more about Lloyd's than he did about HIH, told the Royal Commission that 'the price wasn't influenced by the purchases that I or any other director made' but like so many things that happened at HIH, it looked absolutely horrible.

While Lloyd's handles only about 3 per cent of overall general insurance worldwide, it has specialities in which it has a much stronger global market share. Almost 40 per cent of aviation premiums and more than 60 per cent of offshore gas and oil rig premiums go through Lloyd's, while more than 70 per cent of marine protection and indemnity premiums still go through Lloyd's.

Riddell reported in mid-2002 that although HIH UK believed it had net liabilities shortly before the company collapsed of $308 million, his firm KPMG believed the number was about $560 million.

Of the Cotesworth side he said that HIH (Cotesworth) believed it owed a net $208 million, while his firm concluded that even if all reinsurance was recovered in full, and it seldom is for reasons already shown, the real deficiency was more like $577 million. Which means that KPMG believes that HIH still owes more than $1.1 billion on its UK operations alone. That is $183 million for every year it operated, considerably more than the company was reporting in overall profit, or $15 million a month.

'It is a fair conclusion that the quality of underwriting by the UK branch was poor' was Riddell's laconic conclusion. One had only to recall the UK office's inexplicable decision in 1997 to offer personal accident cover to more than 100,000 members of the Taiwanese armed forces for a premium of £560,000 a year, to realise the accuracy of Riddell's summation.

No one could quite tell the HIH Royal Commission whose idea this was, particularly as there was a house ban in 1997, deleted in 1998, on offering such cover to people in the armed forces. The final payout was not revealed but the list of claims that came in suggests it could have been significant.

Falling from the mast of a ship while in port, being run over by a military vehicle and 'right finger dismemberment from carrying chemical barrels' are a reminder that in the military you don't need to be within earshot of the guns to be in danger. The underwriter was fired and, as Mr Payne put it, the business was high risk 'although the loss sustained was not catastrophic'.

Greg Waters, the internal auditor who had the unenviable task of auditing HIH's operations in the US and the UK, noted that in the HIH operating manuals he saw, 'personal accident insurance ... does not include injury for military personnel'.

Most of HIH's official pronouncements to shareholders through the 1990s were quick to stress that bad times only hit because the company was the victim of the insurance cycle, but the structure of HIH's management and board back in Australia had in fact created a company that was an accident waiting to happen.

Ray Williams was the strong man and driver of the company, big on loyalty and friendship. His two loyal lieutenants were Terry Cassidy and George Sturesteps, both old friends who had worked with him for years. In simplest terms, George was the salesman while Terry Cassidy was the bean-counter. Terry had worked for Price Waterhouse as a trainee auditor but left before taking his accountancy exams, joining Ray Williams instead. By modern standards it was a pretty Dad and Dave sort of operation but it seemed to work all right, give or take that alleged $100 million rescue by the UK parent, in workers' compensation in Victoria. Which was where, in September 1968, Ray Williams found Sturesteps, whom he called 'employee number three' after himself and Michael Payne.

Sturesteps was born in Benalla, Victoria, to a family of Latvian refugees. He had some experience in insurance, having joined the State Accident Insurance Office of Victoria as a clerk in 1958 and stayed until 1965. But by the time Williams hired him, he had a quarter share in a business that did what Sturesteps called 'circumstantial investigation surrounding motor vehicle and workers' compensation accidents'. That's about spying on claimants to see if they really do have a bad back, although he said he was 'more involved in the circumstantial side of things', which sounds as though he spent more time in the office than he did in the back of the van cradling a camera with a long lens.

There was nobody in the company at that stage who had any background at all in actuarial work, the mathematical business of calculating how much claims might cost. And whereas life insurance actuaries are the butt of jokes about knowing almost exactly how long people will live, general insurance actuaries have a much harder job. How do you know when the next foolish swimmer is going to make a successful claim against a local council after breaking his neck or back in the shallows? And how on earth are you going to work out how much it will cost?

But the 1960s had yet to meet the 1990s. Williams hired Sturesteps two months before the boss took his first trip overseas, to London and Lloyd's, and two years before CE Heath got behind the fledgling insurer PLA, Payne Liability Agencies.

Terry Cassidy was a relative latecomer, joining CE Heath Australia's broking business in May 1972 and joining Ray Williams' underwriting group as financial controller in June of 1973.

They were the two key players in Ray's growing empire and, as Williams put it, 'Cassidy did a superb job and his duties expanded over the years. When George Sturesteps effectively moved to the US in 1987, Terry Cassidy was appointed managing director, Australia.'

Cassidy clearly had a better time in insurance than he had as a trainee chartered accountant. He told the Royal Commission that before 1973 he worked at Price Waterhouse as an auditor but he was still the best qualified person at PLA and Heath in Australia. Even Michael Payne, doyen of the industry in the UK, never went to university. He left prestigious Dulwich College in London aged eighteen shortly after the Second World War to do his national service as ground crew in the Royal Air Force, working on a cargo and passenger-carrying variant of the Lancaster bomber called an Avro York.

Leaving aside Payne, who was already a legend at Lloyd's for his successful underwriting, HIH wasn't even the bones of a successful international insurance company.

CHAPTER 5

WINTERTHUR 1995–98

THE ARRIVAL OF the Swiss Winterthur group as a shareholder in CE Heath International Holdings Ltd in 1995 seemed, as streakers are wont to explain, a very good idea at the time. But if the Swiss executives who bought in thought they were acquiring a controlling interest in the corporate equivalent of a honey-loving brown bear, they quickly realised their new pet's behaviour resembled that of a grizzly once they had got it home and wrestled it through the door.

And because the Swiss found the management of HIH really hard to handle, they took the first good opportunity they could to sell out in 1998, thus unknowingly signing a death warrant for the undercapitalised Australian insurer.

Amid all the finger pointing in 2001 and 2002 about how the FAI purchase and the UK and US operations 'did' for HIH, former finance director Dominic Fodera made a very telling point on Monday, 2 September 2002 when he was answering Justice Neville Owen's question: why did HIH collapse?

After going through the usual suspects such as FAI, the US, and the UK, he was the first witness to place the blame squarely on Winterthur's decision to sell out in 1998. He said that if HIH had had a major shareholder 'of the ilk of Winterthur' to take it through the bad times which struck in 2000, then HIH would have survived.

He was half right. There are plenty of reasons to conclude that by

1999 HIH was already heading for disaster, particularly because of its chronic lack of reserving.

You could make a case that by about 1995 HIH was no better than a Ponzi scheme. Taking that analogy, you could say that almost every single action the management took thereafter was designed to pull in as much premium income as possible, without regard for what would have to be paid out to that much neglected group of people, HIH's policyholders.

It wasn't a calculated deception, or at least it didn't start out as one. It was the behaviour you would expect from a group of people whose drive exceeded their predictive skill, and whose ability to sell a policy was way ahead of their ability to work out what claims were going to look like five years down the track.

Lawyers Blake Dawson Waldron put it pretty well in 1995 when they were asked to take a look at HIH by CIC, the insurer HIH was merging with: 'Our overall impression of HIH is that of a company which has not yet made a complete transition from an entrepreneurially run company influenced strongly by senior management and from which senior management benefits significantly, to that of an ASX listed company run primarily in the interests of shareholders.' In his report Justice Owen drily noted, 'To this statement I would add, "and policy holders".'

At no time in the company's listed life was there a proper independent, conservative actuarial assessment of reserves. Arthur Andersen were the auditors but had no specialist actuaries to do that job, so they had to either take the numbers from HIH's resident consulting actuary, David Slee, or take an educated guess. Doubting Slee's independence from the company which by 2000 was giving him 80 per cent of his business, they took the latter course.

It is dead easy to say in retrospect, as Fodera did, that the company could have survived if it had a big brother to help, but it is a fact that HIH had one and treated it with such contempt that it sold out after only three years. Fodera told the judge that if the HIH board had gone along with Winterthur's desire not to let HIH expand internationally, then the Swiss insurer might have stayed on board.

Instead of which, and he did not say this, Ray Williams led HIH on a splendid but disastrous charge into the two markets which made the Swiss most uneasy: the UK and the US. In his report the judge noted that Williams' 'thirst for continued expansion' was a primary cause of HIH's collapse.

The Swiss knew the US was a highly competitive market because Winterthur was there already, and they did not need an upstart subsidiary undercutting them. Their own conservative approach to insurance left them vulnerable to competition anyway, never mind from a company they part-owned already.

Meanwhile Winterthur had done so badly at Lloyd's in London in the early 1990s that the management had effectively black-banned any re-entry to the Lloyd's market. Winterthur had been badly hammered by the LMX spiral. Aside from the underwriters passing risk around in circles, many did the same with their own professional indemnity insurance. Not only did they lay off all the reinsurance risk they could with each other, but they also insured their own competence with each other, which you would have to conclude is the ultimate exercise in cynicism.

In other words, if they took risks that paid off they would keep the profits, but if they made a mistake and got sued, their fellow underwriters would carry the loss. It's not far from those old definitions of socialism and communism using cows and bulls.

The effect was predictably disastrous: instead of being Cuthbert Heath's ideal world in which the worries of the few were shared around the shoulders of the many, the worries of the few ended up on the shoulders of the even fewer.

The Swiss, meanwhile, were their own worst enemy in the way they dealt with HIH. Instead of being cynical sceptics, as an Anglo-Saxon organisation might have behaved, the Swiss behaved with scrupulous propriety in dealing with Ray Williams, even though he needed them a great deal more than they needed him.

Not only did they allow Williams to leave their representation on the HIH board at three seats out of a possible thirteen, but they adhered with touching pedantry to a section of the Australian Corporations Act which states that company directors have to make decisions in the interests of all of that company's shareholders, rather than just the shareholders of the parent company back home.

Australia is full of companies in which the wishes of the biggest shareholder stand head and shoulders above the interests of minority shareholders — FAI was a shining example, the Adler family holding 30 per cent — but the Swiss directors' adherence to the letter of the law was the undoing of what could have been an insurance powerhouse.

But when it all started out, it was a marriage made in heaven. The

Swiss company was a 67 per cent shareholder in CIC Insurance, a well-regarded but lowly performing general insurer in Australia which was 30 per cent owned by Norwich Union of the UK and 3 per cent owned by the Chiyoda group of Japan.

CIC was well provisioned: indeed it even had prudential margins, or what the Swiss like to call 'cushions', but it had run up several years of underwriting losses that were not covered by any good investment results. In its last year of operations, in calendar 1994, CIC lost $9 million on its insurance operations in Australia and topped that off with a $20 million loss on its investments.

And SG Hambros, the Anglo-French investment bank that had muscled in on the HIH float via connections with HIH's UK parent, had its day in the sun over CIC. In 1993 SG Hambros' English import, Colin Richardson, put a proposal to Winterthur on behalf of HIH. He had had the logical idea of putting CIC and HIH together to create a mixed insurer with a good balance of short-tail insurance (CIC was big in household and automotive insurance) and long-tail insurance (HIH, with its emphasis on workers' compensation).

Not many deals offer a 'win–win' to both sides but there was plenty of upside for both the UK and local sides of CE Heath, and for Winterthur.

The most obvious winner was Winterthur since it was going to end up with 51 per cent of a bigger entity than CIC. CE Heath plc, which was still trying to extricate itself from anything resembling a risky business around the world, would sell its remaining 22 per cent stake in HIH to CIC Insurance at $1.52 a share. Given that the business in Australia was floated at $1.50 a share, that was a very political number although in fact CE Heath had never had to subscribe for the shares in the first place.

The deal, dated 13 April 1995, was a complex one whereby Winterthur would buy out its partners in CIC, Norwich Union and Chiyoda, thus acquiring 100 per cent of CIC. Then HIH would buy CIC Insurance from Winterthur in exchange for an issue of 97.6 million new HIH shares, and Winterthur would buy out CE Heath plc, which still held 22 per cent of HIH.

CE Heath plc had quietly sold down from 44.5 per cent to 25 per cent a year after listing, in August 1993, when Macquarie Equities lined up a group of institutions to take the stock at $1.40 a share, a discount of 5c on the current price and 10c on the listing price. Although CE Heath had said at listing time that it would hold onto its stake for two years until

April 1994, Ray Williams brought his usual relentless optimism to bear on the sceptics by saying local institutions in Australia had been precluded from acquiring Heath stock in Australia 'due to scarcity of scrip'.

If that was something of a whopper, Williams was no more culpable than the group finance director of CE Heath in the UK, Paul Hughes, who said that Heath's selling down was 'enhancing shareholder value in the company'. Hughes does not appear to have identified which particular group of shareholders were enjoying the benefit — most likely his own — and neither man was forced to explain himself.

So in 1995 CE Heath plc removed itself quietly from its Australian adventure with a nice cheque for $63 million for those 42 million shares (the 22 per cent), and CIC was backed into HIH at about its book value of $159.2 million.

Sitting on the combination of CE Heath plc shares and the new issue of shares, Winterthur would finish up with 48 per cent of HIH's 288 million shares, compared with what had previously been Heath plc's controlling interest of 42 million of the original 190 million shares on issue. Without actually changing at all in size, the public holding in HIH would drop from 70 per cent to 52 per cent. And Winterthur would therefore get the wonderful-looking deal of shedding a controlling interest in an unlisted, low-performing insurer in exchange for what quickly became control of an aggressive, listed, high-profile operation that certainly promised a lot more excitement than boring old CIC.

CIC, for the historically minded, was a merger in the 1980s of the Co-Operative Insurance Company, Carlingford Australia Insurance and the National Insurance Company of New Zealand. Its business was not exciting: private motor insurance, compulsory third party, household and commercial motor made up some 60 per cent of revenue. CIC also had a substantial workers' compensation business which could be easily absorbed into HIH. But it was all good solid local business, and a perfect counterweight to HIH's expansionary adventures based on long-tail, workers' comp-style cover.

After the deal went through, Winterthur would be able to add to its 49 per cent share by buying the 6.5 million shares that Ray Williams had bought when the HIH float was looking shaky back in 1992, taking the Winterthur stake to a more comfortable 51 per cent.

CE Heath plc must have been over the moon, since the ruling price of $1.40 for HIH shares on the day of the deal meant that Winterthur was accepting $133 million worth of relatively illiquid shares in HIH in exchange for an asset worth $26 million more.

The Australian company's name had to change since there was a clause demanding a change if CE Heath plc's shareholding dropped below 20 per cent. That certainly wasn't a big issue in Australia, where Cuthbert Eden Heath had never been a household name. The tag chosen was Heath International Holdings or HIH. The analysts certainly liked the deal, particularly amid the ruling wisdom which was that insurance companies had to get big or get out. Rationalisation was the analysts' pet word.

Since then almost all major insurers in Australia have suffered everything from a bad time, such as QBE, to an absolutely disastrous one, such as GIO, which made an annual loss of $743 million in 1998–99. Mergers have been of minimal use, except as financial salvation to the shareholders of the companies being taken over. The best possible fate for FAI shareholders in 1998 was for someone to buy them out, as HIH obligingly did. For GIO shareholders it was to be bought out by AMP Ltd, which AMP kindly did as well. The only variant that GIO shareholders missed out on was a brief brainstorm called Project Fish, in which HIH planned to take over GIO in 1997.

In case you were beginning to think HIH ended up taking over everything that wasn't bolted down, that idea was deemed too outrageous even for HIH. Considering that after AMP took over GIO in a messy two-part action that started in 1998 and finished in 1999, it found an $800 million hole in GIO caused by some ill-considered reinsurance ventures in the UK market, that deal would have sunk HIH even faster than FAI did. To give Colin Richardson and SG Hambros their due, they spotted the risk in GIO's reinsurance very early and spiked the deal before it went anywhere.

The combined HIH Winterthur operation, as it was now called, saw employee numbers jump from 740 (earning annual premiums of about $420 million net) to about 1500, post merger, with annual net premiums now closer to $760 million. Gross premiums broke through the $1 billion mark to around $1.2 billion, a fact that Ray Williams made much of in' press announcements. The difference between gross and net is caused by reinsurance. Williams had always said that he favoured reinsurance over prudential margins, which is why the company was paying some $440 million to reinsurers annually.

What Ray Williams was not telling the analysts or his shareholders about, however, was a due diligence report that Ernst & Young did on

HIH on behalf of CIC, since technically CIC was taking control of HIH. The Ernst & Young people were looking for holes in HIH's story and they found some doozies.

Their actuaries calculated that HIH's central estimate of its outstanding liabilities had been understated by $18 million, or in other words, it had previously underestimated how much it would be paying out. They also suggested that HIH should have a $41 million prudential margin or 'cushion', as the Swiss liked to call it, since most other insurance companies liked to have something put away for a stormy day. The catch in that, at least for Ray Williams, was that every dollar that an insurer allocates to reserves is a dollar less profit that it can claim.

The Ernst & Young analysis also found another hole in HIH on the asset side: it calculated that the HIH property portfolio was $15 million overvalued. (FAI had exactly the same problems, overvaluation of assets and underestimation of liabilities, as Williams was to find in 1998.)

HIH's problem was, as the report pointed out, a 'very aggressive' reserving methodology. In the boilerplate world of due diligence reports, that is a damning accusation and it turned out to be absolutely true. HIH was effectively too optimistic about what reserves it would need to keep, and the problem built up and built up until by 1998 the company's own auditors were talking internally about the company's 'rape and pillage attitude'. HIH's own consulting actuary, David Slee, worked out that HIH had underestimated reserves (and thus overestimated profits) by $930 million.

Just to provide an idea of how critically important the reserving issue is, that number greatly exceeds all the profit the company declared during the period between the float in 1992 and 31 December 1998.

Back in 1995, when Ernst & Young was shining an unwelcome torch on the inner workings of HIH, they did not know exactly how badly under-reserved the company was but they did not like what they saw. They worked out that HIH would need to write off $87.7 million from its claimed assets, at a time when its stated net asset value was only $200 million. That meant in fact that HIH was statutorily insolvent even then, since it did not have net assets equivalent to at least 20 per cent of premium income.

There are degrees of insolvency: the Insurance and Superannuation Commission (which became the Australian Prudential Regulation Authority on 1 July 1998) had higher definitions of insolvency than the Corporations Act, which merely demands that a company must be able to pay its bills as and when they fall due.

The Ernst & Young report noted that HIH's auditors, Andersen, had assessed the job of auditing the company as one of 'maximum audit risk' because the management had the ability to 'manage' its reported results and to adopt what it called 'potentially invalid positions and policies'. There are much ruder ways of saying that, for instance that the company's results have been rigged.

(For all that, Andersen kept on auditing HIH until the bitter end in March 2001. If there is one thing worse than having a shaky audit client, it appears to be having no audit client. Justin Gardener, who ended up auditing HIH for seventeen years before he retired from Andersen in 1998 and then very quickly became a director of HIH, was asked by barrister Simon White why he did not pass the audit of HIH on to a colleague. There was no one with the competence to do it, replied Gardener.)

As happens in these situations, the Ernst & Young report's circulation was as small as its contents were punchy. It was done on behalf of CIC, which was to be 100 per cent owned by Winterthur, and it never even got to the management of HIH. It was however read by Ray Williams, who not surprisingly objected strongly to it, and by the Winterthur executives who joined the HIH board, Werner Heri, Willi Schürpf and Randolph Wein. In a remarkable twist of fate, Wein ended up being the man chosen to run HIH after Ray Williams resigned in late 2000.

Williams wrote a note (that was never sent) saying that the report should be ignored and that prudential reserves were unnecessary. He is also reported to have barred the report's two authors from HIH's offices, which would put them in esteemed company.

The actuary's report was thrown across the room at its author when it was presented to Williams.

The worst aspect of the whole 'mutual due diligence' affair is that after HIH discovered that CIC was under-reserved by $43 million on its workers' compensation business, the two sparring insurers concluded that since they both 'had' something on each other, then the two negatives cancelled each other out.

In fact CIC's problems were less severe and the company was clearly over-reserved in other areas, but CIC managing director Randolph Wein let it go and the merger went ahead.

The problem with that logic is that two wrongs don't make a right. Shareholders were never told about the problems, particularly HIH shareholders, and if they had read the Ernst & Young report they would probably have called their broker and shouted 'sell'.

They would have read, for instance, that 'The Marine portfolio has changed significantly over 1994. The new business appears more weighted towards longer duration liabilities and bigger risks than the old business. The reserving methodology adopted by HIH is very aggressive and appears to have already proven inadequate. The nature of this portfolio would appear to warrant a more prudent approach to reserving than has been adopted.'

An interesting and unreported twist to the story is that an indemnity agreement was put in place between Winterthur and HIH regarding the adequacy of CIC's and HIH's reserves at the date of sale. The agreement was unconcerned about whether both sets were inadequate but it stated that if the difference in the deterioration of the claims reserves at 31 December 1994, recalculated at 30 June 1997, was greater than $25 million, then a payment of $25 million would have to be made. Neither party expected the indemnity to be triggered but in fact HIH's reserves fell by $66 million and CIC's by less than $10 million — a gap of $56 million. Strangely, Wintherthur allowed HIH off the hook by allowing it to use a $32 million tax benefit to offset the hole, leaving a gap of only $24 million. So the indemnity was not triggered.

The only explanation for that action must be that if the indemnity had been triggered, any potential buyer of Winterthur's shares would have been scared away. It is an interesting point that the auditors of both Winterthur and HIH went along with the tax benefit accounting treatment, something that might provide legal ammunition to any of the institutional investors who ended up buying those shares in 1998 when Winterthur sold out of HIH.

As Wayne Martin, QC, put it in his introduction to the 1995–98 'Winterthur Period' at HIH, 'through close attention to some of the events and documents that were generated in the course of that transaction, one can arguably see the seeds of the problems that led to the demise of HIH'.

But if the two parties had just discovered enough of a guilty secret to embarrass each other significantly, none of the bad news got even close to ordinary shareholders. They were merely treated to some of Ray Williams' patent 'jam tomorrow' optimism. On 14 April 1995 he told the *Australian Financial Review* that 'We see some tremendous opportunities with the Winterthur relationship. We think we are able to do some things offshore.

They are wanting to do something in China and I think that at the appropriate time we would piggy-back on that.'

If the local analysts liked the deal, the optimistic Swiss believed that in a year or two they could move to full control of HIH. Schürpf noted that 'Winterthur's intention would be to assume control of any combined operation after a transitional period of 12 to 24 months. The ability to assume control was a prerequisite for Winterthur. Towards the end of January 1995, Randolph Wein informed me that he had received confirmation from HIH that its board was happy with the prospect of Winterthur assuming control in due course.'

Ray Williams took a different view in his evidence to the Royal Commission, saying that there was never any intention by his board to cede control to the Swiss group in that way.

It certainly didn't look to Williams like a plot to ease him out, since he had effectively been given the company cheque book — and a much higher credit rating — by a group of Swiss insurers who were dazzled by the logic of the deal they had just done and seemed entirely happy to leave him alone.

They certainly had reason to be indulgent with Williams in particular: it was his personal sale of a parcel of 6.5 million shares in HIH that allowed Winterthur to get from 48 to 51 per cent.

He did the deal after the major acquisition, and declared to the board that he had done the deal. The origin of the shares was not a mystery: it was almost exactly the parcel of shares which he had sub-underwritten back in March 1992 to support the float, and he had been borrowing some $10 million from SG Hambros in London for three years to do so. But what he did not declare was a profit-sharing arrangement which he struck with Winterthur at that time, whereby he would be paid a bonus if the business cleared certain hurdles.

On 9 June 1998, when Winterthur was in the throes of selling out of HIH, he sent the Swiss company a bill for $610,000 as settlement of the deal, which was duly paid.

Williams had negotiated a complex put and call option over his shares with CIC Insurance, 49 per cent owned by Winterthur, whereby Winterthur paid a price of $2.05 a share for his 6 million shares, which by a genuine accident was almost exactly the right number required to take Winterthur past 50 per cent of HIH. As Williams noted on his last day of evidence at the Royal Commission, the price was in line with the market even though he had Winterthur over a barrel. All the other directors' shares were still in escrow — they were not allowed to sell them — and Winterthur were not keen to make a bid for ordinary shareholders' stock, so Williams' line was that his shares were the only ones they could buy. To add to the oddity of the deal, some time later Winterthur gave Williams a bonus of $650,000, which was related to the performance of the shares after they bought them.

The upshot of that was that Hambros got their money back, Williams made an eventual small profit (Winterthur paid $1.52 a share for CE Heath's 49 per cent stake but Williams got $2.05 a share because his deal happened later and the share price had risen) and Winterthur exchanged a 49 per cent stake in a small insurer, CIC, for a 51 per cent stake in a bigger one in the shape of HIH Winterthur.

Justice Owen certainly had his doubts about what happened, although in his report he stopped short of accusing Williams of being dishonest.

He said he found it 'difficult to accommodate' the proposition Williams put in evidence that buying his stock was the only way for Winterthur to get the 2 per cent, rather than on the market. He added that, 'It must be remembered that at the very time Williams was negotiating the sale of his own shares at a price in excess of $2.00, he was negotiating the sale of the parcel held by CE Health at a price of $1.52.'

The extra 2 per cent certainly allowed Winterthur to consolidate its HIH accounts but getting management control of the company that Ray Williams ran as a personal fiefdom was a different matter entirely.

And the episode left a bad taste with HIH directors and shareholders because, as HIH's corporate adviser, Colin Richardson, told the HIH Royal Commission, the option arrangement was not disclosed to the HIH board, nor was it apparently ratified by HIH shareholders at a shareholders' meeting. 'My recollection is that this option agreement was approved by the shareholders at the HIH shareholders meeting,' Richardson said to Wayne Martin, QC.

'How strong is that recollection?' asked Martin.

'Obviously not strong enough,' conceded Richardson.

Richardson sent a very prescient note to his London-based boss, Christopher Sporborg, in April 1995 after the original 49 per cent Winterthur buyout of CE Heath's stake had been announced.

He noted how positive the Australian insurance analysts' reaction had been to the fact that the deal gave HIH control of CIC Insurance, lifting its annual premium income from around $350 million to a much more impressive $1.2 billion or almost four times as much. 'Unfortunately Ray is already talking about acquiring one of his competitors!' he noted almost as a throwaway line.

He was talking about FAI Insurance, which remains one of the biggest single reasons for the HIH collapse.

As Kerry Packer notably stated when he bought back Channel Nine from Bond Corp for about one-third of what he sold it for originally to the mercurial businessman, 'You only need one Alan Bond in your life.'

Ray Williams only ever needed one Winterthur, not that he would ever get another.

By getting the Winterthur management offside, almost straightaway it seems, he missed the perfect opportunity to turn HIH from a thinly spread, flimsy and aggressive insurer into a well-reserved and well-regarded core operation that might well still be operating today.

Werner Heri and Willi Schürpf, two of Winterthur's three nominees to the HIH board, told a dire tale in the witness statements that they supplied to the HIH Royal Commission. The official reason that Winterthur sold out of HIH in 1998 was because Winterthur was taken over by Credit Suisse, one of the world's largest banks, in late 1997.

But Dr Heri noted that the real catalyst for the decison was what he called Winterthur's 'consistent sense of frustration' at its inability to influence the strategy and principal decisions of HIH. That was a reference to HIH's habit of buying or setting up businesses in geographical areas that brought the Winterthur management out in hives.

'As a conservative entity by nature, Winterthur was "uncomfortable" having a majority interest in, but very limited effective control over, an entrepreneurial acquisitive company like HIH,' he said.

He noted that as early as August 1996 'a number of concerns were raised' at the Winterthur senior management level about HIH, including its reserving practices, its UK operations and 'its international activities in general'. Indeed he suggested that since the share price of HIH had risen, it might be a good chance for Winterthur to sell out.

Mr Schürpf noted that within six months of the deal going through, the management of Winterthur in Switzerland were uneasy about the close links between the auditors and HIH.

Dominic Fodera joined HIH and became chief financial officer in September 1995, within two weeks of leaving Andersen, having been lured across with a complex 'golden hello' payment package that was intended to cost HIH $1.2 million but ended up costing more like $1.6 million, because it was linked to the HIH share price. Details of Fodera's package were never made clear to the HIH board, although the practice was in no way illegal. What would now be much harder, if not illegal, would be Fodera's almost instant transition from auditor to executive of the same company. Professor Ian Ramsay, director of the Centre for Corporate Law at Melbourne University, wrote a report in 2001 on the independence of auditors which recommended a gap of at least two years between two such jobs. The judge went further in recommending a four-year gap. That is likely to become law in Australia as part of the cumbersomely named CLERP process, the Corporate Law Economic Reform Program.

If Ray Williams couldn't see a problem in hiring Fodera, Winterthur certainly could. Winterthur wanted Andersen to be replaced because Fodera had been an Andersen partner involved in auditing HIH.

'Winterthur was concerned that there was a real risk that ... position and independence may be, or may be seen to be compromised,' Schürpf wrote. He said that Winterthur suggested using Ernst & Young (not, as would fit neatly, because of its excellent due diligence report on HIH but because E&Y was Winterthur's auditor in Switzerland).

But they got the first of many clear indications of how the land lay. They put it to Ray Williams in January 1996 but subsequently caved in to his argument that Andersen should be kept on as it was one of the Big Six accounting firms. As was Ernst & Young, by the way.

Meanwhile, there was the little matter of being Swiss-based directors of an Australian group. The men nominated local directors as their alternates, Heri naming CIC director Charles Abbott and Schürpf naming former Norwich director Alex Gorrie, but they still needed to know what was going on. That was easier said than done.

'By the time I received board papers in Switzerland, it was common for me to have only about twenty-four hours or less to review significant and voluminous materials. Requests by Mr Schürpf and me for earlier distribution of papers was largely unproductive,' Heri said.

If Winterthur were alarmed at what Ray Williams was doing, they were even more alarmed about how little they were being told by HIH management. Mr Schürpf said that his colleague Erwin Sieber, who was in 1996 the head of internal audit at Winterthur, 'experienced difficulty in obtaining access to information he required and/or requested from HIH'.

An internal Winterthur memo in August 1996 called HIH management 'a closely knit and related club where one is either part of it or "out"'. It said Williams' leadership was 'charismatic and somewhat patriarchal'.

In late 1997 Sieber told Schürpf that he still could not evaluate HIH's internal systems and controls despite having been sent some eighty HIH internal audit reports between late 1995 and late 1997. That highlighted another great weakness at HIH which directors Justin Gardener and Neville Head mentioned in 1998: there was lots of information coming to them, a deluge of it in some ways, but they found that not a lot of it was relevant.

(Rodney Adler was the master of the art of drowning people in information: FAI insurance probably sent more reports to the ASX than any other comparable listed company in Australia, but very few of them revealed anything of consequence about the company and some reports, like Adler's claim on 1 May 1998 that the St Moritz Hotel in New York had been sold for $180 million, were just plain misleading.)

The consequence of all this was that the Winterthur people concluded internally as early as 1996 that they wanted out, or they wanted full control of HIH.

Giant Swiss bank Credit Suisse had been sniffing around Winterthur and in that year they started a joint marketing alliance. Banks and insurers enjoy the fantasy that they can create a one-stop shop and halve their costs, and in 1997 the bank and the insurer went serious and merged fully. Credit Suisse was facing a problem in the US that dates back to the Glass–Steagall Act, whereby you can be a bank or an insurer but not both. The solution was to sell insurance assets and, according to Mr Schürpf, the Winterthur people would make sure that HIH was not forced to sell any assets too cheap. Winterthur may have wanted out of HIH, but they weren't shouting it to Credit Suisse and they didn't want to rock the boat.

The really hard part was that underneath the boilerplate statements, HIH was carrying on as though nothing was happening. Winterthur wanted to centralise all its international activities so that offshoots did not tread on each other's toes, and HIH kept on ignoring such ideas.

A prize example of HIH ignoring Winterthur was when it bought back into California in late 1996, in clear breach of Winterthur's intentions. Winterthur's representatives on the HIH board all voted against it, but because there were only three of them they were overruled. Not only did it cause organisational complications in a company that was already well established in the US, but it was also in clear breach of Winterthur's plans. Lastly, and most importantly, HIH had not done its homework properly and between 1997 and 2000 HIH managed to lose an estimated $620 million in the US. The operations were closed down or placed in run-off in that year.

On 1 December 1997 Dr Thomas Wellauer was made CEO of the Winterthur operation and two days later an internal workshop resolved that the company had three options in regard to HIH: obtain majority control of the board, sell out, or buy 100 per cent.

The first and last were ruled out, the first because it would probably run into Ray Williams and Michael Payne's desire to keep doing business in the UK, and the last because 'it was not thought that HIH was a good fit with Winterthur's businesses and the group's other interests'. Quite apart from the fact that they would have to ask a Swiss Bank for some 700 to 800 million Swiss francs to help buy an Australian insurer who wouldn't tell them what was going on.

Another sharp conclusion was reached: since Australia was no longer a growth market, HIH would inevitably look overseas where it was likely to come into increasing conflict with the activities of Winterthur and Credit Suisse.

In case you think the rumour mill is slower in Switzerland than elsewhere, it is worth noting that the Winterthur management made the 'sell' decision on 5 December 1997 on a top-secret basis, and in just over a month Ray Williams sent a note to Randolph Wein of Winterthur protesting about 'the rumour now flying back to the company that Winterthur intends to dispose of its shareholding in HIH Winterthur. Randolph, to date I have denied that the rumour has any substance. However, if there is any truth to the rumour, I am entitled to be informed.'

Williams was told the next day that Winterthur was indeed looking to sell, but that was the easy bit. The sale process tore up every single remaining shred of goodwill that existed between the two sides, and ended up owing more to the Keystone Cops than Wall Street.

The problem was that the simplest exit strategy for Winterthur, a trade sale to a fellow insurance group, would mean a due diligence investigation by the buyer. The Swiss had done one on HIH in 1995, via Ernst & Young, and then ignored it. Three years later they must have suspected that things at HIH had probably got worse, although they did not even know.

Winterthur's chief financial officer, Dr Gerhard Christen, got a note from Wein that it would be impossible to find a buyer in secret and Wein suggested 'a forward strategy to consider a sort of tender procedure which will give us an opportunity to embrace the entire potential buyer's contingent'. Perhaps that phrase suffered in translation. Even though the share price of HIH had by now risen to a near-record price of $3.25 a share at the start of 1998, there was not what anyone would call a 'contingent' looking to buy HIH.

The other option was an institutional bookbuild, whereby major investors in Australia and around the world are tested by enterprising stockbrokers trying to find a discounted price at which the brokers could sell the entire line.

Indeed in early 1998 Peter Curry, head of the institutional dealing desk at Macquarie Equities, nearly pulled off a major coup by lining up a group of institutions to take out Winterthur's holding at $2.75 a share when the market price was around $3.10. Opinions vary about why Winterthur said no. One view is that Werner Heri, who received the bid, could not make up his mind in time, but a kinder view is that the Winterthur people may still at that point have had the brave hope that they might be able to obtain a premium to the ruling share price by selling to a major international insurer for, say, $3.50 a share.

One thing that is clear in retrospect is that two major international insurers did actually want to make trade bids for some or all of HIH but the Winterthur management, perhaps fearful of legal consequences, concealed them from Ray Williams.

The most farcical episode came on 20 April 1998, when Ray Williams effectively banned a team of twenty executives from Belgian group Fortis who had come all the way to Australia to take a close look at HIH and who were already installed in Sydney's Regent Hotel. Ray Williams took the view that they should make a bid before he offered them a look at HIH's books. They took the view, not surprisingly, that they wanted a due diligence look at the books before they made a bid.

What Williams did not know was that three days before, on 17 April, Fortis had told Alan Highet of Credit Suisse First Boston in Melbourne that it was prepared to pay 'up to $A1.3 billion' for all of HIH, which was the equivalent of $3.57 a share. And on the exact same day Liberty

International of Boston in the US noted that it was interested in bidding 'up to $3.60' for all of Winterthur's 169 million shares, or 53 per cent of HIH.

If either of those bids had been allowed to go ahead, HIH would probably still be here today. But because the relationship between Winterthur and HIH management had by that stage degenerated into an atmosphere of mutual distrust, Winterthur did not even tell Ray Williams about the bids. It is quite probable, not that Winterthur executives have ever said it, that they did not go ahead with the sale to a major insurer because they knew it would all fall apart when the buyer got a good look at the target via the due diligence process.

So on the one hand Ray Williams was sending people away because he did not believe they were serious buyers, and on the other, the vendor was not even telling him the buyers had actually made an indicative bid. He told the Royal Commission that when he was finally shown evidence of the Fortis and Liberty bids, he felt sick and almost wept.

It was a hopeless situation for anyone expecting a top price from a serious international insurer, particularly with Ray Williams acting for the vendor but actually having interests that were nowhere near the vendor's. He clearly had his heart set on a breakup of the parcel and a sale to Australian and overseas institutions, on the premise that full control of a small organisation is better than having a major partner in a bigger one. If that is so, he was to be totally wrong.

Winterthur ended up getting substantially less for its stake than it might otherwise have done and, more ominously, the stage was set for HIH to start sliding down the slope to its eventual collapse.

Instead of selling to a major insurer in April 1998 at, say, $3.50 a share, Winterthur ended up selling down via a 'bookbuild' organised by related investment bank Credit Suisse First Boston in August 1998 at a nominal $2.58 a share, or 92c a share less.

At least Winterthur's desire to 'do the right thing' in the sale process produced an information memorandum that now stands as the first clear warning that HIH was badly under-reserved. There were plenty more warnings in 1999 and 2000, but page 50 of the document prepared by CSFB in 1998 contains a table which shows the situation getting worse as soon as HIH listed in 1992.

The table was an actuary's tool called a 'triangulation', and shows that HIH consistently underestimated how much it would need to keep aside as reserves. In 1992, for instance, HIH thought it had $2.8 million *more* than it needed to cover that year, but by 1997 that figure turned out to have actually been $14.1 million too little. The following years all started out inadequate — unlike 1992 — and got worse. 1993 started out as being $25.3 million short of what it should have been, but by 1997 the real experience of claims from 1993 showed that the reserves for 1993 had been short by $39.6 million. Fortunately for the vendors, no one noticed this public bout of self-flagellation, and the shares were all quickly sold. But it proved beyond doubt that HIH's estimates did not have a 50 per cent chance of being adequate. After a brief burst of adequate reserving in 1992, their probability of being adequate fell to a figure that looks a lot like zero.

But after all that, Winterthur did not actually sell all of its shares.

Winterthur Holdings Australia Ltd sold 146 million of its 169 million shares in HIH via a two-stage system called instalment receipts. The shares were sold at $2.58 each, with an initial instalment of $1.60 and the balance (98 cents) payable on 30 June 1999.

Winterthur kept 22.8 million HIH shares as a market stabiliser and ended up with a pile of worthless paper including 9.355 million 1996 convertible notes. Winterthur Swiss Insurance Company, the parent company, also holds 3.7 million HIH 1996 convertible notes, which are also worthless.

Worst served of all were the institutions, which by a twist of irony are often owned by insurance companies, which bought the shares.

By the time the second instalment fell due and payable, the price of HIH shares had dropped to $1.75 and was still falling. That meant the institutional fund managers were paying 98 cents for something worth 15 cents, a painful experience for any investor.

They had several options, all of them painful: forfeit the shares for non-payment of the instalment receipt, sell at a nasty loss or hold on and hope things got better. Most opted for the latter course, to their eventual despair.

CHAPTER 6

UK, US AND CHINA

THE UK BUSINESS started in 1993 with the best of motives but the worst of timing. Michael Payne had steered his Lloyd's syndicates successfully past the shoals of the 1991 catastrophe but instead of picking up, as rates are meant to do after an insurance 'bust', insurance rates stayed resolutely low. The difference was that there were just as many insurance companies, if not more, chasing the same amount of business as before, not the least of them being HIH's ancestor CE Heath Australia. Heath was going to have to break the promises it made in its prospectus to get the business it decided it needed to write.

In the 1992 prospectus Ray Williams had made it clear that although HIH was going to buy what is called 'outwards' reinsurance instead of keeping what he regarded as big and lazy reserves, the company would not be accepting what is called inwards reinsurance. That is the sort that brought FAI undone, accepting part of other people's risks on the assumption that it will behave a bit like an investment, supplying nice premiums instead of dividends, and then ideally ending with the insurer keeping all the premiums and paying out very little in claims.

The 1992 prospectus noted with great prescience that 'The CE Heath group believes that the writing of reinsurance inwards business lacks the necessary information on the risks underwritten and control of claims.'

But that was before Michael Payne wrote to Ray Williams and asked for a job. Inwards reinsurance was his forte. Payne was a gent of the old

74

school for whom personal trust was a big part of business success but for whom back office record-keeping came a poor second, as he later admitted.

Ten years later he told the Royal Commission that HIH's UK operations were dogged by a major international downturn in rates, poor management and internal controls, personality differences and careless underwriting in areas where he lacked expertise.

The latter was a reference to Syndicate 488 at Lloyd's, more commonly known as the Charman syndicate, into which HIH UK sank millions of dollars in the mid–1990s. The category was called 'marine whole of account insurance', a phrase that is likely to be etched on Payne's gravestone since it was to bring him so much grief.

It was named after John Charman, who had been something of a legend at Lloyd's as a successful syndicate manager. He was also deputy chairman of Lloyd's. But as Michael Payne found out, nothing lasts for ever and, instead of diversifying out of high-risk into low-risk business, Charman appears to have diversified out of high-risk into higher. The explosion, fire and collapse of the Piper Alpha oil production platform into the North Sea in July 1988 with the loss of 167 lives was a catastrophe for the Charman syndicate on its own, but Charman's sidebar venture into aircraft insurance made things worse instead of better. When Payne thought he was picking up Syndicate 488 risks involving airlines like Swissair, he was actually taking risks in Ethiopian Airlines and China Airlines, which were considerably more hazard-prone.

Payne admitted to the Royal Commission that he had been 'wrong' to get involved with Charman in 1996 and it had been 'an error of underwriting judgement' by HIH to offer reinsurance to Syndicate 488 via brokers.

Payne blamed brokers Jardine Lloyd Thompson for misrepresentation, rather than Charman himself. He said that when HIH took the risk in 1996 it was shown numbers which were very different to what the broker then showed him in 1997, referring to past claims. An inquiry by Peter Thompson, HIH UK's resident bulldog, and London lawyers Ince & Co discovered that no less than eleven of the sixteen reinsurance layers that HIH had taken on were firmly in the category of 'to be avoided'.

The shocker for HIH UK was that it had taken on what is called 'unprotected aggregate exposure', an insurance euphemism for unlimited liability, on what were always going to be big claims out of Charman. By

October 1996 HIH's internal auditor Greg Waters was already writing internal reports about how the company's involvement with Charman had expanded without appropriate infrastructure or management control systems.

And because the London market is one where bad news travels fast, HIH had to pay ever-higher costs to reinsure its exposure to Charman. Everyone knew that HIH was desperate and the downside for potential reinsurers was big.

Payne wrote in a memo to Williams at that time that if Winterthur got hold of that information, he would have no option but to resign. 'I know this will hurt and upset you, Ray ... I just don't feel I have the stomach for it any more,' he wrote.

Once internal auditor Waters had written a further report in early November 1997 pointing to the lack of back office controls, Payne groaned in a note to Thompson that 'this would be literal dynamite in the hands of the Swiss'. It was the Swiss who had asked Waters to do the report and they clearly got it in due course. It was almost certainly pressure from the Swiss that subsequently compelled Ray Williams to have Michael Payne removed from the post of chief executive after he had a series of minor strokes in late 1997.

By HIH's standards Payne was in fact a very forthright man, not only about other people's weaknesses but also his own, and for that reason the HIH Royal Commission spent a lot less time on HIH's UK operations than it did on areas where there was any suggestion of a cover-up. Unfortunately, Thompson's skill at tracking down external threats was accompanied by a tendency to get his own colleagues offside.

Payne's health was clearly affected by the stresses of Charman and the film-financing fiasco, which cost HIH more than $500 million. Peter Thompson, an Englishman who has spent much of his life in Australia, was made acting head of the UK operation while Payne was ill.

Ray Williams — ever the loyal old friend — asked for Payne's removal to be done with sensitivity. Accordingly, HIH management took the opportunity to make Payne non-executive chairman, no doubt on the assumption that he would retire. But when he recovered in early 1998, Payne resumed his habit of spending a great deal of time in HIH's London office.

Like Ray Williams, he was a man who did not take kindly to being kicked upstairs. And since he was kicked two years before his old mate

Williams was, he kept tight links with the company's undisputed boss. 'He got in before us and left after us, and meanwhile was in daily communication with Ray,' said one former employee.

Payne pulled no punches in assessing his own performance. In a note to Thompson in March 1998 he supplied a list of his own shortcomings and added: 'I quite clearly lost the plot ... it is difficult to see how I can have any role going forward.'

Payne's relationship with Thompson was clearly an unusual one. Payne realised he had blown it significantly but he believed he was the only person in the office who could sort out the Charman mess, which by May 1997 was expected to result in an ultimate loss to HIH of $US24 million.

Current corporate governance practice says that it is wrong to have a former chief executive promoted to the chair of his company, as effectively happened with Payne. Why? Because it makes life hard for the new chief executive.

But if Payne was exceeding his brief by 'dealing round' the UK office's full-time management, his presence was much less alarming than Peter Thompson's. Thompson was still nominally based in Australia but was put in charge of HIH UK.

Payne's measured statement about this disastrous period is a model of English understatement.

> As time went by, including when I became non executive director, I received several and frequent complaints from directors and senior staff in the UK branch about Peter Thompson's bizarre and irrational behaviour. On a number of occasions I had lunch with Peter Thompson. He would often complain to me about the staff and on occasion, I would attempt to politely inform him that he was having a deleterious effect on staff morale. I also raised with Ray Williams the issue of Peter Thompson's relationship with staff after I became non executive chairman. This reached a crescendo during my time on the board of Cotesworth [the Lloyd's operation that HIH bought control of in 1998].

He said that Norman Britten, the aptly named English chief executive of Cotesworth, had told Ray Williams that if Thompson did not resign as non-executive chairman of Cotesworth, all the other directors would resign. 'Peter Thompson thereafter resigned from the board at the request of Ray Williams. He took this very badly and communicated this to me in a telephone conversation,' concluded Payne with admirable but frustrating economy.

Ray Williams described it with uncharacteristic candour on 8 August 2002 when he said: 'Peter Thompson had a style about him that upset a lot of people, very mercurial. Sort of friendly with you today and not very friendly with you tomorrow, but I think over a period of time it became even more so.'

Williams admitted that some of the follies involving breaches of underwriting guidelines were part of 'the harsh reality of business'. But Justice Neville Owen picked him up on that and Williams later admitted that it was still his responsibility.

Even before HIH dived into the Charman adventure, the Winterthur executives hated the UK market with a passion, having lost millions of Swiss francs via the LMX spiral in 1993. Lack of transparency towards outsiders, which the Swiss were clearly considered, left them feeling that London was a place where bunnies were skinned and that if they were ill-prepared, HIH was to fare no better.

And if Charman was bad, the film-financing mess was far worse. Wayne Martin, QC, claimed that HIH had blown $500 million on it alone, although Payne claimed that it would end up being much less. Unfortunately, and this was to become a familiar refrain, the affair is still in litigation and we may not know for some years what the final loss number was. In his summing up, Martin said that the UK office may have made total losses of about $1.2 billion. In his report the judge noted that by December 2002 HIH's total deficiency in the UK was more than $1.7 billion, which in dollar terms was the largest single contributor to the collapse of HIH.

Another e-mail that might never have seen the light of day was from Garth Hackshall, an auditor in Andersen's UK office, warning his Australian colleagues that HIH's UK operations were under-reserved. He wrote in October 1998 that the latest UK result was 'poor to average, due to prior year deterioration in reserves and the reserves are said to be a factor of HIH's typical Rape and Pillage attitude'. (Ray Williams objected strongly to Hackshall's Hagar the Horrible comparison, stressing to the Commission that he always believed that HIH in the UK was fully reserved.)

There were many shining examples of why Winterthur was nervous of HIH's offshore expansion plans in the mid–1990s, both in the US and the UK.

WHILE IN THE UK HIH stumbled from one crisis to another, its adventures in the US in general and California in particular would make a case study of how buying a 'bargain' without thorough examination can be a costly experience.

HIH had done everything right in California from 1987 until 1994, building up a workers' compensation business, 'Heath Cal', from almost nothing and then accepting an offer worth $119 million for it in March 1994. Ray Williams announced the sale deal on 9 March of that year, a day when his company was announcing its best-ever result: a net profit of $37.99 million, more than twice the 1992–93 figure of $16.2 million.

He made all the right upbeat noises about how funds from the sale would be used to earn higher returns when invested in Australia rather than California, and played down the fact that the US business made up 30 per cent of gross revenue for his company for the year and 38 per cent of net revenue. The sale was in fact perfectly timed for HIH, since the $29 million of abnormal profit the company was able to book on the sale went some way in the March 1995 result to making up for $25.9 million of unrealised investment losses suffered during 1994, plus $30.1 million of realised losses.

The company announced an $11.8 million net profit, well below a third of the number recorded in the previous year, but it had been badly hammered by a change in accounting rules in Australia which demanded that unrealised losses, as well as realised ones, should be declared. It is in fact a 'swings and roundabouts' system, since if an insurer has to mark down the value of its portfolio to the real market during a downturn, it can mark it up again when the market improves.

Had it not been for the sale of the US business, CE Heath would have had to declare a loss of about $15 million in March 1995, which would have wrecked Australian investors' fragile confidence in the company only three years after listing, and during a major share market downturn. The analysts that Ray Williams had been so carefully squiring would have taken a very negative view, particularly since the gain was only one-off and the losses were continuing.

The sale of the Californian business was a wonderful deal all the same, since it had always been a 'skinny' business for CE Heath. It had turned a $10 million a year business into a $100 million business in five years between 1987 and 1992, but Californian claims jumped sharply in 1991 and before it even listed in Australia, Heath made an underwriting loss of

$11.1 million in 1991, compared with a loss of $3.29 million in 1990, and profits in its first three years.

And if that was ominous, the future was looking catastrophic.

In mid–1994 the Californian State Legislature in Sacramento was about to introduce rule changes which were to make it much harder for insurers to make a profit. To make money, rates have to be comfortably high and payouts manageable. For reasons that can only relate to local politics, California scrapped the minimum-rate rule, meaning there was no longer a floor below which no insurer would drop its rates. California has the same separation of powers that Australia enjoys, which means that just because the legislature is pushing in one direction, the courts are under no obligation to go the same way.

While the legislature was pushing insurers' premium income down by removing the floor, the Californian courts simultaneously started lifting the cap by increasing payouts to workers' compensation claimants. And just to top things off, the insurers lost some of their powers to 'manage' claims, particularly in terms of deciding who was and was not permanently incapacitated. More of those powers were given to doctors, who might be better qualified to decide but who had less incentive to nurse injured claimants back into the workforce.

None of this disaster struck HIH in 1995, since the insurer was well and truly out of the market. HIH did offer CareAmerica, the health insurer which bought its Californian business, an indemnity against cost blowouts in previous years, but that was relatively straightforward.

HIH's problems began when CareAmerica offered HIH back the business in late 1996 for less than HIH sold out for. Any businessman's first reaction would be to at least consider the idea, particularly since the staff had remained relatively unchanged, but that was as far as the similarity went. The 1996 *Annual Report* of HIH makes it clear the company had blundered happily back into California with high hopes and minimal research. 'Late in 1996 we became aware of a unique opportunity which we moved very quickly to capitalise upon. Subsequent to negotiations, on 6 January 1997 we were able to announce that we had re-purchased our former United States workers' compensation business,' the chief executive's report trumpeted. He noted it was 'for a price of $US59 million which represented a figure close to net asset value and compared with the 1994 sale price of $US93 million'.

He patted the company on the back for selling out when it did:

'Developments within the California compensation market in recent years have thoroughly vindicated our decision to exit the market,' he said, but there was no explanation of how HIH would be able to prosper when CareAmerica was obviously keen to cut its losses.

'Current conditions are, however, encouraging and we are re-entering a familiar operation, founded and built up by us from 1987 to 1994 and with the same high calibre management team still in place ... We have therefore added what will be a critical foundation for future growth,' he said. What the report did not say was that Ray Williams knew that US insurance companies did not discount their liabilities in the way that Australian insurers did, thus providing some tempting reserves for Australian buyers. In this case there was zero benefit to HIH but another smaller company HIH bought, Great States Insurance, supplied $US11 million. HIH paid $US14 million for the company and then on Williams' orders hijacked $US11 million of what should have been policy holder dividends.

Within a short time HIH was singing a different tune to shareholders, since everything that could have gone wrong at CareAmerica did. The 1998–99 *Annual Report*, which carried the ominous subheading 'Weathering the Storms' on the front cover, was a lot more candid. 'The imperative for downsizing the California business is due to the continued deterioration of the California workers' compensation market. Premium rates achievable have simply not been allowed to adequately reflect steadily increasing claims costs,' said the CEO. 'Fortunately, there are now some signs of improvement in California,' he continued, with no more justification for optimism than he had had two years before.

Williams' corporate advisor Colin Richardson should have been playing the role of Cassandra, questioning the merits of the deal, but a report he prepared for HIH management in December 1996 was embarrassingly optimistic. 'CareAmerica is essentially the same asset as that sold by HIH Winterthur in 1994,' it began. 'It has, however, increased the number of licences held to 25,' it added. Nothing about the · alarming new regulatory regime in California at all.

After stating correctly that the most important consideration was the prognosis for the California workers' compensation market in the next five years, Richardson's report then takes the same tack as Williams about the so-called improving conditions. 'Anecdotal evidence, supported by senior management of CareAmerica, suggests improving market conditions,' his report stated.

It later used the carrot of saying that the acquisition 'will provide a significant increase in group premium'. Not surprisingly, HIH management swallowed the report like an oyster and the deal duly went ahead. Richardson claimed his report was never intended to advise on the desirability of the deal, but the judge said its effect was to 'engender a belief that he had an advisory role in relation to the transaction'. This also became a familiar refrain, particularly when Richardson advised HIH on its takeover of FAI in 1998.

Williams subsequently stood Richardson and his family (two children and nanny included) a $17,000 trip to Europe. This was on top of the fees HIH was already paying, as a personal recompense, and without any evident approval by the HIH board.

Richardson appears to have spotted early that it was not a job where outspoken scepticism was going to be the line to take. A clue to his approach is that when he came to give evidence to the Royal Commission, he was the only witness who used Williams' honorary title 'Doctor', much to the mirth of the spectators.

And meanwhile, although it looked as though HIH was buying back into the Californian business for much less than it sold out for, there was a critical and ultimately disastrous difference. When HIH sold the business in 1994 it guaranteed it would indemnify the buyer in the case of what is called 'prior year deterioration': if the company's claims provisions on its pre–1994 policies were inadequate and the cost of claims blew out.

But when it bought the business back in 1997, it got no such indemnity from the vendors. The next three years turned out to be absolute shockers for HIH's US operation, while the prior year policy payouts blew out spectacularly.

HIH's manager international, George Sturesteps, the horse fancier from Benalla, admitted to the Royal Commission that it was a 'serious oversight' by HIH management in 1996 in not arranging a full due diligence examination of the CareAmerica group in California. It paid $120 million Australian for it and within eighteen months it was $100 million underwater. Not that the irrepressible Ray Williams wanted to hear how bad things were.

In a bid to find out the state of its reserves in the US in March 2000, HIH hired Los Angeles-based actuaries Milliman & Robertson to check them and the report came back that there was a $US55 million shortfall.

'Gorgeous George' Sturesteps, who had been bought his $US200,000 apartment in San Francisco by Ray Williams in 1995 as a bonus for selling the Californian business, was in no hurry to believe that the reacquired company had turned out to be a dud. He concluded that M&R, as they were called, were being conservative because they were being sued as a consequence of an earlier report for another client. He convinced Dominic Fodera of his view.

'The results that M&R had come up with were materially higher than what we had booked and ... [HIH's] US management had lost faith in what M&R were doing,' Fodera testified. So they sacked M&R. They then hired rival actuaries Towers Perrin Tillinghast to do a report on the same reserves, but using different methodology. The conclusion? A $US55 million shortfall again. (It is worth noting that the Californian Department of Insurance checked in 1999, the year before. You will not be surprised to hear the department concluded the gap was $US57.75 million which is so close as to make no difference.)

This called for David Slee, the Melbourne-based actuary who went back a very long way with Ray Williams and who had an eerily good record in arriving at numbers which pleased his old friend. Surely David Slee would show them all the error of their ways.

But even Slee baulked at the numbers he saw. He too recommended a lift in reserves, although no one thought to tell the HIH board about it. This was an awkward piece of timing because HIH was about to announce its June 2000 results and a $US55 million hole was worth almost exactly $100 million Australian. It just never seemed to get mentioned loudly enough to make it into the accounts. Like a big gorilla asleep in the front hall, everyone seemed to tiptoe past it.

Sturesteps said he had told Williams 'at some stage or other' about this teensy-weensy problemette and said that he had not told the other HIH directors because Mr Williams knew. And did he tell the company's auditors? That was not his responsibility, he explained to barrister Simon White, counsel assisting, on 20 September. 'Slipped between the cracks, didn't it?' suggested White.

It couldn't stay hidden for ever.

In September 2000 Arthur Andersen's US office asked to see the Milliman & Robertson report which showed that HIH's reserves in the US had a $US55 million shortfall in them.

HIH's US chief executive, Gary Castro, had sent a note to his finance manager, Bill Howard, in Sydney reporting the Andersen request. When

Howard passed it on to his finance director, Dominic Fodera, Howard appended a note: 'The s..t is about to hit the fan by the look of it.'

Although Andersen never did get to see the report, Howard's prediction certainly came true eventually.

In his final report the judge concluded that Williams might have broken section 180(1) of the Corporations Law (as it was in 2000) by not showing the Milliman & Robertson report to HIH's auditors or to HIH's board. That is a civil charge which carries a maximum financial penalty of $200,000. He also found that Williams might have been responsible for a criminal offence in allowing misleading information to appear in HIH's financial reports, in not recording the $US55 million shortfall in HIH's June 2000 results. That offence carries a maximum prison sentence of one year and is one of four instances in the HIH affair in which Williams may be indicted for an offence that carries a prison term. (The others relate to a deal he did between April and September 2000 with Brad Cooper to pay an inflated price of $17.5 million for half of Ness, a burglar alarm manufacturer, and to two alleged instances of misleading conduct relating to reinsurance contracts that HIH took out with Hannover Re in August 1999.)

Back on the Milliman & Robertson issue, the judge put up the lesser possibility that Williams might have committed a breach of sections 180(1) or 181(1), both of which carry the same $200,000 maximum penalty. The civil breaches may also attract disqualification from managing a company and could oblige him to provide possible financial compensation.

IF THE US AND THE UK operations were giving the Swiss palpitations, HIH's 1997 adventure in China turned into an explosion in a fireworks factory.

Like most companies outside China, HIH had been eyeing it up as a potential goldmine but needed to find a partner there who already had a general insurance licence. The Chinese central government had decided against allowing foreign companies to come in and set up shop without local partners, so when a Chinese insurance delegation came to Sydney in 1995 that included a Mr Wang Jin Cai, chairman of the Yong An property insurance company in the ancient Chinese capital of Xi'an, interest mounted. The rules were liberalised in October 1995 to allow foreign investment in Chinese insurers. Mr Wang, an imposing figure almost 2 metres tall, made all the right noises to HIH management when he came to visit them. They were awed but unshaken when they took him to a Chinese restaurant in Sydney where he ate every single abalone dish on the menu.

By the end of 1996 HIH had deposited $US30 million into an account at the People's Bank of China for a joint venture with Yong An, and in that year Ray Williams and Terry Cassidy visited China three times.

Mr Wang not only had a licence but he had all the right connections with the Communist Party and also the Chinese People's Army. When the two Australians first arrived at Xi'an airport in October 1995 they were met by a Rolls-Royce limousine and a military escort to see them to their hotel with sirens wailing. This is apparently standard fare for foreign corporate visitors in China, as Mr Cassidy made clear in his evidence, but there was more.

Two days later, at a banquet in their honour in the Great Hall of the People in Beijing, Williams and Cassidy got a strong message from Mr Wang Hanbin, vice chairman of the People's National Congress. He 'expressed his desire for HIH to co-operate with Wang Jin Cai in establishing his insurance company'. This information emerged in a report done by Sydney lawyer Stephen Parry on behalf of HIH in late 1997, by which time HIH had been lucky to escape with most of its wallet intact.

Mr Wang had made much to the visitors of his new building in Xi'an, which was under construction at all times when they came. It turned out that the two events were related since as Mr Parry reported, HIH's initial $US30 million investment was used to help pay for the building. The whole HIH involvement was 'a planned fraudulent exercise on the part of Mr Wang', Parry reported.

HIH had tried to find out a bit more about Mr Wang but when word of the inquiries reached his ears, the imposing Mr Wang turned less than diplomatic. He was asked for the names of his companies in Hong Kong, the USA and Europe, but declined to answer, for what he called 'political' reasons.

Ray Williams, ever the optimist, told the *Australian Financial Review* in December 1996 that 'the one thing you learn about China is that it's all to do with relationships, and with people getting on well together, having respect for one another'.

The Winterthur management never got to hear about this until afterwards, even though at that time their company owned 51 per cent of HIH's shares. HIH's investment was never reported back to the HIH board and it was only because the $US30 million was in the People's Bank of China that HIH ever got that money back.

HIH had $A7 million in sunk set-up costs, but an embarrassed Chinese government made sure the $US30 million went back to Australia when Yong An was put in the Chinese equivalent of liquidation in late 1997. HIH took the bold step of capitalising the $7 million in its accounts, effectively calling the money an investment. The judge noted that it should have been written off.

Terry Cassidy was philosophical when the HIH Royal Commission took him through the Yong An adventure on 8 September. 'The view of the board was that this was China in the mid to late 90s,' he said.

At least by then they knew. The HIH 1997 *Annual Report* noted merely that 'Some difficulties were experienced with our joint venture in China ... deposit for the future.'

Wayne Martin, QC, asked Terry Cassidy whether the company had thought 'about telling the shareholders that $US30 million of their money has been invested in reliance on somebody who you believed to be a fraudster?'

'No,' was Cassidy's characteristically honest reply.

CHAPTER 7

PUBLIC LIABILITY AND PROFESSIONAL INDEMNITY INSURANCE

A GOOD INSURANCE professional knows that various categories of insurance are subject to cyclical variations.

Downturns occur when there are too many insurers out there offering to cover the same risks for lower premiums, or when the cost of payouts jumps to new highs because of more generous settlements coming from the courts. For instance, between 1983 and 1988 in London, the capacity of Lloyd's increased by an average 15 per cent a year while premiums grew by only 3 per cent. The inevitable consequence was that insurance rates came down as underwriters struggled for new risks to insure, while the risks themselves grew by far more than the premiums.

When premiums start to get to suicidal levels general insurers groan about a 'crash' and newspapers run banner headlines about the demise of normal life. In Australia in 2002 there were many articles about how local councils were looking at padlocking the swings in the playground and how the church fete was going to have to be cancelled because the organisers could not obtain public liability insurance.

None of this is actually new.

In March 1986 *Time* magazine ran a cover story entitled 'Sorry America: Your Insurance has been cancelled'. It said that after years of huge jury awards, buyers of insurance liability policies faced crippling bills, with increases in premiums ranging as high as 5000 per cent.

It said that the New York City tramway system had had its annual insurance bill lifted from $US800,000 to $US9 million. A sporting goods manufacturer had been paying $US8000 a year for $25 million of product liability insurance; its renewal notice demanded a $US200,000 premium for $US1 million of insurance, and so on.

Public liability, in which HIH had a market share in Australia of more than 50 per cent, had a 'double bottom' that was another major factor in the undoing of HIH.

Public liability insurance has always been led by the US, home of the liability lawyer, and it went through a trough there between 1986 and 1989. But what caught industry veteran Ray Williams off guard after 1992, when HIH listed, was that public liability had another downturn in the mid–1990s and this time it was global. Most analysts now believe that it was unprofitable for most companies from around 1995 until rates kicked up sharply in the wake of the al-Qaeda attack of 11 September 2001.

Meanwhile, there was another related category of insurance taking off in the late 1980s that was making so much profit for its underwriters that Australian insurance companies were lining up to get a slice of the reinsurance action: professional indemnity insurance.

If public liability is about what gets paid out when a chain breaks on a swing in a park, professional indemnity is about what gets paid out after an accountant, lawyer or doctor makes a professional error.

ALAS and ALAC were two very presciently named categories of PI insurance in the US which were reinsured both by FAI and HIH in the late 1980s. Premiums seemed to be higher than previous claims had appeared to justify so the Attorneys' Liability Assurance Society (ALAS) and its sister organisation, Accountants' Liability Assurance Company (ALAC), were a honeypot for international insurance companies looking for a bit of what is called 'inwards reinsurance'. Minet International Professional Indemnity (MIPI), the offshore arm of a UK-based reinsurance broker, was a particularly heavy acceptor of the US risk, which it then offered around the world to conventional insurance companies and professional investors alike. MIPI covered what were called the 'Big Six' accounting firms, including FAI and HIH's auditors, Arthur Andersen, specifically covering the period from 1988 to 1992.

Reinsurance in its simplest form is a wholesale version of ordinary insurance and the two Australian insurers were in this case tempted to take on a small slice of someone else's risk, in order to make a profit.

The big appeal to accepting companies was that premium revenue was about seven years ahead of the average payout date.

Unfortunately, the US professional indemnity goldmine was a short-lived affair. Policies written in 1987 and 1988 were among the worst hit since the share market crash of 1987 produced a storm of lawsuits against professional advisers for malpractice.

The US professional indemnity business was not a disaster on the scale of the asbestos and pollution claims blowouts that almost crippled Lloyd's, but its effect on FAI in particular was enormous. By the time FAI was taken over by HIH in late 1998 the size of the reserve shortfall in FAI's Commercial and Professional Insurance Division (CPID) was around $130 million because the claims against US accountants and lawyers had snowballed through the 1990s.

Angus Maciver, an Anglo-Scottish lawyer who had travelled out overland to Australia in the early 1970s and joined FAI in 1974, was head of FAI's CPID at the time the US risks were taken on, so he had honorary status at FAI in later years as the 'Cause of the Disaster'. This was despite the fact that Larry Adler would have known all about the US business. A kind of 'Blame Gus Club' sprang up inside FAI after he left in 1997, which was well aired at the Royal Commission. Former FAI chief executive Rodney Adler, whose father Larry had invited Maciver's uncle Eric Atkinson to become an FAI director in the early 1970s, portrayed Maciver to the Royal Commission as a man reluctant to embrace the exciting new management culture that he was trying to impose on FAI. But no one at FAI seemed to want to wrestle with the bigger question posed by the long-tail professional indemnity exposure: what to do about it?

One of the best efforts to stiffen FAI came in 1995, when Rodney Adler hired accountant Daniel Wilkie from blue chip insurer NRMA as potential chief operating officer. 'It is not unfair to say that FAI suffered a poor reputation, and part of my job as chief executive of the company was to change that reputation in a claims-paying sense and in a quality of management sense,' Adler told the Royal Commission. 'We did not have the quality of people that I felt comfortable with, nor did the insurance market feel comfortable,' he said.

Wilkie was not exactly slavering at the prospect. 'He was not keen initially,' Adler told the commission. 'He felt that we were an under-reserved and poorly performing company and that he did not wish to join us.'

But Wilkie, who was offered around $400,000 a year to jump ship, was prevailed upon to take charge of one of the two insurance divisions. Wilkie was a man who did not like to say no to a challenge. A stocky and moustachioed petrol-head and 'rugger bugger' from central casting, he had a diary that was liberally sprinkled with lunches and dinners involving sporting speakers, to the extent at times that observers might have been pressed to work out when he was actually running the company.

Wilkie took on FAI's retail division, which sold classes like car, home contents, workers' compensation and compulsory third-party accident cover, and operated profitably. But Adler later widened his role to include the much more dangerous Corporate and Professional Insurance Division (CPID), which mainly sold public liability and professional indemnity in Australia and overseas.

Although the policies had been taken out in the late 1980s, it was not until 1997 that anyone at FAI appears to have tried to do anything to tackle the problem or even admit to it.

There are several versions of who spotted it first. Actuary Peter Moran joined FAI in mid–1996 with a range of briefs including spending half his time reviewing the company's international claims and by the middle of 1997 was able to tell accountant Tony Boulden about 'significant under reserving' in the area.

Boulden, who had been working at FAI for seven years and was a financial controller of CPID, already had some idea because he noticed in the April 1997 monthly management accounts that FAI's policyholder claims were running $9.7 million worse than budget. He also found a report by consulting actuaries Coopers & Lybrand dated 15 May 1997 which said that the loss ratio for the international professional indemnity book at FAI was running at 173 per cent.

In simple terms, that meant that in that area FAI was paying out $1.73 for every dollar coming through the door in premiums. The insurance world has a lexicon of euphemisms for such situations, the most common being 'claims history deterioration'. Boulden used the least varnished word, deterioration, then did something else which is a comparative rarity in this saga: he did something about it.

He asked Ashraf Kamha, who took over as head of CPID after Angus Maciver left, if he could investigate the US PI problem further. Kamha, who was later to play a major role as whistle-blower, agreed.

Boulden started out in a small way as he could only spare one day a week in mid–1997 to crosscheck between pooled claim files called 'bordereaux' and the reserve case estimates kept on Aegis, which was FAI's supposedly foolproof computerised system. They did not tally.

At about the same time Moran was making his own inquiries and also concluded that Aegis did not square with the bordereaux that were coming to Australia twice a year from the US. That could have been going on for years, he admitted to the Royal Commission, which in itself is a startling remark. An insurance company that does not reconcile its cash flow with its long-term liabilities is inevitably heading for disaster unless by some quirk of fate it has been overcharging on premiums. Given that there seems to be a 'race to the bottom' in premium levels every fifteen years or so, overcharging is rare and anyway, it never lasts long enough to get a stretched insurer out of trouble.

In October 1997, Boulden reported back to Kamha. Kamha told the commission he learnt from Boulden of 'a general state of disorganisation' in the international CPID portfolio. 'The staff concerned did not have the experience to realise what is required to be done and they were not properly instructed or trained,' he said. 'As a result, increases in claims reserves reported by brokers were not entered on FAI's computer system and were not accounted for.'

Junior claims officers were simply sitting on advice about claims until the time came to pay them out. That was contrary to accounting standards, which demand that claims provisions must be lifted and changed as soon as it becomes apparent they are inadequate. Understating claims provisions is to the insurance world what understating your liabilities is to the mainstream commercial world.

By December 1997 Tony Boulden was able to report to a horrified Ashraf Kamha, a thirty-year veteran in the insurance industry, that there was a $112 million shortfall in FAI's reserves for that US business alone.

Warren Buffett, the Oracle of Omaha, memorably noted after 11 September 2001 that when insurers start talking about 'reserve deterioration', that is just a euphemism for saying that they overstated their previous profits. In that vein, FAI had reported losses in four of the previous five years and even in a good year a $20 million net profit was quite an achievement.

If it was correct that FAI had overstated profits by $112 million (and under HIH that number later climbed to some $178 million) then you would have to make some dire conclusions about FAI. Aside from the popular line that the company may never have been solvent since Larry Adler founded it in 1960, it may not have been genuinely profitable since it started accepting US professional insurance risk in the late 1980s.

The best that can be said was that Larry Adler made a profit of around $300 million for FAI in 1986 by selling out a big stake in Pioneer Concrete to corporate raider Robert Holmes à Court. It would be churlish to suggest the company was insolvent then, when it had a market capitalisation of around $2.8 billion.

Anyway, fast forward to 1997. Kamha took his concerns straight to chief executive Rodney Adler in December of that year and, according to his evidence, Adler became 'extremely alarmed and concerned' and told Kamha to treat the matter as confidential.

Adler then told him not to discuss the shortfall until a 'review' had been completed, a response of which any politician would have been proud. This was to happen as soon as possible, Adler told him. 'I think they were words to the effect that "until the review is completed and the full magnitude and nature of the problem is ascertained, this is a serious enough matter to, you know ... be confidential",' is how he described the conversation.

At one level Adler's response was a logical one, but at another it was very dangerous since the information was a major threat to the company's 1997–98 accounts. Any failure to act on known negative information would be artificially inflating the accounts.

Certainly the executive team at FAI appeared to have a good idea of what was going on. Daniel Wilkie, who by then was FAI's chief operating officer and had been promoted above Ashraf Kamha in 1997, knew more than he would have liked to know and also said that finance director Tim Mainprize had also talked to him about the shortfall at the time.

Niran Peiris, the company's financial controller, gave some awesomely dull evidence to the Royal Commission but a report of a conversation he had in 2000 with an HIH accountant looking for a job change, Robert Martin, added some much needed colour to the picture. Peiris was by then a senior manager at the Allianz group and Martin had had to spend eighteen months in 1999 and 2000 trying to clear up the mess of FAI's lack of reserves. Martin was looking at a move to Allianz but wanted to clear the air with Peiris first, so he set up an informal meeting with him.

Martin told the commission that Peiris had said, 'CPID was like a minefield. A good day was walking in and not getting a leg blown off.' Unfortunately, it is one thing to know about a problem, but quite another to do something constructive about it.

In the statement Ashraf Kamha gave to the Royal Commission, he said he had been told in September 1997 that the main cause of the under-reserving problem was the transfer of experienced underwriting staff to FAI's London office.

In November 1995, an executive called Mark Bonnar transferred from Sydney to FAI's London office. In November 1996 Angus Maciver resigned from FAI, latterly as head of CPID, after twenty-two years there.

Some of Bonnar's responsibilities were picked up by others in Sydney, but it seems no one took over his critical role of setting claims reserves — predicting how much money should be set aside to pay future claims — in CPID's international portfolio. If CPID was a minefield, the man with the only map had just got up and gone.

Meanwhile, quite apart from running the risk of overstating its profits, by this point FAI was also back on the tightrope of risking insolvency. The company only had a financial 'buffer' of $22 million in cash in December 1997, since most of its major assets were illiquid real estate investments such as the St Moritz Hotel in New York and the Emu Brewery site in Perth. Both required expenditure before they had a chance of being sold for anything approaching their book value.

In November 1997 Rodney Adler appointed Daniel Wilkie to the job of chief operating officer, which put him above the older and more experienced Kamha. Adler had been told by Wilkie, a man noted for his direct approach, that he would not work under Kamha. Adler did what most executives do at times: he went along with Wilkie's edict, putting him in charge not only of the general insurance division but also CPID, and then gave Kamha a special project investigating the purchase in London of a Lloyd's syndicate on behalf of FAI.

And just as the skeleton in the CPID cupboard was starting to emerge in front of Kamha, Adler had handed it to Wilkie. 'At that time, I explained to him that he would have to take over the review that Mr

Kamha had been conducting at my request,' Adler said later, although he kept well away from messy details such as reserve shortfalls. Kamha had known the 'hole' was $112 million on 2 or 3 December, when Boulden had told him.

Boulden's working papers were in a special file, by now known to one and all as the Boulden File, and to which the password was 'Rodent'.

Both Boulden and Kamha knew that the hole might become even bigger. It consisted of claims that had been incurred but not provided for, but there is another extra category in long-tail insurance called IBNR, 'incurred but not reported', which should also be considered by a prudent insurer.

Say, for example, a US accounting firm had made five significant and inexcusable errors in auditing five different companies' accounts, and for which they were likely to be sued. Legal actions happen in haphazard time frames and it might be that they had been successfully sued in three of them but that in the case of the other two, the claims had not even been lodged. Those two future cases, if the insurer was prudent, would be classified as IBNR.

Kamha told the commission that he was 'shocked by the magnitude of the figures' and gave Wilkie, his new direct superior, a detailed briefing 'almost five minutes' after Boulden had handed him the 'Rodent' spreadsheet. He described Wilkie's reaction as 'very concerned'.

Wilkie told the Commission that at the time he had not yet taken over responsibility for CPID and also denied hearing anything about a $112 million shortfall. The judge said he 'preferred the evidence of Kamha' about the conversation.

Wilkie appears to have had the same reaction as Adler to the bad news. He wanted a review and he wanted it soon, but the actuary he wanted to do that job, Geoff Trahair, was still employed at NRMA (where Wilkie used to work) and would not be available to start work on the CPID reserving problem until February 1998. The magician still had to finish one party before he could come to this one.

Meanwhile, Wilkie went with the Adler line that until they knew the size of the problem, there would be no merit in making a fuss. If there was a polar bear eating all their provisions, they seemed to be more concerned with deciding how big it was than looking in the cupboard for the rifle.

Adler told the commission: 'Within two, three weeks of [his promotion], Mr Wilkie came back to me and said, based on his preliminary review, that there was not a problem that concerned him greatly, but he would like to employ a much more qualified actuary than we currently possessed to analyse the CPID area specifically and that, unfortunately, that person would only be able to arrive around February.' That was one of his shorter sentences. He also told the commission that it would have been 'so absurd' to ask for details before the review had been completed.

Wilkie told the commission that while waiting for the new actuary, Geoff Trahair, to start work, he did not ask Boulden, Moran or Kamha anything about the under-reserving issue in his new domain. 'Looking back now, I guess four years after the event, perhaps more could have been done at the time, but at that particular point in time I thought that was a reasonable course of action,' Wilkie said.

But if Wilkie and Adler were waiting for Geoff Trahair to quantify the problem conveniently for them, the passage of time had a fortuitous benefit. If Trahair could not start until February, that meant his inevitably negative report would miss the 31 December 1997 half-year results deadline, which was signed off on 19 February. The company reported a pre-tax profit of $3 million. And if FAI executives affected an air of studied unconcern in the last weeks of 1997 about the CPID monster, they were simultaneously working flat out to squeeze every last drop of positive financial numbers out of the books.

The 31 December half year ends at a very inconvenient date if you are trying to get things done in a hurry, and the first thing that happened was that Ashraf Kamha's Christmas holiday was comprehensively ruined. Between 22 and 25 December 1997 he got a series of calls from Adler, Wilkie and Mainprize, on a variety of subjects.

Top of the list was a request by Wilkie to provide an 'adjusted' list of claims estimates in the CPID, which he managed, and they had to be processed before 31 December. For 'adjust', you can read 'reduce'. The lower the claims estimates, the more the sorely needed resources of FAI could be spread around where they were more obviously needed.

Adler rang him about a Lloyd's syndicate proposal but, he said, didn't mention the $112 million problem. And Mainprize rang to make sure he knew to get Wilkie's list through ASAP.

Kamha later told the commission he had not understood the magnitude of the $25 million worth of reserve reductions he made at the time but, in preparing to give evidence to the Royal Commission, he had realised Mr Wilkie's instructions were 'improper'.

Tony Boulden was also involved in the process, sending a message on 21 January 1998 to a colleague in Sydney that 'all the adjustments should bring the result to under $20 million'. And on 23 January he was squarely in the middle of another lemon-squeezing exercise, asking colleague Graeme King in Hong Kong to see if he could reduce a medical malpractice reserve there from its December 1997 level of $59.22 million back to its 30 June 1997 level of $49.26 million. The effect of such an action is to improve half-year top-line profits by almost $10 million without anyone actually doing anything. The catch of course is that whichever actuary decided that $59.22 million was the reserve required had been completely ignored.

King wrote back: 'I must say I am reluctant to reduce in view of the requirements in HK by the Insurance Authority,' he said. 'To reduce the figure at December will only add to the various problems we are facing here in this financial year.'

Hong Kong would appear to have had a more vigilant insurance regulator than Australia did, to judge by the lack of similar mentions in any of those FAI internal e-mails of the Insurance and Superannuation Commission, as it was until 30 June 1998.

As it happened, FAI was in such dire straits that it ended up grabbing up-front all the $57 million worth of financial benefit of the two major reinsurance contracts it did line up in 1998, and concentrated much of its efforts on fooling auditors Andersen that the deals were real reinsurance and were not what an FAI manager called them: a rental of the balance sheet of stronger insurers.

If the auditors were fooled, Australia's insurance regulator was almost entirely in the dark.

For years Australia had chugged along with the Canberra-based Insurance and Superannuation Commission (ISC) but after 1 July 1998 senior staff with the commission were asked to join the new Australian Prudential Regulation Authority (APRA). The framework of the reinsurance side of APRA carried on much as before, using ISC staff until August 1999 when 'New APRA' was created.

This was a brainchild of the *Wallis Report* of 1997 on Australia's financial system, and the notion of replacing eleven different regulatory bodies with one, APRA, was an excellent idea.

But there were two disasters in the transition from Old to New APRA. One, all the records on Australia's insurance companies were transferred to single page 'handover sheets' which, for instance, classed HIH's main insurance company, HIH Casualty & General, as low risk. The other, worse problem was that there was a huge turnover of staff because APRA was going to be based in Sydney.

Most of the senior staff were ex-Department of Treasury and were very well established in Canberra, where schools are good and housing is not expensive. A request for financial help in moving to Sydney was turned down and most of the senior staff merely moved to other senior jobs in the public service in Canberra, in departments that were only too pleased to have them, in preference to moving.

Two of the three most experienced insurance regulators, Russell Stenhouse and Richard Smith, left, and the third, Michael Saliba, followed just over a year later. Stenhouse had a particularly strong desire to stay in Canberra, not for any of those domestic reasons but because he is a do-it-yourself engineering fanatic with a penchant for having bits of car and motorcycle engine stored all around his house.

'There is a case that the cost of real estate in Sydney caused the insurance regulator to be effectively impotent in Australia for three years,' remarked one barrister familiar with the Royal Commission. He has yet to be proved significantly wrong.

The Insurance and Superannuation Commission was certainly on FAI's case through the 1990s, noting for instance that in 1993 the company was $553 million below the required solvency margin. Things got marginally better in 1995 after some pressure from the ISC on FAI to restructure itself, although that was arguably just a way to use the company's few resources to make it look better. Nothing much had actually changed.

A Mr Armstrong of the ISC and then APRA wrote a note in mid–1998 to say that FAI's lack of a prudential margin 'requires desperate attention'. It never really got anything more than a minor cosmetic touch-up.

At the time an APRA internal note said: 'Officers within APRA considered FAI was under-provisioned to an extent which would have placed that company in breach of the minimum solvency standards.'

There are two sorts of solvency standard: the regulator's standard, which demands that an insurer has surplus reserves sufficient to pay out 20 per cent of its premiums in any given year, and there is commercial solvency, which is less demanding. That merely asks that a company should be able to pay its debts as and when they fall due. FAI not only failed the harder test through the second half of the 1990s but almost certainly failed the easier test too.

Peter Thompson, a senior HIH executive who was asked to sort out the FAI mess after HIH took it over, noted to his colleagues that he believed FAI was insolvent at 30 June 1998. HIH started taking it over three months later.

FAI was in good company. John Palmer, the Canadian chartered accountant and former prudential regulator who wrote a report for APRA in late 2001 on its poor performance in supervising HIH, came to the same conclusion about HIH on the very same date.

Alan Cameron, the man who chaired APRA's sister organisation, ASIC (the Australian Securities and Investments Commission), for eight years, summed up APRA's problem very well when he gave evidence to the commission on 12 November 2002. He said APRA had a passive culture that it had inherited from its predecessor the ISC, while ASIC had been founded with what he called an 'enforcement culture' in the early 1990s.

He told Justice Neville Owen that APRA had 'almost the London tea and biscuits approach to supervision' and that while ASIC was not afraid to have a confrontation, APRA had 'the bedside manner of the doctor' in the way it looked after institutions like insurers.

The old hands who attended the HIH Royal Commission took a harsher view. One, retired actuary John Corbett, said that most people in the Australian insurance business were amazed when federal Treasurer John Howard granted FAI a licence to operate in 1978. For them, APRA was merely trying to clear up a mess that had started twenty years before. A telling footnote is that in the tightening up of insurance prudential regulations that happened in July 2002, federal treasurers in Australia would no longer have the discretion they had to grant insurance licences without the support of the regulator.

CHAPTER 8

HEADS IN THE SAND

WHEN GEOFF TRAHAIR did finally arrive at FAI in early 1998 he found that all the contentious evidence was in the Tony Boulden file, accessed by the password 'Rodent'. With the understatement that appears to be a badge of honour in the actuarial profession, he subsequently described the situation as 'rather remarkable'.

He said the only explanation he was given for the failure to include the results of offshore brokers' bordereaux (policy summaries) in the Aegis system was that it had been on the instructions of the previous divisional head, Gus Maciver.

On 19 March 1998 Trahair produced a report for his new bosses at FAI which said there was a shortfall of $91.9 million in the professional indemnity area. Considering how few people knew exactly what was going on, it was a very solid fit with Tony Boulden's calculations. The worst affected portfolios were called Attorneys' Liability Assurance Society (ALAS) and Minet International Professional Indemnity (MIPI) which, on Trahair's first inspection, appeared to have paid out more than 200 per cent of premiums, although he later reduced that number. MIPI covered the Big Six accounting firms (including PwC and Andersen) and specifically covered the period from 1988 to 1992.

Where the story now gets really strange is that Daniel Wilkie, the man who hired Geoff Trahair, said he had no recollection of receiving Trahair's report. Commissioning it was transparently the act of a wise man, but taking delivery of it quite another matter.

We do know that Trahair physically told Wilkie on 19 March that there was a $65 million shortfall relating to two international CPID portfolios, which was just part of the story. And we also know that Wilkie told Adler in the same month that FAI had 'a $50 million to $60 million problem', in a conversation that Adler described as 'unpleasant'. Adler said he was 'shocked' by the news and it was the first time he had heard of it. To give him the benefit of the doubt, Kamha had not been very specific about numbers when he first spoke to Adler about the hole. Adler told the commission that in his December 1997 conversation with Kamha the shortfall was somewhere between $5 million and $10 million. (Under cross-examination, he said he had not inquired why the problem had arisen, who was responsible, nor whether proper procedures were in place.)

And Adler seems to have been very incurious about Trahair's much more ominous report, which he too had earlier been so keen to wait for. He told the Royal Commission that he had 'never seen' Trahair's report.

If Trahair could not find anyone willing to read his report among the senior executive triumvirate at FAI, he found others in the actuarial world who would.

Trahair discussed his project with Peter McCarthy, an actuary who had been working in the retail division since 1995 where he had looked at potential under-reserving. In April 1998, McCarthy put the two sets of figures together and calculated that FAI was $250 million short of adequate provisions. He was 'shattered', he told the commission. 'The only hope was for FAI to find capital or be sold.'

McCarthy says the pair went to see Wilkie. After McCarthy wrote a list of the problems on the whiteboard in Wilkie's office and told him they added up to $250 million, Wilkie apparently made two comments: 'It's all over', and 'we are creators of our own demise'.

Trahair remembered the meeting too, although his recollection of the number was that it was only 'more than $100 million'. He says Wilkie said he would have to go and see Adler.

Wilkie told the commission, by contrast, that he did not recall the meeting ever taking place. And even if it had taken place, he would have taken any information provided with a grain of salt because McCarthy was 'a noted alarmist'. 'Mr McCarthy's initial position is always to overreact to anything and then come back subsequently with the passage of time and more information,' Wilkie said.

Whiteboards have the awkward problem that they never give up their secrets afterwards, unlike e-mails, so history never recorded what the grand total of shortfall was. The most conservative estimate is around $130 million.

Simon White, barrister assisting the Royal Commission, summed up FAI's problem nicely by using a bad pun: 'This was truly a case of a very long tail wagging a very sick dog.'

But not only did Wilkie deny ever getting Trahair's formal report, he said Trahair was effectively unable to form a view on FAI's troubles: 'Mr Trahair told me that he had all sorts of troubles actually coming to a quantum for the liability. There was missing bits of information and it was getting to the stage where the amount of effort required was beyond his resources ... To the best of my recollection, that was all he told me.'

And Adler didn't seem to be a great deal wiser about FAI's giant and growing professional indemnity problem than Wilkie was. Shown a copy of Trahair's $91 million shortfall report by the HIH Royal Commission, Adler said it was the first time he had seen it, adding airily that 'under-reserving was not my mandate'. He also said he had never seen internal FAI documents suggesting a shortfall of more than $150 million.

In one day of his evidence he started by saying that FAI's reserves had been adequate, but later he said: 'I wouldn't want to define that [$50 million to $60 million problem] as under-reserving ... my understanding was that we were adequately reserved and this problem was manifesting itself in the future.' That was the ultimate disingenuous statement, since all insurance reserves relate to the future.

But if the management's attitude to a nasty number was a passable impression of synchronised ostrich head burying, things took on an air of messy farce when FAI Insurance's external actuaries, PricewaterhouseCoopers (PwC), were brought in in June 1997 and June 1998 for their annual examination of possible reserve shortfalls. In 1997 they examined public liability and in 1998, professional indemnity.

Unfortunately, all the people who would have been most able to help PwC produce a worthwhile report were kept away from Chris Latham, the PwC actuary who was asked to run the review.

Geoff Trahair said in evidence that Daniel Wilkie had told him that Ashraf Kamha would be responsible for supplying information to PwC in

1998 and that 'specifically, this information [his report on the $91 million shortfall] was not to be provided'.

He was also told the information should not be provided to FAI's usual auditor, Andersen, either. Since auditors are hired to make sure companies produce financial numbers that are a true and fair picture of their financial situation, keeping the auditors away is the ultimate short-term solution to a problem.

And meanwhile, in July 1997 actuary Rodney Hoskinson of FAI's research department had almost finished working out future claims calculations on FAI's Australian public liability insurance to help PwC when Ashraf Kamha told him he should do no further work on the CPID loss provisions and that the work he had done was confidential.

So, a few days later, Hoskinson had to tell the auditors he was not doing that work when he had previously told them he was. He spoke to Anita Lee and Daniel Vanderkemp of Andersen, possibly the only two auditors in this entire affair to emerge at the end with reputations actually enhanced.

But back then they appear to have been taken in. Hoskinson wrote to FAI's financial controller, Niran Peiris, on 31 July 1997 that 'they were a bit surprised because we had previously told them I would be doing this valuation. I told them that a decision had been made several weeks ago that CPID would use Coopers, and that I thought it was perfectly reasonable for Ashraf to choose where he seeks his advice. They are not aware of the difference in my figures and those of Coopers,' he confided.

He appeared to be accepting of the situation since he also told Peiris that the auditors would get a 'completely separate document, not referred to in any of my other reports'.

He explained that his report would be 'a draft only for their information, without further discussions with CPID. The auditors won't know of its existence from the Research Department.'

Mervyn King, a retired South African Supreme Court judge who visited Australia in mid–2002 to lecture on corporate governance, said of such affairs: 'I wish that companies could realise how much intellectual effort is wasted by management looking at ways to conceal information rather than just getting on with running their business as efficiently and transparently as possible.'

The e-mails brought out from the FAI records show how a startling transformation had overcome well-educated and rational people. A financial problem that was not of their making, followed by the high-handed decision to ration information to the consultants who were actually being paid to help, snowballed very quickly into a full-blown cover-up. Throw in the perennial issue of whether to obey an instruction from a superior or make a fuss in front of them, and you have a classic moral 'slippery slope'.

Television adverts always seem to portray the corporate world as a place where individual endeavour, a sharp suit and a taste for good coffee will take you anywhere. There is of course a grain of truth in that but in the insurance industry in the 1990s, it seems to have been more about dealing with other people's previous miscalculations than making some new conquest of your own.

In FAI's case, the situation was compounded by the fact that management had gone 'actuary shopping' to PricewaterhouseCoopers in the hope of recording lower reserve requirements. Research department actuary Rodney Hoskinson decided to try to do something about it.

Hoskinson was something of a wag, by actuarial standards at least. Asked in July 1997 to see what he could shave from his central reserve estimates, he made it clear that all the spare reserves had long ago been spotted and used elsewhere. 'There is more fat on Kate Moss [a waif-like supermodel] than there is in the estimates for NSW CTP [Compulsory Third Party] and WA and Tassie Workers' Comp,' he said.

He sent a message to his colleague, FAI accountant Marc Gross, just before the first Coopers report was released to FAI. The Coopers report for 1997 had calculated that FAI would need $28 million in outstanding claims in total reserves for public liability in Australia, while Hoskinson had worked out that the company's exposure would be $39.86 million. The ultimate figure turned out to be closer to $60 million, in fact.

'Whose provision are we booking for the CPID liability?' he asked FAI executive Marc Gross in July 1997.

'Mine ($39.86 million) or Coopers' ($28 million)? I think I can guess. It makes me sick to the stomach that Coopers can produce such a figure,' he told Gross.

Hoskinson was clearly embarrassed to see such a personal letter put up on the screen at the Royal Commission since he told Richard Lancaster, counsel for auditors Andersen, that he had been 'reacting emotionally' when he wrote that, but offered little more explanation.

Hoskinson told Richard White, SC, counsel assisting the commission: 'The numbers that they [Coopers] had come up with, with the benefit of hindsight, were clearly too low.'

Hoskinson said he did not think it was up to him to tell Andersen's auditors about the difference between the two numbers. 'I probably felt that was an issue for management to deal with the auditors,' he said.

A letter that Rodney Adler sent on 1 August 1997 to Ian Heppell on the reserving issue was a clear reaction to Hoskinson's criticism. Adler praised the work of Heppell's department but made it clear FAI staff had to work together and that sometimes management had to take a different view from researchers. 'The world is not black and white,' he said. 'Different opinions do arise and sometimes decisions will be taken in the best interest of FAI which may contradict and/or be in opposition with certain executives in certain departments,' he continued. 'Bad luck, that is life,' he concluded. He then ordered that there be 'no discussion' between Heppell's research department and Coopers, which is about as logical as making sure your spouse does not talk to the real estate agent while you are trying to sell your house.

Giving evidence to the Royal Commission in early July, he took a very different tack. He said that if he had been informed that FAI's case-by-case data relating to claims reserves was being manipulated and that executives were being 'less than frank' with Coopers, then 'retrenchments of some significance' would have occurred.

Those 'retrenchments of some significance' ended up happening at HIH, where after 15 March 2001 some 1000 staff lost their jobs.

After all the internal anxieties he had been hearing, Adler would have been pleased that the report from PwC in mid–1998 merely recommended that FAI should lift its reserves by $13.1 million. That was, as he announced at the time, the result of a decision 'in the best interests of FAI', by which he meant the decision to keep the research department well away from Coopers.

Since he ended up selling his company to HIH for $300 million in late 1998 when at least two informed views estimated its real value at about $20 million, he can always claim that his philosophy worked. But as a blueprint for corporate governance, the amount of fudging and evasion that had gone on at FAI was appalling.

Heppell tried his best to highlight the research department–Coopers charade by asking Ashraf Kamha to show Rodney Hoskinson's draft June 1997 report to FAI's finance director, Tim Mainprize. He too had run the white flag of surrender most of the way up the flagpole by writing to Kamha on 31 July 1997 and saying Rodney Hoskinson's report would be entirely separate. 'It will not be attached to or mentioned in the report to the General Insurance division,' he said, adding that it would remain a 'draft' unless Kamha said otherwise. A draft report, and this must have come up dozens of times in the commission, is what reports tend to be called when someone wants to disclaim ownership of them if anything goes wrong.

Heppell's main dash for the moral high ground, in his letter, came later and was impressive in its way. 'In Rodney's [Hoskinson's] opinion, if you set the provisions on Coopers' advice the portfolio will be under-reserved,' he wrote. 'Further, if you were to set premiums in line with that advice, losses would result. Rodney and I are employees of FAI General Insurance Company Ltd and, I believe, carry some responsibility to the shareholders to press his views. We would like to provide a copy of the report to Tim Mainprize as well as Tony and yourself to clearly satisfy this responsibility.' He asked Kamha's permission to do that.

Sadly, his protest seems to have had as much success as Hoskinson's, even though they both elected to point the problem out to senior executives. Not only was Adler a 30 per cent shareholder in the company but he was its chief executive, and Tim Mainprize was the only executive other than Adler to be on the insurer's board.

And if you tell a small corporate fib one year and it seems to work, what do you do the next year? The overwhelming temptation is to tell a bigger one.

There was little short of a conspiracy among FAI's management almost a year later about how to handle the annual visit of Chris Latham, the PwC point man on the job.

David Cheal, a technology specialist contracted to the HIH Royal Commission in late 2001, discovered that an e-mail message he was looking at from that period had a password-protected attachment that began like this: 'What does Chris need to know? What does he suspect? Will he react badly if he is now told something that he only previously suspected?'

E-mail messages were the lifeblood of the Royal Commission because they always seemed to be written by people who were not expecting those messages ever to see the light of day ... even though computer hard discs keep copies or 'shadows' of all manner of careless communications.

The password-protected message was wonderful stuff, complaining of the same old 'Kate Moss' problem: the manipulation of case estimates to improve results.

Geoff Trahair owned up to co-authoring at least one version of the document with fellow actuary Peter McCarthy, to prepare chief operating officer Daniel Wilkie for his meeting with Mr Latham. Wilkie was the third man in Rodney Adler's ruling triumvirate at FAI and the man who was always given the hard yards to run.

The meeting was given extra spice by the fact that FAI was three months off announcing its 1997–98 results and the memo stated that there was between $57 million and $64 million of deliberate under-estimation of future claims on other FAI policies, or in other words manipulated case estimates.

These were in addition to a reserve shortfall of some $100 million in FAI's US professional indemnity business.

'We need to make sure that all FAI staff dealing with Coopers are seen to have the utmost credibility [in Coopers' eyes].' It went on, 'and it may be possible to sell Tony Boulden as the scapegoat, although this begs the question as to whose directions he was carrying out'.

There was a lot more on how FAI's actuaries and research staff should present themselves to Mr Latham since, as the document noted, 'If Daniel [Wilkie] or Research's credibility is in doubt in Coopers' eyes then we are really stuffed.'

In simple terms, FAI had hired PricewaterhouseCoopers as external actuaries to come in and advise on how to advise on provisioning when by this time it was apparent there was an overall shortfall in the company of between $150 million and $220 million, depending on how much overlap you allowed between Boulden and Moran's brave expeditions into the Stygian depths of FAI's already notorious data.

The advice the two actuaries offered to Wilkie was not all evasive, suggesting they 'be upfront as much as we can with Chris' about manipulation of case estimates in CPID and how the company was going to stop writing some types of insurance policies and stop operating in some countries. They sound sacrificial rather than core offerings, though: 'Fiji, Guam, Saipan, construction, personal accident, public liability'... The first three are a test of identifying dots in a lot of blue on the map, usually in a box in the top right-hand corner, while the three insurance categories were all a disaster for FAI anyway. Telling your consulting actuary that you are about to stop doing something geographically difficult or financially nasty is a step in the right direction, but it could also be construed as an attempt to put him off the scent by offering a statement of the bleeding obvious.

The note also stated: 'we cannot increase the reserves to their level in one step: it will take a few years to get there'. That is a major howler in the pantheon of atrocities that insurance companies can commit. If a company's reserves are inadequate, its management has to 'fess up straightaway and increase its reserves, even if that means wiping out all the profit it had been hoping to declare. In simple terms, money made by insurers can be put to reserves or profit, but not both.

(It is worth remembering that the best run of the old mutual insurance companies always did their reserving first. Rather than picking a planned profit number and then bending the reserve numbers to get there, which is what both FAI and then HIH turned into an art form, they used to work out what the worst outcome was in the payout column, reserve for that and then start looking at the profit numbers. If all of that fitted then maybe there was a dividend payable, but not until all the other issues were covered.)

Where Trahair and McCarthy's briefing document gets baroque is in its suggestion to shift the onus of blame onto PwC for not seeing how FAI's reserving policy had been heading previously before things got this bad. 'Perhaps they were not as thorough as they should have been,' is how the memo put it.

Quite how bad things were is shown by how MIPI was 'developing' year by year. 'Payments over the last several years have been $6 million, $11 million, $10 million, $7 million and now $18 million for the year to May,' it noted, with the month of June threatening to make the total higher still.

'Chris commented in his last report that development had slowed in 1996–97,' the note read, referring to the not-so-nasty $7 million number.

The Byzantine conclusion the note reached was that because Coopers had previously valued the MIPI exposure using FAI's data alone, they could be accused of not having been thorough enough.

'Had they examined our exposures, they would have realised the extent of the under-reserving before now. Chris should be amenable to some form of face-saving solution,' it concluded darkly.

Simon White, counsel assisting the commission, made a useful classical reference in describing how the whole relationship between insiders, outsiders and relevant information had been turned on its head.

'Aegis was the name given to the shield of Zeus in Greek mythology and is symbolic of divine protection,' he said. 'Regrettably, in the events that occurred, the only protection the Aegis database gave FAI was preventing its external actuaries becoming aware of significant under-reserving within the company.'

History does not provide the full story of what happened when Chris Latham came to FAI but it is apparent that he was given a lousy set of numbers to work from. His report to FAI said that the company should add only $13 million to its claims reserves in what we know was the stricken CPID area.

Geoff Trahair admitted to the Royal Commission that Mr Latham had been dishonestly given inadequate information for his review but that he, Trahair, had been 'overridden' by his superiors. 'I was operating under the instructions I had been given,' said Trahair, who said he had been told that any disclosure to Latham of shortfalls in FAI's case estimates should be made by FAI senior executives, Ashraf Kamha or Daniel Wilkie. Daniel Wilkie had told his two actuaries, Geoff Trahair and Peter McCarthy, that all dealings had to be via Ashraf Kamha and, just to reinforce that, Trahair was instructed on 14 June 1998 to actually sit at Ashraf Kamha's computer to send information to Latham. Trahair did as he was told.

'I was unhappy with the situation, yes, but I was being over-ridden,' he said.

He said Kamha had also been aware that the information was incomplete, being the same as what had been supplied to Coopers the year before.

Any analysis of this chapter shows that by 1997 and 1998 the senior executives of FAI appeared to spend more time working out how to keep important information from their consulting actuaries and auditors than they did actually trying to run an insurance company.

And it got worse rather than better.

In his report the judge exonerated Trahair and McCarthy, noting for instance that McCarthy could not satisfy both his boss and Coopers, and that he could not approach Coopers without his employer's consent anyway. 'They were in a difficult position,' he said of the two actuaries. But he referred Tony Boulden's activities, which related to his infamous file, to ASIC. 'The omission of genuine case estimates totalling $112 million in the data forwarded to PwC is a serious matter,' he wrote, noting that it affected FAI's reported profit as at 31 December 1997 and had a bearing on whether FAI was statutorily solvent. The relevant section on fraudulent alterations carries a maximum prison sentence of two years.

The judge saved most of the criticism, however, for Daniel Wilkie. He made no less than three referrals for possible criminal behaviour. The first was for telling McCarthy and Trahair not to discuss the reserve problem with the actuaries from PricewaterhouseCoopers, the second was for failing to tell the FAI board between March and June 1998 what Ashraf Kamha had told him, that the under-reserving was 'of the order of $100 million'. He got an identical referral for providing reports to the board between July and December 1998 which were false and misleading, because they omitted details of under-reserving.

The judge framed his referrals by beginning 'if, as I have found ...' and then explained the alleged breach, often offering two possible acts that it might have contravened. The main criminal provision is section 1309 of the Corporations Law, which covers providing information known to be false, or not checked for falsity. In many cases he provided a 'back-up' provision by giving ASIC the chance of launching a civil case, which has a lower burden of proof. Section 1309 has maximum theoretical penalties of two years in prison.

The ASIC civil penalty provisions do not allow for gaol but they can ban a person from managing a company, fine them up to $200,000 and oblige them to pay compensation where that applies.

In this instance Rodney Adler got a 'civil' referral for failing to ask the right questions of Kamha and Wilkie about the reserve shortfall, but he got a section 1309 'criminal' referral for failing to tell the FAI board between March and June that the shortfall was between $50 and $60 million.

Tim Mainprize was found to have failed to tell the board at that time of what the judge called a 'significant' shortfall, which earned him the first of four criminal referrals to ASIC.

CHAPTER 9

THE JOYS OF REINSURANCE

CONTRARY TO POPULAR belief, these days it is surprisingly difficult for a company to rig its annual result. Enron and WorldCom make that claim look hollow, but they were scandals that were detected.

The Enron case saw senior executives devising all manner of fake accounts and invoices to cloud the company's real earnings numbers, but at WorldCom, which at one stage was some ten times bigger, executives had adopted the suicidally obvious tactic of booking certain calls costs in the capital account.

Sooner or later it was going to come out — and it did — that someone was pretending that the company's daily business was an investment. It would be wonderful if all accounting could be reduced to a 'money in, money out' system, but it remains that businesses have to separate out their daily business from the longer-term productive investments that they are supposed to make.

Why were the scandals bigger in the US? Because the US quarterly reporting system places a huge onus on company finance directors to come up with a better number than the previous quarter. Throw in what analysts like to call 'nosebleed price–earnings ratios' — where the price of a stock often anticipates more than twenty and often forty years' earnings — and you have a mindset in which US corporate executives would have been tempted to pour concrete into a volcano crater so they could say that volatile market conditions had quietened down.

Australia has a system of continuous disclosure whereby companies must inform the Australian Stock Exchange (ASX) immediately if they have any information that is likely to move the share price. There are exceptions allowed, such as when the company has yet to start exploratory merger talks, but in general terms it allows companies to let the bad news out at different times from when they announce their results every six months.

On paper, giving out the financial numbers four times a year rather than two seems logical, but in reality the double load in the US seems to allow financial managers no room for anything but good news. Not only do they have the vital 'top-line' earnings number to consider, but there is what analysts call the 'whisper number', that is, the consensus view among analysts of what the company *ought* to be reporting.

It means that in uncertain times there is a microscopic focus on the top line but often a limited focus on what is called the quality of earnings: whether they are real and sustainable or whether they have been propped by a management pulling assets out of every hollow log to manufacture a good number.

And that is where FAI Insurance and HIH Insurance were just as guilty in the late 1990s as any of those overblown US corporates mentioned above, since their skimpy and often downright contrived financial reporting was mostly done US-style, from the reported earnings number backwards.

Insurance company accounting has always been an arcane affair anyway, in almost every country, because there is an extra dimension overlying the traditional system of accounting: the future.

Few other types of organisations are compelled to look into the crystal ball and work out what will happen to claims and cash flow in five years' time.

At 30 June every year there are myriad incomplete events at an insurance company that have to be considered if it is ruling off its books on that day.

Just at the most basic level, what of an annual public liability policy that runs from 1 July to 30 June? Claims on this policy are unlikely to be known for several years but at 30 June the insurer needs to make an estimate for those expected claims. It has to set aside reserves for what might be reported to it.

Actuaries make a life's study of the more complex areas of prediction, since reserves are a critical element. They know they won't be 100 per cent right every time but what they strive for is to be right over several years: perhaps 10 per cent over-reserved in year 1 and 10 per cent under-reserved in year 2, or vice versa.

If the company persistently underestimates how much it will need by way of reserves, it will be able to spend several years claiming every dollar of under-reserving as a dollar of profit. Until it collapses, anyway.

Say, for instance, an insurer expects to pay out $500 million this year in claims and $550 million next year, but that actually the claims come in at $30 million more than that each year, at $530 million and $580 million. On a percentage of claims basis that does not look too alarming — a 6 per cent miscalculation — but as a percentage of net profits it would make a much more significant difference. If the company was recording an investment surplus of $30 million a year, then in year 1 it would be claiming a gross earnings figure of $30 million when in fact it was probably not breaking even.

FAI had a triple handicap in the late 1990s. Not only were its major assets failing to perform, but it was heavily invested in a number of very volatile stocks and it was horribly under-reserved in the US inwards reinsurance business that it had picked up in the mid to late 1980s as a nice little earner and which had turned into a monster. Opinion is divided as to whether it was Gus Maciver or Larry Adler who opened the door to it, but the door was by then a piece of wreckage swinging unhappily on its hinges.

The net effect by the middle of 1998 was that FAI was heading for a $50 million loss, with very little prospect of business turning round.

FAI's accounts for the year to 30 June 1998 were propped up by two reinsurance deals that were actually done either as the books were closing or indeed after they closed, and which enabled FAI to claim an extra $57 million in pre-tax profit for the year just ended.

Welcome to the world of financial reinsurance, where all the usual rules of logic are turned on their head. A nasty combination of desperate insurance companies in dire need of cash and cash-rich reinsurers looking for minimal risks and big fees has spawned an industry which has vocal claims to legitimacy but which in reality tends to blow huge clouds of smoke across the supposed transparency of insurance company accounts.

Juergen Graeber, a senior executive of Hannover Re, put financial reinsurance into some sort of perspective when he was giving evidence to the Royal Commission. A brisk, business-like man, he was asked by Justice Neville Owen for some sort of background on 'Fin Re'.

Graeber pointed out proudly that his company had invented it in the late 1970s.

What was it for?

He made it clear that in his view, financial reinsurance was all about big companies helping out smaller companies by smoothing out the peaks and troughs that occur in the traditional operations of insurance companies. The insurance industry certainly knows and agrees it can be useful if the big reinsurers put up their balance sheets as a guarantee to help fill the gaps. The other benefit is that financial reinsurance can confer tax benefits not only on the company that buys the policy, but also on the company that puts up the money.

It works like this. Say, for instance, a small insurer is having a bad year with one type of claim. If that insurer can be reasonably sure that the setback is a one-off occurrence, then the bigger company will take on some of that risk and basically offer a generous 'recovery' or payout in the first year, but with a clear promise by the smaller insurer to pay that recovery back by way of premiums in future years.

It's insurance in reverse. You have the problem, you get the payout, then you pay the premium. Unfortunately, like fire and gunpowder, potentially useful discoveries can sometimes produce unfortunate results if they fall into the wrong hands.

What if the reinsurer is not actually taking on much risk? The US regulator has what is called the 10/10 rule, which is that if there is a less than 10 per cent chance of the reinsurer having to pay back 10 per cent or more of the premium by way of a claim, then it is not reinsurance. Take one look at your car insurance history and you will see that is not a high hurdle.

And what if the insurance company buying the policy is not actually having a temporary blip so much as a fall off the precipice?

Accounting treatments make all the difference. FAI and HIH used to include notes to their accounts to the effect that they had reinsurance policies in place but there was nothing as vulgar as numbers in the notes.

Colin Richardson, the corporate adviser who will forever be known as the man who advised HIH, told the Royal Commission that when he read a note to the FAI accounts in 1998 which stated that the company had 'entered into a number of long-term reinsurance contracts whose premium will be expensed in future periods in accordance with the pattern of reinsurance services received', he concluded that there would be a match between the money FAI was getting and what it would be paying back. There wasn't.

Like those anodyne notes that investment advisers are obliged to trot out that 'shares may go down as well as up in value', they tell you almost nothing about what was going on but the reality was that they were papering over a giant crack in FAI's reserves.

The price of papering that crack was fierce if taken upfront but because FAI's accounting arrangements did not actually book the full amount of premium in the first year on the other side, the scheme produced a dramatic improvement in the appearance of FAI's books.

And HIH was worse. After it bought FAI in late 1998 and then found that FAI's underlying financial numbers were a shambles covered over by two smartly constructed financial reinsurance policies, HIH management went out and organised a similar policy with Hannover Re. The only major difference was that the Hannover Re deal was bigger.

How did the disease begin at FAI?

Rodney Adler started out very carefully, sounding out not only reinsurers but also reinsurance brokers as he looked for access to what he knew was FAI's only real hope. You may have noticed there was very little said about increasing FAI's business: by late 1997 it was all about keeping the ship afloat.

Rodney Adler testified at length about how he was aiming to obtain reinsurance cover against future adverse developments, but that was the sort of guff you find in annual reports. His real and depressingly understandable intention was to obtain enough financial reinsurance cover for FAI to be able to turn its back on the offshore long-tail black hole, and to do it in such a way that shareholders — indeed maybe even buyers — would not go into a dead faint on hearing about it.

It quickly became obvious that you don't throw your weight around when you are trying to buy reinsurance without actually paying anything for it. As FAI's group reinsurance manager Stephen Burroughs put it when sounding out brokers Willis Faber & Dumas Ltd in Sydney in February 1998, FAI was looking for 'a transaction involving minimal frictional cost and close to zero cash-flow ... our aim is not to physically borrow cash from the reinsurer, rather rent their balance sheet.'

And meanwhile, 'Daniel [Wilkie] has already made it clear to me that FAI is not prepared to pledge any assets as a form of guarantee.'

Burroughs, who became a classic case of the middle-ranking employee

Bonegilla Migrant Camp near Albury, where Larry Adler was sent on his arrival in Australia from Hungary in 1949. The huts seemed to have been designed to be as cold as possible in winter and hotter than Hades in summer.

Larry Adler made an almost textbook transition from migrant to man of substance, from train cleaner and taxi driver to finance, insurance and investment entrepreneur. On 15 November 1960, Fire and All Risks Insurance opened its doors. The Rolls Royce came later.

Peter Rae, *Sydney Morning Herald*

David Trood, John Fairfax Photographic Library

Both images: Jon Lindsay, *Sun Herald*

Rodney and his wife Lyndi in the social pages in 2001 as HIH crumbles. In an interview taped in 1999 by Brad Cooper, Rodney said: 'Dad marketed me as if I was great ... If it wasn't for my Dad, I wouldn't be where I am today.'

OPPOSITE: Larry and then Rodney in the director's office at FAI. Larry Adler's approach to the established insurance cartel when he founded FAI has been compared to farting in a cathedral. Rodney joined the business as investments manager in 1984 and was made a director in January 1988. He took over as managing director on 15 December 1988, less than a week after his father's death.

Colin Richardson, the HIH corporate adviser who moved from SG Hambros to Deutsche Bank in 2000 and who described his role in the FAI takeover as 'purely executionary'.

Rodney Adler giving a door-stop interview at the Supreme Court hearing into the Pacific Eagle Equities affair. Adler was disqualified from acting as a company director for 20 years.

Dean Sewell, Australian Financial Review

Ray Williams, former HIH chief executive, liked to hear it said that he had forgotten more about insurance than most people in Australia would ever learn.

Rob Homer, Australian Financial Review

Ray Williams leaves the HIH Royal Commission pursued by media. Although Williams carefully avoided making any comment, on one occasion he re-crossed the street for the cameras without even being asked to do so.

Steven Siewert

Stefan Moore

Ray Williams' Balmoral mansion and his extensive waterfront property on Lake Macquarie. Ray Williams oversaw the biggest spending spree by the executive office that the company had ever seen, in 2000 spending $32 million on a huge number of items that might have merited an embarrassed smile in a company that was doing well, but looked like crass waste in a company that was close to insolvency.

As a pair of wide boys whose sole focus at HIH seemed to be the cash side of the business, Rodney Adler and his friend Brad Cooper carved a shocking swathe through the cosy, non-confrontational culture of HIH in 1999 and 2000. Cooper apparently exerted a Svengali-like influence on Adler, who in turn had the previously autocratic Ray Williams wrapped around his little finger.

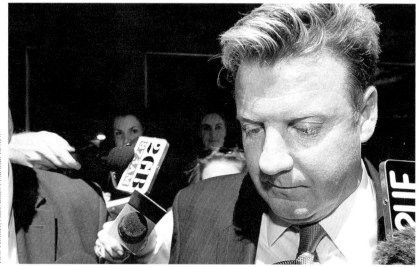

Brad Cooper leaves the Supreme Court in November 2002 after being arrested at his Balmoral home. His great skill, despite his lack of syntax, was to establish 'facts' by a mixture of talking, confusing people's recollections, extracting promises and drafting letters.

Rachel Donnan, Australian Financial Review

Randolph Wein took over as HIH chief executive after Ray Williams' resignation in October 2000, only two months before the end. The rumour at HIH was that he got the top job because the headhunters had to find someone with the initials RW to match the monogrammed towels in the executive washroom, reinforced by the fact that Ray Willing, a former chief executive of NRMA Insurance, had also been approached for the job but had declined very quickly. Wein was killed in a motorcycle accident in Hong Kong in October 2002.

OPPOSITE: Brad Cooper at home. Of all the people who might figure in a book about an insurance company, Cooper is almost certainly the least likely. Not only was this former motivational speaker and burglar-alarm salesman the biggest risk taker in a risk-averse business, but he knew the least about insurance of anybody in this whole sorry tale. By the time it collapsed, Cooper had extracted some $11 million from HIH.

Rob Homer, *Australian Financial Review*

Charles Abbott, HIH non-executive director and former partner at lawyers Blake Dawson Waldron, leaves the HIH Royal Commission. Abbott failed to disclose to the HIH board that he had made an arrangement with Blake's which would pay him 10 per cent of any legal work he could push their way.

Rob Homer, *Australian Financial Review*

On 13 March 2001, Bill Howard, investment manager and chief general manager finance HIH, authorised the payment of a $1.9 million spotter's fee to business partners Brad Cooper and Ben Tilley for having introduced the Packer family as potential buyers of HIH's property portfolio. The liquidation was announced one day later.

Peter Morris, Sydney Morning Herald

Geoffrey Cohen, pictured in 1996, was HIH's chairman and non-executive director from 1992, and one of several former Arthur Andersen employees. Like most of the other directors, Cohen knew very little about insurance. The official term used in counsel's summing-up of the evidence was that he was 'utterly ineffective'.

Virginia Star, Australian Financial Review

Tony McGrath of KPMG, appointed provisional liquidator of HIH, at the creditors' meeting in early 2002. He estimated that HIH's liabilities might reach $5.3 billion, making it the biggest corporate failure in Australian history.

Jane Dyson, Sydney Morning Herald

Ben Tilley leaving court after testifying at the Royal Commission. He, with Brad Cooper, was the recipient of the $1.9 million 'spotter's fee', paid by telegraphic transfer on the last day before HIH announced liquidation. The fee went to Cooper and Tilley's Goodwill Group Pty Ltd, founded to foster 'random acts of kindness'.

Martine Perret, Australian Financial Review

Ray Williams believed that auditor Alan Davies (pictured) gave him a 'nod and a wink' that there were no nasty surprises in the FAI accounts. Davies was known as an 'old-fashioned auditor' — he was so traditional in his guardianship of FAI's secrets that, even after HIH had obtained control of FAI, he still did not reveal anything about FAI that was not publicly available.

John Buttle, the Andersen partner parachuted in to replace Alan Davies as leader of the HIH audit, was the prime mover in bringing the whole nasty Pacific Eagles Equities mess to light.

An experienced auditor with Arthur Andersen, Martyn Scrivens' (pictured here leaving the Royal Commission) first encounter with reinsurance was at FAI. He was persuaded at a meeting with all the major players in the reinsurance deals in August 1998 that the way FAI had accounted for the deals was 'in conformity with industry practice'.

FAI finance director Tim Mainprize (left, with Adler in 1996) was the only executive other than Adler to be on the insurer's board. He won the press-room competition at the Royal Commission for most regular use of the phrase 'I can't recall'. He was also found to have failed to tell the FAI board of what the judge called a 'significant' shortfall of between $50 and $60 million, earning him the first of four criminal referrals to the Australian Securities and Investment Commission.

Kate Callas, Sydney Morning Herald

Peter Rae, Sydney Morning Herald

Daniel Wilkie, FAI's chief operating officer, was offered around $400,000 a year to jump ship from blue-chip insurer NRMA. In his evidence to the Royal Commission he conceded he knew about a $70 million shortfall in FAI's reserves but didn't tell the external actuaries.

Reinsurance broker John Tuckfield's magnificently candid 'secret squirrel' e-mails made the Royal Commission investigators' task infinitely easier.

Niran Peiris, FAI's financial controller, was quoted at the Royal Commission as saying that FAI's troubled Commercial and Professional Indemnity Division was 'like a minefield. A good day was walking in and not getting a leg blown off.'

Dominic Fodera became HIH chief financial officer in September 1995, within two weeks of leaving Andersen, lured across with a 'golden hello' package that was intended to cost HIH $1.2 million but ended up costing more like $1.6 million, because it was linked to the HIH share price. The Royal Commission recommended no less than six separate sets of charges against Fodera, five of them potentially criminal.

Vince Caligiuri, *The Age*

Collingwood Football Club president Eddie McGuire, a former newspaper copyboy who is jokingly dubbed 'Eddie Everywhere' for his multiple media and Australian Rules football interests, convinced Brad Cooper to join the club's board, and Cooper in turn engineered a $250,000 FAI sponsorship deal for Collingwood.

Daniel Vanderkemp is one of the few auditors in this entire affair to emerge at the end with a reputation actually enhanced. In 1998, as a relatively junior auditor for Andersen, he spotted that the FAI reinsurance contracts were not 'kosher' and told his managers, most of whom were partners. No less than five of them, including Martyn Scrivens, overruled him.

Tanya Lake, *Australian Financial Review*

taking the rap for carrying out his bosses' instructions, explained the balance sheet renting comment to the Royal Commission by saying 'when reinsurance managers get a bit verbose, they like to throw in a few cliches'. Unfortunately for him, he was the one drafting the letter. He was the junior man in what has been called a conspiracy by counsel assisting the Royal Commission, in which only five executives of FAI were to have anything to do with these policies: Rodney Adler (and he only in emergencies), Tim Mainprize, Daniel Wilkie, Niran Peiris and Burroughs. Adler even stated several times that Burroughs did not report to him, perhaps because Burroughs had been much more revealing in his evidence than some of his immediate bosses.

So FAI was essentially a car with a steaming radiator and a clanking motor pulling in at the brokers' and reinsurers' hypothetical service-station mechanic's forecourt, driven by a man whose first comment through the driver's window might have been that he was after some help but didn't actually have any money.

But the financial *garagistes* were surprisingly interested. To continue the analogy, they were not just looking at fixing the radiator and having a look inside the engine. If there was more money to be made by getting a promise of future payment from the hapless owner in exchange for more work, then that was what was going to happen. This car was well past justifying any serious repairs.

What were the reinsurers thinking when they took a look? They knew that FAI needed them more than they needed FAI and that the grumpy driver had to get to 30 June 1998 with all the right certificates — in FAI's case, enough revenue to turn a looming $50 million loss into what Rodney Adler had promised shareholders would be a $20 million profit.

And what was Adler actually doing? Early evidence to the Royal Commission was that like any good general he was sending his best man, but it was also clear whose fingerprints were going to be on any deals that FAI had to do to stay afloat.

And they were not the fingerprints of Rodney Adler. One of the strongest candidates for the 'smoking gun' trophy was a letter dated 1 May 1998, drafted by Stephen Burroughs and signed by Wilkie and Mainprize, which promised that no claim would be made on a specific reinsurance policy. That is what is known as a 'side letter' and its function is to remove all risk from the reinsurer, which in this case was General Cologne Reinsurance.

The existence of side letters highlights the worst element in financial reinsurance. Their effect is to leave the bigger company with nothing more ominous than what it records as a reinsurance policy on its books, and little or no risk, while on the buyer's side a big hole has been filled by a lump of money that can easily be got up as a reinsurance policy, even though it is actually a disguised loan.

The real shocker of such actions is the effect on the buying company's books. Instead of, say, getting a $57 million loan which has to be accounted for as a liability, the buying insurer can park that $57 million loan straight onto the revenue side of the profit and loss account.

Confused?

You are not alone. Some of the best auditors in Australia, and no doubt in other countries, have been talked into accepting such measures as legitimate even though they can be thoroughly dodgy if used in the wrong way.

Try this analogy involving an insurance company that suddenly goes mad and starts offering financial reinsurance. Your house has been slightly damaged because a man up the road rented a van last Saturday that hit the overhead cables, shorted out half the neighbourhood and pulled the bargeboard off your roof. (That much is a true story, in case you believe the line that the human race is getting more intelligent.)

The bill to fix it is $1500 but because you have other financial problems you ask the insurer to lend you another $10,000. If they were playing the reinsurer in the financial reinsurance game, they would examine your household accounts and see that you are a good risk having a bad year. They would construct the loan and terms, dress it up as a roof repair and maybe even backdate it and write you a nice policy insuring you against all sorts of unlikely events to your house, to make it look more like insurance. But you would know exactly what it was and if as a householder you were asked to list your recent earnings, you would baulk at putting that $10,000 on the list. It is of course a loan. The same goes for calling it an asset. But that is exactly what FAI managed to do in 1998, using an expanded version of that strategy.

Wilkie came as close to admitting it as anyone, as he closed his evidence to the HIH Royal Commission on 8 March. He had conceded he knew about a $70 million shortfall in FAI's reserves but didn't tell the external actuaries who calculated the reserves that the FAI directors relied on for the 1997–98 *Annual Report*.

He had also acknowledged knowing that FAI's auditor, Andersen, was not shown the GCR side letters which largely invalidated the GCR reinsurance contracts. But he passed responsibility for them onto Mainprize and Niran Peiris, the two senior finance executives at FAI.

When Richard White, SC, counsel assisting, suggested Wilkie knew that FAI's accounts were 'false in material particulars', he replied: 'I didn't realise I had become the chief financial officer.'

Mr White: 'You knew the accounts were likely to mislead any user of them.'

Mr Wilkie: 'That was a matter for Mr Mainprize and Mr Peiris.'

Mr White: 'You were prepared to allow them to present misleading accounts to be signed off by the directors?'

Mr Wilkie: 'Mr Mainprize is a director himself. He understands exactly what was in the accounts.'

Mr White: 'So you were prepared to allow that to go ahead, because Mr Mainprize was the person responsible, is that the position?'

Mr Wilkie: 'I guess if you want to put it like that, yes.'

The FAI accounts, which had been converted by the alchemy of reinsurance from a $50 million pre-tax loss into an $8.6 million profit, were published on 9 September 1998.

HIH financial controller Robert Martin stated in evidence that by October 2000 he believed FAI's reserves at 30 June 1998 were understated by $500 million, enough of a problem on its own to almost sink HIH.

CHAPTER 10

IGNORANCE IS BLISS

RODNEY ADLER CHOSE his chief operating officer Daniel Wilkie as the best man to be sent off to London in March 1998 to get reinsurance cover. His colleagues back in Sydney watched him from afar with a mixture of awe and anxiety.

Tough as a wounded bull and about as subtle, Wilkie was the man who could get them out of a jam but who could also land them in a bigger one than they were in already. The fact that FAI had a problem with under-reserving was a short-fuse issue, since management should have informed the board and the shareholders about it. They hadn't, and here was Wilkie striding the international stage looking to put together a rescue package.

Wilkie wasn't exactly carried shoulder high around London, despite the fact that he wanted to do some business. One of the first reinsurers he tried, Hannover Re, set up a meeting with him at Heathrow Airport but imposed such stringent conditions on him that Wilkie walked away,

Conditions included that FAI should provide Hannover Re with full details of its 'long-tail' exposure, which is a long-winded way of saying 'no'. Aside from the cost and complexity of what was being asked for in the other demands, FAI's long-tail exposure was such a mess that it took HIH a year and a half to even get an idea of its scale after it took over FAI in 1998. Giving full details to Hannover Re was out of the question. Wilkie had been sent to London not to explain the size of the hole but to acquire enough reinsurance that he did not have to. 'I think what we offered did not find the attraction,' said Juergen Graeber of Hannover Re later, in a nice piece of Germanic understatement and unidiomatic English.

Graeber had in fact had a nasty verbal run-in with Rodney Adler's father Larry about twelve years previously which may have forced the terms higher. 'I'm observing this company a long time and about fifteen years ago the CEO, Mr Larry Adler, said that reinsurance is just an investment,' he told the commission, flattening the last 'v' into an 'f'. 'I discontinued all commitments with that company at that time and cautioned all my underwriters for the rest of their life.'

Wilkie did better with the Americans. He lined up a $50 million policy with Warren Buffett's Omaha-based National Indemnity group, via reinsurance brokers Carpenter Bowring in London. The brokers certainly knew early on that FAI had good reason to seek out new reinsurers.

Those policies have all sorts of names but they are known in the insurance world by one simple name: 'time and distance' policies. You buy them to buy time, and the distance you want is the distance you gain from your next crisis. For a group of people who make their money out of other people's fear of misfortune, they can sell a cruel brand of optimism. It was John Tuckfield of Carpenter Bowring who told his colleague Geoff Bromley in an e-mail on 2 June 1998 that Rodney Adler wanted to talk time and distance.

Bromley, a Melburnian who now lives in London, responded to Tuckfield as soon as he had spoken to Adler and, for a man who wanted to have as little to do with reinsurance as possible, Adler had been very candid. Bromley told Tuckfield that FAI was under-provisioned by $100 million in the professional indemnity area alone.

He wrote to Tuckfield: 'Spoke to Rodney at 5.45 a.m. your time this morning. He was a bit late going to work. He needs a stop loss cover and wants it fast. He needs $20 million of cover for each of the 1997–98 and 1998–99 years to ensure his earnings meet expectations. He notes that it is the 1990 and prior years that have caused the slight problem and losses from those years have certainly affected the results for 1997–98 and are expected to also potentially cause a problem in 1998–99 ... Rodney would like to finance these losses over the next six or seven years. We need to get this in place by June 30 ... '

Tuckfield made a note at the time which makes it very clear he knew he was doing something that FAI wanted to keep a lid on. 'Rodney to be brought in as and when necessary. All discussion to be with Daniel.'

Tuckfield and Bromley had the sort of e-mail relationship that does not mince words but goes straight to things that really matter, thus making the Royal Commission investigators' task infinitely easier.

Tuckfield wrote to Bromley that Wilkie 'has promised to kiss our collective butts' if they could line up a reinsurance deal that could be used to prop FAI's June 1998 results.

The problem was made worse in that Wilkie had spent weeks in May and June negotiating with Swiss Re, one of the biggest reinsurers in the world, only to be told that any deal would have to be shown to the Australian insurance regulator, which at the time was called the Insurance and Superannuation Commission (ISC). That was not how those at FAI were planning it. 'Red rag to a bull' was Bromley's dry comment to Tuckfield about how Wilkie reacted when Swiss Re's name was mentioned.

By the time Wilkie gave up on Swiss Re and started serious talks with Carpenter Bowring it was 23 June and he theoretically only had a week to put the deal together, since 30 June 1998 was the last day of the financial year whose results badly needed a boost. FAI was heading for a $50 million pre-tax loss. But when both sides of a deal want to bend the rules a bit, dates can go out of the window.

Wilkie ended up doing a deal with National Indemnity via Carpenter and Bromley actually on 30 June 1998. It offered a simple enough arrangement: reinsurance 'recovery' of $50 million in exchange for a premium expense over five years of $55 million.

A nice touch about the National Indemnity deal was that it did not involve a side letter. Side letters are used in the negotiating process between reinsurer and insurer to minimise the former's risk even further. Although this type of financial reinsurance is a disguised loan, it has to look like a real insurance policy and in that case, there is always the risk that the insurer is going to find something further in the small print and actually make a claim.

The side letter merely promises not to make a claim and the reason there is no side letter relating to that contract is that Geoff Bromley offered one to National Indemnity on 23 June and the latter never mentioned it further.

Berkshire Hathaway, which owns National Indemnity, makes much of the fact that it never proposes reinsurance, merely accepts proposals. The US group was clearly happy enough with a guaranteed $5 million profit.

It is interesting to work out whether Warren Buffett, the Oracle of Omaha, is culpable in this affair. He leaves the negotiation of reinsurance to Ajit Jain, his hard-driving reinsurance expert, whose job is to do deals that make the most money for Berkshire Hathaway and incur the least risk. This one fitted the bill nicely. What was also supposed to happen, according to National Indemnity, was that the deal was ratified by the relevant authorities. In fact it never was, or not in Australia anyway.

The National Indemnity policy contained a clause to say that FAI could claim a further $30 million of recovery in case Australia was hit by one or more earthquakes, each with a damage bill of $5 billion or more, during the life of the policy. To illustrate how likely a $5 billion earthquake is in this country, the one that hit Newcastle in 1997 had a bill of $1.7 billion and was by far the biggest this country has ever seen. In fact, National Indemnity was facing almost no risk at all, and the clause was merely a confection to make it look as though it was.

Bromley as much as admitted that in August 1999, a year later, when HIH had taken over FAI and HIH finance director Dominic Fodera was looking to cut down on the raft of high-cost horrors that HIH had unwittingly bought in FAI. The policy was costing $600,000 a year in premiums. He lit on the earthquake clause and quickly sent a note to Bromley asking for it to be removed.

Bromley sent one of his famous candid e-mails to Tuckfield saying: 'Would he not be worried that by cancelling the section, he highlights the sham of the contract?'

That was to come back and haunt Bromley at the Royal Commission. Tested on what that meant, he said he was describing what the reinsurance contract would become if the earthquake component was removed.

There were some other little pieces of 'common industry practice' brought to bear on the National Indemnity contract by the brokers, which all had the effect of making it look as though more risk was being taken by the reinsurer than actually was. Although the agreement was struck about midnight on 30 June 1998, Tuckfield asked Bromley to backdate the cover note to 4 July 1997, thus adding a year of manifestly earthquake-free time to the policy.

The cover note was issued on old letterhead as well.

A slight setback was that the policy's placement slip, the other half of the vital documentation, was actually signed and dated by National

Indemnity officer Scott Stirling on the correct day, 30 June 1998, which meant some interesting adventures when auditors Arthur Andersen were to be shown the documentation. They were not shown the correctly dated placement slip, which would have made clear that National Indemnity was not taking as much risk as the backdated slip suggested.

John Tuckfield was clearly relieved by the turn of events, since he sent a magnificently candid e-mail to a colleague a week later. On 6 July he told his New York colleague James Fitzpatrick: 'Have done a secret squirrel deal with FAI, which has made them eternally grateful, especially Daniel Wilkie, who has promised us a minimum five-year appointment.' He later explained to Lucy McCallum, counsel assisting the Royal Commission, that 'I wanted to convey to him the understanding that I couldn't discuss it.' Ms McCallum replied that that was 'an absurd construction of that sentence'.

A year later Tuckfield wrote to Geoffrey Bromley that the FAI deal 'had nothing to do with reinsurance really', a proposition that no one at the Royal Commission even bothered to ask him to explain. He had summed it up all too well.

Wilkie was 'eternally grateful' because the deal would allow FAI to claim a profit of $29 million on its annual results, by booking a recovery of $34.57 million and a premium expense of only $5.5 million. The bad news, as HIH was to find out after it took over FAI three months later, was that FAI still owed National Indemnity four annual payments of $12.75 million each.

The deal was wonderful for FAI, which was heading for a $50 million loss on that very day. Nothing had actually changed except that FAI suddenly looked a lot healthier. Almost nothing of the deal was disclosed in the FAI accounts apart from a note under the deathless heading 'Premium Income and Outwards Reinsurance' which said: 'The economic entity has entered into a number of long term reinsurance contracts whose premium will be expensed in future periods in accordance with the pattern of reinsurance services received. Reinsurance recoveries on long term reinsurance contracts are recognised on the same basis.'

Richard White, SC, counsel assisting the commission, asked FAI's financial controller Niran Peiris whether 'these notes would tell any reader anything about the impact which these two reinsurance contracts had on FAI's profit and loss, or on its financial position?'

Peiris, a qualified lawyer and accountant, replied 'No'. He had drafted the note and admitted that it gave no indication that FAI would be guaranteeing future accounting losses of more than $23 million in future years because of the reinsurance contracts.

Rodney Adler certainly reacted with irritation to any suggestion that in doing those deals, FAI had done anything wrong. During the Royal Commission he sent out a statement saying 'all reinsurance policies entered into at FAI involved an exacting approval process, involving the ISC, auditors and many other interested parties'. More ominously, he noted that 'FAI did not enter into any reinsurance contracts which were not typical of the industry.'

That was intended to look like a defence, but could also be construed as a blistering indictment of a global reinsurance industry that has lost sight of what reinsurance is actually for. If reinsurers are advancing disguised loans to nervous insurance companies to cover events that in most cases have already happened, they might as well call themselves banks.

Wilkie's other coup was to do a direct deal with General Cologne Reinsurance (GCR), which has since become another wholly owned subsidiary of Warren Buffett's Berkshire Hathaway.

He did it with a group which used to call itself the Financial Reinsurance division at GCR but since 1997 has allowed itself the more mysterious title 'Alternative Solutions'. The three musketeers of this enterprise, Milan Vukelic, John Houldsorth and Tore Ellingsen, worked in the department variously in Cologne, London and Dublin.

That deal was signed originally on 18 March 1998 and offered what was called 'aggregate excess of loss' cover of up to $65 million for a premium, again payable in instalments afterwards, of $55 million.

The arithmetic clearly didn't fit, at least from the GCR point of view, even without worrying about risk. Since FAI badly needed a payout, the premium had to be greater than the payout. But that situation brings auditors out in spots and is called a 'premium overhang'. This time there was no guff about an earthquake to make the payout look bigger than the premium.

GCR's worries about making money were allayed by a contract called the 'Six Slips', dated 1 May 1998, which asked FAI to pay $12.5 million over two years, thus bringing $65 million of recovery for $67.5 million of premium.

To avoid the appearance of overhang the two reinsurance contracts were not booked in the same way: they were dated differently and the auditors were never shown the Six Slips. Rodney Adler was later to claim in his evidence in June 2002 that he had no knowledge of the Six Slips at the time the contract was entered into and that he believed there was no relation between the Six Slips and the main GCR contract. 'I don't think I even met any individual from GCR,' he said, leaving Daniel Wilkie firmly in the frame as the main driver of the deals.

Unfortunately, FAI's insurance book was in such dire straits that even that impressive $65 million of 'recovery' was not going to be enough. The deal had to be pumped up slightly in September 1998 to $84 million worth of recoveries and $89 million worth of premium.

The deal was subject to at least two side letters, copies of which were recovered by the HIH Royal Commission and posted for all to see. One was dated 1 May 1998 and stated FAI would make no claim on the Six Slips and the other, dated 26 June 1998, said of one section in the bigger policy that 'unless mutually agreed by both parties, FAI Insurance Group will not seek reinsurance recoveries under this section of the reinsurance contract'. In other words, FAI would not be making a claim on a policy for which it was paying more than $75 million.

Jeff Simpson, a former deputy general manager finance at HIH who resigned in 1999 after watching HIH take out a remarkably similar policy with Hannover Re, noted that the clause was 'really a disguising section'. That remark, made in a file note to himself, does not sound like much but when Simpson appeared at the Royal Commission for the first time on 14 March 2002, his evidence was galvanising. He followed a number of witnesses who were close to the reinsurance deals and whose evidence had at times set new standards in prevarication.

Simpson had by then retreated to a lower profile but less ethically demanding job at Wyong Shire Council, north of Sydney. He said both FAI and HIH had exploited 'deficient' accounting requirements for reinsurance contracts, which enabled them to hide the arrangements, adding the reassuring note that he thought it would not be possible to design similar deals today. 'I think the objective was to get them past auditors and if they approved it as reinsurance, then that was their objective,' Mr Simpson said.

He was certainly more helpful than the three musketeers of GCR, whose lawyers in London wrote a letter to the Royal Commission in April 2002 saying they would not be coming.

GCR had provided a number of local witnesses but the three who declined to come were the men who actually designed the financial reinsurance. Clyde & Co of Eastcheap wrote to say that 'it has been suggested that if our clients do not attend to give evidence voluntarily, there is a risk that His Honour Mr Justice Owen will draw inferences that are adverse to our clients' interests'. It went on to say that the commission had already had a lot of evidence about GCR so 'in our view it would be unfair to draw any inferences adverse to our client's interest, simply from the fact of their non-attendance'.

That got a wry cheer from the *cognoscenti*, but was a reminder that a Royal Commission's powers are limited. Inside Australia, a commission can subpoena witnesses and evidence, but if witnesses overseas don't want to come, things get too cumbersome to be worth pursuing.

The most incriminating documents, the side letters, were not signed by GCR executives anyway. They were both signed by the two most senior executives of FAI below Rodney Adler: Daniel Wilkie and Tim Mainprize.

Mainprize, who was the first accountant to be hired by FAI when he joined in 1970, won the press room competition at the Royal Commission for most regular use of the phrase 'I can't recall'. At the commission he acquired perverse fame for having no recollection of having had dinner in Sydney with Jeffrey Pokross, a New York share ramper with proved connections to the Mafia, on a visit Pokross and his wife made in April 1998.

Adler was a long way from the action and said later he knew nothing about the side letters, having merely instructed Daniel Wilkie to get the reinsurance policies in place. This defence was quickly tagged the 'reverse Nuremberg', but it is clear that Adler knew exactly what was needed. In most of his evidence to the Royal Commission he stressed that Wilkie's errand was to put reinsurance in place in case of problems in the future, not the past. Worrying about the future in insurance is fine, but covering up the sins of the past is not.

Adler conceded that FAI had experienced problems with bigger than expected claims from policies written in the late 1980s and early 1990s by its corporate and professional division. Informing the board of continuing losses in these 'hot areas for FAI' was embarrassing and frustrating, so he had asked Daniel Wilkie to find reinsurance cover to, as Adler put it, 'quarantine' those policies. 'I said to him eventually I would really like to put these claims/policies to one side, a so-called bad bank, good bank scenario, have them properly reserved, properly provided for, quarantine them and in that way I won't have this constant embarrassment in front of the board.'

But Adler said he had played no direct role in seeking reinsurance, leaving the negotiations to Mr Wilkie, who 'had my absolute support and trust', and other senior executives.

That noble notion took a caning on 20 June 2002, under questioning from David Williams, counsel for Guy Carpenter.

When Williams asked him if he had other plans if the reinsurance hadn't worked, Adler said that FAI would just have to look for 'millions of dollars elsewhere'.

The GCR side letters were never shown to FAI's auditors, since the auditors would immediately have had to categorise the reinsurance deals as deposit arrangements — which is what they actually were — and not reinsurance, thus eliminating $57 million worth of claimed recoveries — financial Spakfilla, as one lawyer quietly called the money — for that 1997–98 year.

Even without being shown the side letters, the junior member of the Andersen audit group, Daniel Vanderkemp, concluded they were not proper reinsurance anyway since there was not enough transfer of risk.

Vanderkemp's evidence is perhaps the single biggest problem that Andersen had in the entire HIH saga. The defunct chartered accounting and auditing company is tightly intertwined through the story, having been auditor both of FAI and then HIH. Vanderkemp is long gone, not surprisingly, having concluded in 1999 that his talents might get a bit more room to move at AMP Ltd.

Another problem for Andersen is that, having ticked off the way FAI accounted for its financial reinsurance which was, as Jeff Simpson put it in his evidence, 'pushing it to the limit', it then had to give the nod to slightly less alarming examples at HIH.

If you give a tick to financial reinsurance for one company, you can hardly turn around and disallow something similar in the other company. Indeed, when Andersen started asking difficult questions at HIH in late 2000 about some items in the accounts of FAI, by then an HIH subsidiary, they got more than they bargained for. HIH group manager reinsurance Peter Thompson, who had quite a reputation in HIH for writing snarky notes, wrote back: 'you must have looked at these issues when auditing FAI'.

Andersen sent him a list of questions and they certainly got a list of answers. One question was: 'This is a very significant matter for which FAI had no reserves. Why wasn't the matter properly audited previously?'

In boxing parlance, that is called 'leading with your chin'. Thompson duly swung a haymaker: 'You should answer your own questions. You must have audited this matter when auditing FAI.' He ended by referring them to their own audit work papers on FAI from previous years.

Where Andersen's position was much stronger is in the amount of concealment and obfuscation its auditors had to put up with, both at FAI and HIH.

In the case of FAI, the Andersen auditors were not shown side letters which entirely invalidated the real force of most of the General Cologne Re policy, and in the case of National Indemnity they were shown a cover note which had been backdated by almost a year.

And in the case of HIH, which in 1999 recovered sufficiently from the shock of seeing what FAI had done with reinsurance to do a bigger deal on very similar lines with Hannover Re, there was a side letter and other measures put in place to make sure the policy was never claimed on. This policy allowed HIH to claim an extra $92.45 million in reinsurance recovery for the year ended 30 June 1999, allowing it to turn a modest pre-tax profit of $9.6 million into a very well-received figure of $103.45 million.

But where Andersen stands particularly exposed is in the fact that Daniel Vanderkemp, a relatively junior auditor, hit a brick wall when he reported the reinsurance as suspect.

No less than five of his managers overruled him. His immediate boss, Martyn Scrivens, was invited to a meeting with all the major players in the reinsurance deals on 26 August 1998; they persuaded him with arguments from all sides that the way FAI had accounted for the deals was 'in conformity with industry practice'.

All the dice were loaded against Scrivens. Rodney Adler said to him on 25 August: 'Why don't we arrange for you to meet the underwriters?'

Hey presto, at 9.00 a.m. the next day Scrivens found himself on one side of an argument about whether reinsurance could be accounted for in the way FAI wanted, or in the way he wanted.

The meeting was Rodney Adler's idea but, as the big picture man who was only giving orders, it was not quite his scene. FAI's finance director, Tim Mainprize, and its financial controller, Niran Peiris, were his nominees, while Geoff Barnum, chief executive of General Cologne Re in Australia, represented his company, and John Tuckfield of 'secret squirrel' fame represented Guy Carpenter, the UK-based reinsurance broker which arranged the National Indemnity deal.

It is easy to say it now, but four against one was never much of a contest.

Scrivens is an experienced English-born auditor who had spent fourteen years as a partner at what was then Arthur Andersen in Geneva. He had tackled insurance company audits before but FAI was his first encounter with reinsurance, a much more complicated animal, particularly when it is almost designed to be complicated.

Scrivens had been pitchforked into his first encounter with reinsurance while doing the audit at FAI in 1998, and wrote a note to file the next day which said that 'FAI has consistently contended that we do not understand industry practice in this area.'

Such a statement, if correct, would have been vintage Rodney: at first glance a whiff of righteous indignation, but on closer examination a carefully crafted excuse that didn't mean much at all.

After HIH collapsed Adler summoned a meeting of his former FAI lieutenants at Prime Restaurant, part of the development in the basement of Sydney's old GPO building in Martin Place that he had been closely involved in, and which ended up losing Adler and other business partners a significant amount of money.

He wrote a note to file, which is what more devious people might do if they wanted to cover their tail.

On 13 June 2001, less than three months after HIH had collapsed, Adler had summoned Wilkie, Tim Mainprize and Niran Peiris for a 6.00 p.m. meeting. Adler said it was 'basically, in the pursuit of gathering facts and reminding ourselves of events that happened several years ago'. Topic of the day was the side letters. Daniel Wilkie had the most to contribute but said he was very busy elsewhere and only came to the restaurant for a very short time.

The Adler note said: 'Daniel recalled that it was signed at the very last minute due to the pressure of the moment ... he could not recall if it was disclosed to auditors or actuaries but he did recall that Tim Mainprize had co-signed the letter and it was more a letter that was not legally significant due to the fact that it was only concerned with the agreement over the timing of the claims than anything else.'

Tim Mainprize, the man who forgot the Mafia-connected share ramper from New York, remained true to form and 'could not recall ever signing the letter and discussed/disagreed with Daniel that he had ever signed the letter', according to Adler. 'Niran and I could not comment as we had never sighted or knew of any side letter.'

In his report the judge went in almost as hard on Daniel Wilkie as he had over the reserve shortfalls. He recommended what he called 'criminal charges, or civil penalty proceedings, or both' against Wilkie for doing a deal with General Cologne Re 'which could not confer any accounting benefits on FAI unless the accountants were misled'. The worst element, for the judge, was that the deal had to be financially detrimental to FAI because the premiums were higher than the payout, a point of impressive simplicity that was almost never raised anywhere else.

He also recommended a criminal 'false and misleading information' charge against Wilkie for deliberately not telling Adler, the board of FAI or its auditor about the 'Six Slips' contract and two side letters, in a situation where they were all highly relevant to showing whether there was a transfer of risk to the reinsurer, and whether they were correctly accounted for by FAI. FAI had booked everything as reinsurance.

Tim Mainprize got much the same treatment, even though he was not the one negotiating with GCR, plus he got another criminal referral for signing FAI's accounts for 30 June 1998 when he knew they contained a false entry. Burroughs got a lesser 'civil' referral on the basis of sending material to GCR Australia and of knowing why FAI wanted the transaction. 'Burroughs facilitated FAI's entry into the transaction,' the judge said.

The most internationally significant conclusion that the judge arrived at in the whole saga was of possible wrongdoing on the part of broker John Tuckfield and of GCR's offshore operations; its local operation GCR Australia; and of four executives, Tore Ellingsen, Christopher Byatt, Lindsay Self and Andrew Smith. All of the referrals against the individuals are for civil action, as the judge was at pains to point out, but he left it open as to whether criminal charges could be brought by ASIC against GCR or its local offshoot GCRA. That leaves a legal door firmly open.

GCRA's chief executive, Geoff Barnum, was left off the judge's list of referrals even though he was aware that side letters were being used and did not prevent their use. The judge noted there was a technical complication about whether Barnum owed a duty both to his employer and to the Corporations Law, which he said made the issue 'too remote to justify a referral'.

GCR is now a wholly owned subsidiary of one of the biggest reinsurers and best-known ethical companies in the world, Berkshire Hathaway. GCR Australia has a staff of about 50 and writes about 10 per cent of the reinsurance policies in this country.

(Tuckfield's backdating of the National Indemnity cover note from June 1998 to July 1997 earned him a referral to the DPP of a possible breach of the New South Wales Crimes Act of 1900, which can attract a prison sentence.)

The judge was at pains to point out he was not hostile to reinsurance or even to financial reinsurance, but he drew the line at reinsurers knowing they were selling a product that was not reinsurance, but which they knew would be accounted for by the buyer as reinsurance.

The reason there will be a stir in the global reinsurance industry is the same reason why Rodney Adler claimed there was nothing unusual in the policies FAI bought: they were typical of the industry.

What appears to have evolved over the years was that reinsurers concentrated their sales efforts of these 'time and distance' policies in countries where insurers are allowed to discount their reserves, such as Australia, rather than countries like the UK and the US where they are not. That means UK and US insurers generally have stronger reserves and do not need the financial reinsurance being sold. While it might look like a promising market for the overseas reinsurers, it therefore allows unscrupulous local buyers of financial reinsurance to 'double dip', once by discounting their reserves and once by making instant 'recoveries' on those policies.

CHAPTER 11

RODNEY AND MALCOLM

SOME BUSINESS RELATIONSHIPS are a bit like mail order marriages: they are unlikely pairings but there are aspects of the arrangement that suit both parties.

On Christmas Eve 1997 Malcolm Turnbull called Rodney Adler to see if there was any business Goldman Sachs could do with FAI. Adler accepted the overture with alacrity. Neither man has said so since, but both appear to have been pleased and relieved that they might do some business with each other. Adler needed a way out of FAI's inexorable decline and Turnbull badly wanted a deal. Both ended up getting what they wanted, but must latterly have wondered if all the grief they ran into subsequently was worth it.

It was an encounter born of anxiety. Why else would the head of the Australian arm of one of the world's top-ranking investment banks have made an approach to the principal shareholder and chief executive of Australia's least reputable major insurance company on a day when a lot of people are making last-minute Christmas purchases?

Turnbull had been co-chairman and joint chief executive of Goldman Sachs Australia since July 1997, or about five months. He had been chosen by Goldman as a man who might be able to allow Goldman to 'hit the ground running' in deal terms, because of his connections as a lawyer and then merchant banker in Sydney. One deal he had had high hopes for was the privatisation of New South Wales' electricity utility, in the wake of successful similar privatisations in other Australian States, particularly Victoria. Not only was he on good nodding terms with the NSW Labor Premier, Bob Carr, despite Turnbull's growing Liberal Party sympathies, but Turnbull's long-term business associate was the former NSW Labor Premier, Neville Wran.

Carr was not hostile to the idea of privatisation but in October 1997 the ALP State Conference in New South Wales voted overwhelmingly against the proposal.

In US-style investment banking, deals aren't a big thing, they are the only thing. Stockbrokers are people who buy and sell shares on behalf of others but investment bankers, who suffer their fair share of rhyming slang, see themselves as the top end of the stockbroking business because they devise new share issues and offer advice on mergers and acquisitions — company takeovers.

If Goldman wasn't going to get a slice of a multi-billion dollar electricity privatisation, something else had to be found to fill the gap. At that time Goldman had yet to start conventional stockbroking operations in Australia and the fastest way to move was by obtaining 'mandates', as they are called, from companies for advice.

Failing all those possibilities there was Goldman's Principal Investment Arm (PIA), based in New York. At that time Goldman was a partnership — it later became a listed company, to the significant benefit of Turnbull, who became a partner in November 1998 — but even before it was publicly listed it had hundreds of millions of US dollars of its own capital to invest.

Turnbull and his associate, South African-born Russel Pillemer, were approaching Rodney Adler on Christmas Eve 1997 not only as potential advisers but also potential investors. Their line was that they were there 'to discuss potential opportunities for Goldman Sachs to do work for FAI'.

Their records suggest it was mostly Adler doing the talking, which was nothing new for him and which suited them fine. If they couldn't report back to New York that they had a mandate, they could at least call Adler a potential client.

He indicated that he believed FAI and its 43 per cent owned subsidiary FAI Life were both 'significantly undervalued' and that he would ideally like to pass control of the company to his son Jason, who was born in 1989. But he told Turnbull and Pillemer that with all the insurance industry consolidation that was happening, it was more likely that he would have sold out by 2002.

Turnbull, who had known Rodney Adler for some fifteen years after Larry backed merchant bank Whitlam Turnbull, could see that Adler had the insurance equivalent of a field marshal's baton in his rucksack. Adler told Turnbull that insurance was his 'first love' although Turnbull was later to report to colleague James del Favero in Hong Kong that Rodney Adler was a 'tremendous entrepreneur by nature' but 'not the person to run an insurance company on a day-to-day basis'.

One idea that Turnbull and Pillemer put forward to Adler was to take FAI private: to buy out the other shareholders in FAI. That was 70 per cent of the company that Adler didn't own, which would cost $A142 million if he paid a premium of around 20 per cent above the market to buy them out. By that time the FAI share price, which had been above $7 in the pre-crash heyday of 1986, was around 50c and sinking. FAI, which had been worth more than $2.5 billion in the 1980s, was down to around $200 million.

But even Adler blinked at that proposal. 'He said that he thought he could be a billionaire in a few years' time if he was successful in doing this', the Goldman Sachs men noted in their files. But 'his concern was that he would be taking on a very high level of gearing and possibly gambling with his net worth', they added.

Turnbull suggested that to make things easier, Adler could do the deal in stages and start by taking the smaller FAI Life private first and then sell it all. FAI Life was a small, share market-listed life insurance company that had been spun out of FAI and was not in anything like the difficulties being faced by its parent company. But most analysts believed it lacked the scale to operate meaningfully on its own, and should most logically be sold to a bigger insurer. And Adler could also get in an equity partner, Turnbull suggested.

By 6 January 1998 that partner was possibly Goldman Sachs, according to a fifteen-page memo sent from Sydney to New York. Someone hadn't had much of a Christmas break. Headed 'PIA Opportunity', the note from Turnbull, Pillemer and two others said that if Goldman Sachs were to put up, say, $A30 million of its own money in 1998, a stripped-down and recapitalised FAI might be refloated on the Australian share market in June 2001 and might turn Goldman's investment into $66 million, a profit of 120 per cent in three years. While most of Australia's corporate community was still at the beach, those numbers were worked on and by 12 January 1998 another note went to

New York suggesting $70 million might be turned into $216 million, a return this time of just over 200 per cent.

The plan was codenamed 'Project Firelight'. FAI Insurance was 'Fire' and FAI Life was 'Light'.

Leaving aside the numbers, which were very theoretical, it was culturally a very unusual collaboration. Geoff Hill, a veteran Sydney merchant banker who was invited by Rodney Adler onto the FAI board in 1996, put it this way when testifying to the Royal Commission. 'Goldman Sachs were one of the crème de la crème of the industry,' he said on 17 May. 'Whilst I may have been comfortable with FAI as a company, I would not have thought that that sort of company, given the nature of the assets that it had, would first lend itself to somebody of such prestige coming in as a major shareholder in a privatisation,' he added.

Groucho Marx once expressed a similar view about joining the sort of club that would have him as a member.

Firelight was probably always going to be doomed. Turnbull was looking for a deal, and his masters in New York wanted results. It is likely that they were never that keen on Firelight from the outset but if they had canned any idea of PIA getting involved from the outset, then there was even less of a chance of a financial return.

Adler was talking freely to Goldman about what an odd mix of assets FAI had, such as the St Moritz Hotel in New York. Someone at Goldman quickly dubbed them the 'Dog Assets'. But Adler was much quieter about the monster in the cupboard on the other side of his balance sheet — the liabilities — and meanwhile his non-executive directors at FAI were entirely in the dark.

There is nothing illegal in a major shareholder in a company making plans to privatise it. It is his or her money, and risk. But as another FAI director, Ted Harris, pointed out, it did lead to a conflict between what was best for the major shareholder and best for the other directors on the board. 'When you have a representative of a major shareholder who is also the chief executive, he might be looking at things in a slightly different way to non-executive directors,' he said.

Clearly privatisation is an age-old dilemma for many family-controlled companies, but FAI wasn't like most family-controlled companies. Most families step back after a generation or two and let professional management do the day-to-day running, leaving heirs and cousins on the board to consider grand strategy, with as much help as possible from independent directors. Rodney Adler chose to keep the reins in his hand.

Adler told the Royal Commission that he was sure he had told his chairman, John Landerer, about Firelight in early 1998. 'I said to him casually that I had had an approach from Goldman Sachs. We discussed a range of topics and that it was interesting and he said, "Well, that's good, keep me informed".'

'I said, "Sure",' Adler testified.

Landerer, an old friend of Larry Adler who had taken on the 'temporary' chairmanship of FAI after Larry died on 13 December 1988, had a different memory. 'At no stage did Mr Adler advise me during 1997 and 1998 that he had any discussions with either Mr Turnbull or Goldman Sachs in which the topic of privatising FAI or Goldman Sachs investing in FAI was raised.'

This dispute goes to the heart of the corporate governance problem at FAI. Company chairmen have some odd ideas about what they should and should not do — HIH chairman Geoffrey Cohen memorably stated that one of his main jobs was to check the board minutes — but one constant is that they should be able to hire and fire the chief executive. Because this chief executive happened to have 30 per cent of the stock, John Landerer was effectively deprived of what should have been his one inalienable power.

Rodney Adler's purchase of just under a million shares in FAI on 13 January 1998, and the pathetic 'punishment' he got for breaking the rules, are a prize example of the distorted power relationship that existed between Adler and his board.

There were only two periods in the year when FAI directors were not allowed to trade in FAI shares, being between the end of the half-year trading period and the announcement of its results about six weeks later. What Adler would have known was that some expert massaging of FAI's reserves would allow a better than expected result to be posted. It emerged that FAI had reduced its reserves (thus increasing claimed profits) by $24 million at the end of 1997, arranging to restore those reserves quietly in the first half of 1998.

Adler may also have wanted to 'take out' the last of a line of FAI shares that AMP Ltd had been selling via New York.

Questioned by the Royal Commission about the purchase of the million shares, Adler said he 'would imagine' that he informed his chairman, John Landerer, of the purchase, a refrain which sounds familiar.

This time Jim Berry, the head of surveillance at ASX in Sydney, produced records which showed that the shares were bought at 10.03 a.m. and that Adler sent a note to Landerer at 11.10 a.m., more than an hour later, saying he had been offered the stock but not disclosing that he had already bought it.

Landerer later conceded that when he confronted Adler, he had merely promised not to do such a thing again. What Landerer did not know was that Adler was six days away from doing a possible deal with Goldman Sachs which would have prevented him from buying FAI stock for two years.

Norman O'Bryan, SC, counsel assisting, produced two draft letters from Malcolm Turnbull to Rodney Adler, both dated 19 January 1998, offering different business proposals.

One related to a formal mandate to help FAI sell its 47 per cent stake in FAI Life, and the other offered to work on a possible privatisation of FAI Ltd using capital from Goldman Sachs. By way of tying FAI to Goldman, the letter asked Adler to agree not to buy the outstanding shares in FAI 'other than pursuant to an advisory and co-investment agreement with Goldman Sachs Australia'.

The two letters were unsigned by either Turnbull or Adler and there is no evidence they were ever sent.

Another example of the FAI chairman's lack of power occurred on 1 May 1998, when Rodney Adler put out a press release trumpeting that FAI had 'sold' the St Moritz Hotel in New York for $US185 million (around $A330 million). In fact it was a lease rather than an outright sale. The St Moritz was and is a hornet's nest of complicated lease and freehold arrangements, and Landerer realised that the return to FAI was going to be less than a quarter of that, closer to $A70 million.

Landerer queried the release and asked Adler to issue a correction. Adler said to him: 'Should we issue it or should we wait for a query?' He was referring to the system by which the ASX asks for clarification of any potential misunderstanding in a release.

Landerer said he would not wait for a query and that he wanted all mention of the $US185 million removed from the revised press release. Where this story lacks a clear ending is that no revised press release was ever sent out. It was certainly never received by the ASX, and the original incorrect announcement was left to stand.

Aside from Landerer's systemic lack of power to keep a rein on his chief executive, he and his directors had a much bigger problem even than that. Their evidence was that they were not being told more than a skerrick of what was actually going on at FAI.

Exhaustive questioning of advisers, directors and management at FAI in the Royal Commission witness box produced the bizarre scenario that senior management were working on grand strategy with executives of Goldman, who walked in and out of the office regularly in the clear belief that the directors knew what was happening, while the non-executive directors came and went on a monthly basis and were left in complete ignorance.

Since Adler said he had left it to Landerer to tell the other directors about Firelight, and Landerer said they didn't know, the situation inside the FAI board was just above the level of a bedroom farce. The judge noted in his report that 'Whilst it would have been preferable for Turnbull to have personally and directly verified that the non-executive directors of FAI were fully aware of ... the discussions between GSA and Adler and the work GSA performed in connection with Project Firelight, this did not happen. Nonetheless it was not unreasonable for Turnbull to rely on Adler's word.'

Some directors had a serious stab at getting involved. Geoff Hill testified that he was 'astounded' to discover that in 1998 FAI's external actuaries, PricewaterhouseCoopers, had not spoken to its external auditors, Arthur Andersen, about its reserves.

Reserves are the single biggest item in an insurer's balance sheet, and by then FAI's were reportedly about $250 million short of what they should have been, which if properly recorded would have wiped out FAI's shareholders' funds and left it insolvent by every conventional measure.

But the audit committee, which Hill chaired, found itself spending much of 1998 battling with Rodney Adler about related party issues such as Home Security International, Brad Cooper's burglar alarm vendor, in which by then FAI had a 41 per cent stake.

In August 1998 Adler put it to the FAI board that he wanted HSI to spend $25 million to take full control of Ness Securities, which made the alarms in Seven Hills in north-west Sydney. On paper, there was some logic to the idea, except that it was hardly mainstream FAI business, and FAI owned less than half of HSI.

At that time FAI was effectively papering over a $50 million hole in its results, and a possible $250 million hole in its reserves, and here was the board at loggerheads over whether a subsidiary would take full control of a suburban manufacturer of burglar alarms.

FAI director Peter O'Connell, a former partner at Sydney lawyers Gilbert & Tobin and a man who was brought into FAI by Rodney Adler for his knowledge of technology companies, described FAI's July 1998 board meeting over the Ness transaction as 'heated'. He was one of the four directors who voted in favour, along with Adler and Tim Mainprize, and Sir William Keys, the former RSL federal president who resigned from FAI in 1999 and died in 2000.

O'Connell cited 'sound commercial reasons' for his decision, on the basis that a distributor could do worse than control its supplier. But the three who opposed the deal, John Landerer, Ted Harris and Geoff Hill, felt there was something not right about it. The main beneficiary was a shadowy figure called Paul Brown who went to Cranbrook with Rodney Adler and who now lives in Monaco. Brown had invested less than $1 million in Ness and the deal was going to allow him to sell out for $20 million. In turn HSI was going to be able to pay Brown back some $6 million previously lent by him to HSI, but the benefits to FAI shareholders were a great deal less clear.

Brown has noted that he wanted 'no profile whatsoever' in Australia, and clearly had no desire to testify to the Royal Commission. Thus he would not have to explain why a Monaco resident should be so interested in a Sydney burglar-alarm manufacturer. Some of the other directors believed that Brown was merely a warehouser of stock and cash for Rodney Adler, a claim that Adler denied and is impossible to prove. John Landerer testified that he believed Adler was the beneficial owner of assets claimed by Brown.

Adler was very protective of Brown's involvement, tackling Landerer over the latter's questioning of who actually owned Ness. 'Enough is enough. I find this rather humiliating and very time-consuming,' Adler wrote in a letter to Landerer four days before the meeting. For a chief executive, Adler was sounding like a man afraid of losing his grip.

This is not a 'bleeding hearts' letter and this is not a letter from a person who cannot take criticism. It is a letter from a very concerned board member through his chairman and other directors of the company saying that the meetings are becoming mini 'star chambers' where details of the minutia [sic] is discussed at length and other matters are left as we will run out of time.

In other words he didn't want to fight about what he regarded were trivial non-core acquisitions, while his audit committee wanted to know what on earth was exciting him so much about them in the first place. Both sides felt that not enough time was being spent on the serious stuff, but for different reasons.

Ironically, the next FAI board meeting on 11 August was by comparison so friendly that Rodney Adler sent an arch note to Hill afterwards saying, 'I met a very interesting person today at the board meeting. His name was Geoff Hill. I really liked him. I wonder if you could keep introducing me to him. He was very nice.'

Hill had added some comments of his own to the note, including, 'Thank you Rod. Can I double my directors' fees too?' and 'Please have Brad [Cooper] or Paul [Brown] present next week ... failing him Jodee Rich.'

Rich at that time was setting himself up for a second time as a share market *wunderkind* with One.Tel Communications, in which FAI took a seed capital 25 per cent stake of $1 million in 1995 and which by 1998 had turned into $60 million. Adler had profited personally by more than $4 million. Sydney's eastern suburbs fast set was agog at the performance, which sucked in the Packer and Murdoch families. Indeed the Packer interests bought three-quarters of FAI's original stake in 1998 for $43 million, and a 25c rise in the share price shortly after that deal gave FAI's residual stake the encouraging valuation of $32.5 million.

But even then there were FAI directors who remembered too much about Rich's earlier share market disaster in the 1980s, Imagineering Ltd, to be fans.

Ted Harris, another member of the audit committee at FAI, kept his own counsel about One.Tel because he was more worried about what he saw as poor corporate governance at FAI. In 1998 he was 72 and the oldest director, with the rheumy eyes and doughty temperament of a world-weary bulldog. He was also by far the most experienced businessman on the FAI board, having been not only chief executive of Ampol Petroleum but also chairman of TAA, the domestic airline that was later to be subsumed into Qantas.

He noted to the Royal Commission that none of the executive management of FAI had ever explained the company's reinsurance arrangements to its non-executive directors and that, more ominously still, he could not always get the numbers he wanted from the executives.

At the 7 April 1998 board meeting Harris crashed headlong into FAI management over whether the company was going to meet the profit forecast of $21 million for the year to 30 June 1998 that Rodney Adler had made previously. Under Australian Stock Exchange listing rules, a company which is likely to depart from previous forecasts by more than 15 per cent, up or down, must inform its shareholders.

As it turned out the company could only come up with an $8.6 million pre-tax profit, and that was *after* adding in $58 million worth of near-instantaneous reinsurance 'recoveries'. Harris may have been in the dark, but his instinct and concern were fully justified. 'I became a little intolerant at that meeting because I could not get management to give me figures that would satisfy me as to their veracity,' he said.

In the end Rodney Adler signed a note to the ASX on 29 July, more than three months later, to the effect that FAI was not going to meet the $21 million forecast. The $8.6 million pre-tax profit result was published eleven days later. FAI shareholders were about to be rescued by Ray Williams' ill-considered bid, which started on 23 September, but they were given as much information along the way as the proverbial mushrooms.

In summary, there were about four parallel streams of activity going on in the management of FAI by mid–1998, and the board knew about almost none of them. Rodney Adler was living in an unusual world in which his two top lieutenants, Daniel Wilkie and Tim Mainprize, were fixing up the reserves by whatever means they cared to, while he kept his distance. His board, meanwhile, were variously assumed by Malcolm Turnbull and finance director Tim Mainprize to be *au fait* with Project Firelight, but with no one actually checking that they were. And the biggest topics for debate at board meetings were Adler's various non-insurance investment schemes.

Adler complained at one stage to chairman John Landerer about the excessive activity of the audit committee under Geoff Hill. Had Landerer taken it up with the audit committee, asked Norman O'Bryan, SC, at the commission.

'I did not. I was extremely happy that the audit committee was performing in the manner which he was complaining about,' replied Landerer.

But if he was locking horns continually with his own board by mid–1998, Adler knew by then that Ray Williams was getting closer and closer to making a bid for FAI. Williams had fought hard to stop Winterthur making a trade sale of its 51 per cent of HIH, and HIH was about to land back with a thud as a lowly rated Australian domestic insurer. In November 1995, after Winterthur came along, giant US ratings agency Standard & Poor's had lifted HIH's overall rating from BB+ to BBB-, a perfect door-opener to corporate business. Many companies do not allow themselves to buy insurance from low-rated insurers, however low the premium.

But the selldown sent the rating the other way. As soon as Winterthur announced in April 1998 merely that it was reviewing its holding, S&P cut its estimate of HIH's vital 'claims paying' ability from AA- to A. Few moves are more guaranteed to shrink the interest of corporates seeking insurance, particularly if they hope to see a payout on any future claims.

Malcolm Turnbull's approach to Rodney Adler in late 1997 had a logical side effect: Rodney Adler lost interest in merger talks with HIH.

It is now generally conceded that the single act of taking over FAI Insurance did not specifically kill off HIH, since there were more than $2 billion worth of other follies committed in the UK and the US over a much longer period. But it is also fair to suggest that the mess caused by the acquisition was, as Ray Williams put it, the final nail in HIH's coffin.

For eight months in 1998, during the worst of FAI's long series of travails, HIH took no steps to look closely at FAI.

And aside from all the other events so far described, in May 1998 Adler hosted Jeffrey Pokross, a New York banker with proved Mafia connections, on an all-expenses paid visit, and in June of 1998 Daniel Wilkie put all the reinsurance in place to make FAI look like a going concern. Of all the times not to keep an eye on FAI, this was a bad one.

On 7 September 1998 Goldman Sachs concluded formally that it would not be going ahead with Project Firelight, informing Rodney Adler on 12 September. He was, as he put it, 'surprised and disappointed'.

A week or two earlier Rodney Adler had bumped into Ray Williams at an Insurance Council of Australia function. Adler was chairman of the lobby group and Williams deputy chairman. Ever the salesman, Adler suggested to Ray Williams that HIH and FAI should look at some form of collaboration. In that era of consolidation at all costs, that was the message both sides wanted to hear, if for markedly different reasons.

On 9 September 1998, two days after Goldman threw in the towel as buyers, FAI put out its carefully constructed 1997–98 results, declaring a pre-tax profit of $8.6 million.

Examining these results now is like listening to dented cockpit voice recorders from two airliners that have defied the law of probabilities and collided.

We know who was flying the HIH plane — the man who built it — and we know that by then he had sent co-pilot Winterthur back to economy and, while Winterthur was strapping on a parachute and working out how to get safely out of the plane, Williams had locked the cockpit door.

But at FAI the cockpit atmosphere was more of a running scuffle and the non-executive directors in first class had to put the best construction on the lurches, thumps and yells emanating from the other side of the bulkhead. Tim Mainprize, the accountant who must wear the cabin service director's hat in this analogy, said he did not check to see whether FAI's directors were all aware of Project Firelight. 'I didn't feel it was my obligation to separately raise it with the board,' he explained.

A cleft stick would have been more effective. Messages weren't sent, or looked as though they were, and the 'cc' system of 'copying in' extra message recipients added another layer of mystery.

One piece of apparent evidence that Adler told John Landerer about Goldman Sachs' earlier work was a copy of a letter that he sent on 5 February 1998, in the early stages of Project Firelight, to Malcolm Turnbull discussing details. The letter carried the footnote 'cc John Landerer' but the chairman testified that he never got it. The judge accepted that evidence.

By that time Adler was certainly behaving more like an autocrat business owner than anyone bound by the tedious dictates of corporate governance, a trait he unwittingly shared with his fellow-pilot Ray Williams.

He freely gave confidential information to Goldman Sachs, as did Tim Mainprize. Quizzed by the Royal Commission about that breach of the FAI rules, Adler explained without obvious hesitation that 'I believe in my role as chief executive, I had been given that authority.' Ray Williams later said something very similar about his decision to give an eight-year unsecured, interest-free loan of $400,000 to an old friend of his in London, Fred Holland. Holland was a former chairman of CE Heath in the UK but had no role whatever in the Australian company that was floated in 1992.

Can executives act in that way without consulting their board? The FAI code of conduct certainly banned giving away confidential information without board approval.

Adler signed off on the code in 1995, which meant he agreed to the following: to disclose conflicts of interest, not to disclose confidential information without board approval and not to trade in the company's shares during 'blackout' periods without first informing the chairman and company secretary.

Adler admitted on 14 June 2002 that he did not remember reading the code during 1998.

What did his directors think of all this at the time?

Landerer had told the commission on 16 May that he 'might well' have dismissed Adler if he had known about the disclosure of confidential FAI information to Goldman Sachs, which is the strongest comment he made against Adler. Goldman had had access to five years' worth of FAI profit forecasts broken down by product line, not that Goldman placed much faith in them. While the forecasts predicted rising profits, by October 1998 FAI was getting so many claims from its troublesome Commercial and Professional Insurance Division that it was being forced to sell down illiquid stocks to pay the bills.

If FAI was having ethical dilemmas in late 1998, Goldman Sachs came in for criticism both inside and outside the Royal Commission for switching roles from co-investor to sale adviser on 14 September.

The investment bank spent some 650 hours and many thousands of its own dollars on Project Firelight. Rodney Adler and his top lieutenant Daniel Wilkie made a presentation to Goldman's investment committee on 15 June 1998 in New York, evidently without the knowledge of the board. It was customary enough for senior management to do 'roadshows' around the world to institutional investors, so it was not hard to slip in a visit to Goldman. The two did not stay at the St Moritz, incidentally, which at that time charged around $US100 a night for well-located but down-at-heel rooms, but at the much grander Waldorf Astoria.

From that invitation you might construe that Goldman New York was keen on Firelight, but documents supplied to the Royal Commission suggest that the investment committee had gone off the idea even before April 1998.

A series of e-mails between Turnbull and his colleague James Del Favero in Hong Kong in late March and early April suggest that New York baulked at the idea because Rodney Adler was not the 'killer manager' that they felt the top job at FAI required.

By 1 April Turnbull was writing to Del Favero that 'I was disappointed that notwithstanding a strong recommendation from the Sydney office, supported by Singapore, they [Goldman Sachs' investment committee in New York] were not prepared to allow us even to proceed to due diligence [on FAI]. If you don't trust your local management that far, you barely trust them at all,' complained Turnbull, who went on to say that he believed a major reason for the lack of enthusiasm in New York was 'distance from the centre'.

Which is probably why Turnbull helped arrange for Adler to go to New York in June.

A full copy of Adler's presentation survives, and it makes for painful reading when the reader knows that the hardheads at Goldman Sachs in New York were already thoroughly sceptical.

It starts: 'On December 13 1988 my father, the founder of the company, died. Effectively, from that day I became the chief executive of FAI Insurance Ltd.

'Today, at the age of 39, looking back over the previous decade on any financial analysis, on any graph showing share price performance or market capitalisation, it has been a decade of unparalleled failure.

'The market capitalisation of FAI, including converting preference shares, is only $A200 million and the company is a shadow of its former self.'

You get the drift. It is all true, all honest sackcloth and ashes. But it gets worse.

He said that in 1990 FAI was exposed to some $A750 million worth of loans to the following companies: $450 million to Bond Corporation, $100 million to Ariadne, $80 million to Qintex and $30 million to Hooker Corporation.

At least Adler moved quickly on before he had to explain about the reputation of those companies and their chief executives: Alan Bond, Bruce Judge, Christopher Skase and George Herscu.

He raised the pitch gradually then ended with this hopeful claim: 'Our reputation in the insurance industry, which includes the insurance broking industry, is excellent and we are approved by every major broking house throughout the world,' whatever that meant.

'We believe that the value of our brand name alone is worth more than the market capitalisation of FAI today ... Whether you decide to enter into a joint venture with me or not is a decision I am clearly trying to influence but we certainly deserve on the fundamentals, the backing and support of your group.'

He didn't get it.

Norman O'Bryan, SC, counsel assisting the Royal Commission, took no issue with Goldman over its decision to keep its corporate wallet firmly stashed, but he zeroed in on a letter that Goldman Sachs Australia sent to its New York office on 7 September 1998 which reached the same conclusion.

The letter, which Justice Neville Owen said would cause him to 'wake up in the middle of the night screaming in twenty years' time', painted a very dire picture of FAI in explaining why Goldman had decided not to put money into FAI. It said that the 'true' net assets of FAI, after writedowns and unwinding of reinsurance contracts, were approximately $20 million, compared with a stated book value of $200 million.

The note was sent by Malcolm Turnbull, Russel Pillemer and analyst Renaud Haberkorn to colleagues Michael Pruzan and Alec Machiels in New York. The latter two were by now experts in FAI, since they had flown to Sydney in August and had had presentations on FAI in Sydney from Adler and others.

The three-page report was commendably brief, thoroughly relevant and, by almost all subsequent evidence, accurate. The only dissenter in later evidence was Rodney Adler, who held that in paying $300 million for FAI, HIH had got itself a bargain.

The report said, for instance, that FAI's assets were overvalued by more than $100 million, and revealed an incisive understanding of the reinsurance deals that Ray Williams said he did not know about. 'To cover losses generated by the long-tail business in 1998, FAI entered into a reinsurance arrangement that provided an extra income in 1998 and would generate losses over the next four years. The cost of breaking such a treaty is estimated at $A80–$100 million,' the report said.

Williams gave evidence on 13 August that if he had known of a $100 million shortfall in FAI's reserves and about the $57 million reinsurance recovery, then 'figures of that magnitude may well have meant that the company was insolvent'. Williams' $100 million and Goldman Sachs' $100 million are not even the same lumps of cash: if you add Goldman Sachs' overvaluation estimate to Williams' under-reserving number you come to a $200 million hole in FAI, which by a cruel coincidence was the overall share market valuation of FAI at the time.

By 7 September, Goldman Sachs had spent its own money on its own work and come to its own entirely understandable conclusions about FAI.

But it had nothing to show for some 650 hours of mainly executive time, which breaks the great unspoken rule of investment banking. You don't spend your own money for nothing.

A week later the die was cast when Rodney Adler said he had hired Goldman Sachs on behalf of FAI (not just himself) to 'review FAI's options'. When that was hardened up after the HIH bid to a full-scale advisory role, the project name was changed to the coy tag of 'Project Fireside'.

On 14 September Adler told chairman John Landerer and directors Geoff Hill, Ted Harris and Peter O'Connell that he had met with Turnbull the previous week. He apparently said nothing about months of previous work by Goldman Sachs. 'We have appointed Goldman Sachs to review our various options ranging from raising additional equity to selling outright, and all the options in between. The preferred emphasis being a strategic long-term partner via capital injection. Goldman Sachs have accepted the mandate with thanks and relish (however, it is subject to board approval),' he wrote. The directors might as well have been shackled to the walls of the railway tunnel for all they really knew. Aside from Goldman's previous work they also did not know, and Turnbull said he did not know, that Adler was coaxing an already keen Ray Williams towards making a bid in just over two weeks' time.

The FAI–Goldman deal was clearly ad hoc at that stage or, as Turnbull put it with his lawyer's vocabulary, putative. There was no formal agreement signed until just before HIH made its bid on 23 September, and Goldman's fee of $1.5 million was not agreed by the FAI board until 28 September. It was not quite the New South Wales electricity privatisation, but it was a fee. But it meant that Goldman Sachs had emphatically changed roles, from potential co-investor to sales advisor.

Several non-executive directors of FAI were scathing about the change in relationship between Rodney Adler and Goldman Sachs after they found out much later about the eight months of earlier work. John Landerer said that by staying on as chief executive after Goldman Sachs decided not to proceed, Rodney Adler placed himself 'in a position of irreconcilable conflict'.

In a witness statement before he gave evidence, Landerer also took a swipe at Malcolm Turnbull, who had relied on Rodney Adler to inform directors about Project Firelight. 'I am surprised that Mr Turnbull of Goldman Sachs Australia never advised the board of his previous roles and knowledge and I believe it was his obligation to do so,' he wrote.

Ted Harris thought the board would have been very reluctant to appoint Goldman Sachs if it had known on 14 September about its earlier work.

Peter O'Connell said that after Goldman's damning $20 million view of FAI's possible value on 7 September, 'I would have thought it would be difficult for Goldman Sachs to be retained by us as our independent adviser.' He said he would want to ask FAI's auditors why there was a $200 million gap between FAI's and Goldman Sachs' numbers. 'If it turned out that our valuation was wrong, there may be a whole regime of disclosures that we would need to make,' he added.

Geoff Hill, who knew most about the perils of investment banking, was the most forthright. He said he would have told ASIC, Australia's securities regulator, if he had known about Goldman Sachs' change of role because he considered it 'improper'.

He said it was 'not a level playing field' for HIH. 'You would have had Goldman Sachs and Mr Adler spending six months evaluating a takeover and arriving at the conclusion, in Goldman Sachs' case, that it wasn't worth doing, on information that nobody else had had. On the other hand, you had HIH utilising apparently public information and making a takeover.'

If there was a lot of retrospective wisdom being demonstrated by former FAI directors in the Royal Commission in 2002, on 14 September 1998 the information-deprived board did little to question Goldman Sachs' appointment.

Peter O'Connell, the former Gilbert & Tobin partner, remembered saying he thought it was 'not a logical choice'.

'Goldman Sachs were a relatively small shop in Australia,' he noted and added that although he viewed Mr Turnbull as 'a well recognised and extremely competent investment banker' he could recommend executives working in the Australian arms of JP Morgan and Merrill Lynch who 'might be more helpful'. But Adler pressed on, and as O'Connell put it, was 'adamant' that Goldman Sachs was the right choice.

The Royal Commission focused on two issues for Goldman Sachs: accepting a mandate from FAI, and the 7 September '$20 million' note.

Although Goldman placed no valuation on FAI in the Part B response to HIH's offer, it did make a presentation to FAI directors on 10 October 1998 which included possible valuations of FAI at between $157 million and $287 million.

Malcolm Turnbull fought hard against imputing any importance to the $20 million number, from dismissing any notion that it was a valuation, to saying it was an internal note and to disparaging it as being written by 'relatively junior' staff.

His colleague Russel Pillemer used the phrase 'back of the envelope' more than a dozen times in describing the way the $20 million number was arrived at, before Mr Turnbull even took the stand. 'The suggestion that Goldman Sachs valued FAI at $20 million is a false one and it's demonstrably false from the documents that are before the Royal Commission,' Turnbull said.

There was no basis on which you could infer that the valuation of FAI was $20 million, he said, and the allegation that it did 'has caused considerable damage to the reputation of Goldman Sachs and myself and Mr Pillemer', he said.

He also noted in evidence that he had made a presentation to FAI directors on 13 October, after HIH made its bid, in which he and Pillemer had stated 'very starkly and clearly' that it was possible to come up with a negative net tangible asset value for FAI. That is exactly what HIH ended up doing in 2000, booking $400 million to its goodwill account as an indication of the difference between the net asset value of FAI and what HIH paid. The conclusion: FAI was worth minus $100 million.

In other evidence Turnbull said that it was 'irrelevant', as far as Goldman Sachs' advice to the FAI board was concerned, that Goldman had decided not to invest in FAI. 'Goldman Sachs has its own or had its own investment criteria which included … a very, very high hurdle internal rate of return target of around 35 per cent,' he said.

John West, QC, counsel for John Landerer, asked Turnbull whether Goldman's decision not to invest in FAI might be the sort of market-sensitive information that companies should report to the Stock Exchange. Turnbull replied that a statement to the ASX to that effect would be 'meaningless, just stated in those bald terms'.

Russel Pillemer had noted in his evidence that the 7 September note was prepared on the basis of a 'fire sale' of FAI, and not as a going concern.

John Landerer cut through a lot of the hypotheticals when he told the Royal Commission on 14 May that 'It really wouldn't have mattered to me what label you put to their opinion or valuation. What would have mattered to me was that they decided they didn't wish to proceed and what mattered to me was that they came to a decision that the true value was $20 million and I would have asked for that to be investigated by the auditors.'

Although the FAI directors had voted on 28 September to get an independent valuation done on FAI, Mr Turnbull had persuaded them against it, saying it could cause unnecessary delay.

Goldman Sachs ran a major public relations campaign outside the Royal Commission, which unlike any other party at that time included ringing up journalists after the proceedings. Not only did Goldman send down from Hong Kong Edward Naylor, a senior 'house' handler of the media, but it also brought in veteran Sydney public relations man Ian Kortlang, an old friend of Turnbull's, at Goldman Sachs' expense.

Section 995 of the Corporations Act states: 'A person shall not, in connection with the making of, or the making of an evaluation of, or a recommendation in relation to, offers under a takeover bid, engage in conduct that is misleading or deceptive or is likely to mislead or deceive.'

That was the basis of a lot of discussion about FAI's Part B report, although the judge made no finding against Goldman Sachs or Turnbull for any of their conduct at any stage.

FAI's Part B report of 13 November 1998, whose front page carried the names of FAI and Goldman Sachs, was like most Part Bs: a relatively formulaic affair, designed to make a simple recommendation to shareholders — 'SELL' — but it contained a catch-all section called 'Other Material Information'. (Goldman's policy was that legal responsibility for the Part B statement lay with FAI.)

The section stated that apart from the sale by Rodney Adler's private company Lader Pty Ltd of 14.3 per cent of FAI to HIH, much publicised, 'there is no other information material to the making of a decision by FAI shareholders whether or not to accept the offer, being information that is known to any of the directors of FAI and has not previously been disclosed to FAI shareholders in this statement or the Part A Statement'.

Rodney Adler for one knew that one of the biggest investment banks in the world had walked away from investing in FAI just before the HIH bid was made because it didn't believe it was worth it. If FAI shareholders had known they would almost certainly have accepted the HIH bid with even more haste than they did.

A submission from Goldman in January 2003 said it did not 'withhold material information from FAI and which, had it been revealed, would have prompted the FAI directors to take steps effectively to sabotage the very generous and fully priced takeover offer from HIH and thereby severely disadvantage their own shareholders'.

That unusual statement perhaps accidentally encapsulated the inherent conflict that Goldman Sachs had faced in switching roles from potential buyer to adviser of FAI.

What it appears to be saying is that if Goldman had shown every bit of material information to the FAI directors, their reactions might have sabotaged the chances of keeping HIH's very juicy bid. The evidence many of the directors gave, about for instance how they might have informed ASIC if they had known about Goldman's earlier work, or not appointed Goldman as advisers, bears that out.

It was a very difficult situation in which Goldman's legal duties were possibly pulling one way and the huge commercial imperative of getting a good price for FAI shareholders was certainly pulling the other. Goldman's attention was also concentrated by the fact that the $1.5 million fee it was getting for advising FAI on the HIH takeover was only payable if the takeover succeeded.

The judge took a low-key line, choosing to point out only two areas of unease.

On the Part B, he noted that no reference was made in it to the financial implications for FAI of the under-reserving, which was not shown in the recently published FAI accounts. Nor was any mention made of the future adverse impacts of the reinsurance contracts, he said. But he did not raise the issue of whether Goldman's decision not to buy into FAI should have been in the Part B statement.

His only significant criticism of Goldman was over the fact that although Turnbull and Pillemer had made presentations to the FAI board in October 1998 in which they canvassed one proposal that was 'practically identical' to Project Firelight, there had been no mention made to the board either in writing or orally of the amount of work that Goldman had done on Firelight.

He said it was 'regrettable' that those matters were not revealed to the board, particularly so in the light of the evidence some directors gave to the commission that it might have affected their attitude to appointing Goldman as advisers.

CHAPTER 12

THE TAKEOVER

WHY ON EARTH did Ray Williams buy FAI?

It is always dangerous to use the 'retrospectoscope' to look at a deal that long ago died a painful death, but even in 1998 FAI was being treated with disdain by professionals in the Australian insurance industry. They believed (correctly) that the company's reserves were inadequate and that its assets were overvalued, so they steered away and left FAI to its admittedly flourishing retail (house and car) domestic insurance business. Ray Williams, who seemed to know everyone in the industry, must have known.

So why did one of the most experienced players in the Australian insurance business buy the least reputable operation in the place, sight unseen? Take your pick of two theories, both well aired by the *cognoscenti*.

The cynics go for the *desperate* scenario, which goes like this: if HIH was by mid–1998 turning into a dangerous Ponzi scheme with a frightening appetite for money because of the terrible underwriting decisions of previous years, FAI was a lifeline of sorts thanks to the high revenues it got from its domestic business.

And if you construct a scenario where Williams knew that he was cornered and knew he was going to have to tell his shareholders about it sooner or later, FAI was a chance. Buying it would cloud the picture for a while, anyway, as Alan Bond used to manage so well with his empire. If you keep acquiring businesses fast enough, no analyst except the ones in favour will ever be able to keep up. And from there on, there were two possible outcomes: prosperity or oblivion.

Prosperity might come, and this is very much from the drowning man's perspective, if FAI turned out to be solid and the market picked up, and the US recovered, and the UK recovered, and the synergies emerged, and, and, and.

And oblivion? If FAI turned out to be an overpriced dud with inadequate reserves and overstated assets — as it in fact did — then the combined company was going to go to Hell in a handcart.

But it was going that way anyway. Considering the Winterthur group had just made its agonised exit and HIH's credit rating had just dropped, then where was the downside? The worst case scenario was that it could all unravel even faster, but the critical point was that even the act of buying FAI sight unseen was a chance. Half of something is always a lot better than all of nothing.

That is the cynic's scenario, which is in fact borne out by the judge's note in his introduction to his report. It notes that HIH's insurance indemnity performance deteriorated very badly despite a big rise in premium. In the year to December 1997 the company lost $33.8 million on premium of $1233.5 million. The next comparative numbers were a loss of $73 million from premium of $1550 million, then by 2000 it was $103.5 million from $1995.4 million. In just two years the underwriting loss had more than doubled while premium rose by 25 per cent.

Others subscribe to the *optimist's* scenario. This is that Ray Williams actually believed he could do something with FAI. All that hindsight makes such an idea seem pretty laughable but confidants say that is exactly what he believed. 'He reckoned that getting the cautious influence of Winterthur off his back was the best thing that could have happened to him,' said one.

'He had seen that the CIC deal was a good one, and Winterthur came with it, but by 1998 he found they were blocking every move he wanted to make offshore,' said the confidant, who remembers the conversation clearly. 'He saw their departure as the big chance to do all those things offshore he had been wanting to do for years: he had enjoyed their presence when HIH was small, but now he saw the Swiss investors are an impediment.'

It's all about how you look at things. And HIH plus FAI was going to be 'Australia's largest listed general insurer', as Ray Williams was fond of saying. It seems absurd now to see the move in such simple terms, but that is what Ray Williams was telling people. 'He was obsessed with two things: being number one, and the share price of HIH,' said the confidant.

Further investigations revealed that Ray Williams' first question to several people in his office every day was 'What's the share price?', even when other matters were baying round the door. Being number one was even easier to calculate: HIH was number three and FAI was number five, and together they would sneak past one-time roadside help provider NRMA to become the biggest general insurer in Australia.

An irony is that the bid for FAI in September 1998 set the HIH share price back by around 25c from $2.25 back to $2, but by that time the die was cast. If you stick to the present and avoid retrospect, there was perhaps some logic.

Wayne Martin, QC, counsel assisting the commission, took some of the onus off Williams by noting in January 2003 that the board of HIH was just as mercurial as Williams was on the subject of strategy.

'Fundamentally the board had no real strategy or forward plan for the business they were overseeing,' he said, noting as an example the fact that in July 1998 the board announced that it was going to pursue growth in the offshore segment of the business and increase the proportionate share of revenue from offshore. 'Two months later, however, the company announced its bid for FAI which was totally contrary to the strategy which had just been announced,' he added.

(He also noted that when Ray Williams put HIH's major business lines up for sale in late 2000, in what became the Allianz deal, he did not tell directors until after he had done it — having chosen one of Sydney's grandest restaurants, Forty-One, as the place he would tell them.

Martin didn't leave it there. 'Extraordinarily, when board members found out about what had been done by senior management, there was no criticism of management for having taken this step without reference to the board,' he said. 'That fact, in our submission, is very telling in terms of identifying the true source of control of the group.')

So once again it emerged that HIH was an out-of-control empire in the hands of a corporate autocrat with a growing taste for the Big Splash. But for all the confidence, Ray Williams was walking bright-eyed and bushy-tailed into a trap.

He imagined that taking over FAI would be a rerun of the successful CIC transaction back in 1995, but he ended up being totally outmanoeuvred by young upstart Rodney Adler at every turn.

Adler knew the outcome he wanted: a bid worth anything up to $450 million but more likely $300 million. And he knew who might be mad enough to bid: Ray Williams. But if Adler had been a poker player, he was sitting on a pair of threes.

For a start, the FAI share price was little better than horrible. After starting 1998 at 74 cents, its lowest start to a year since 1993, the price of FAI shares had slumped to 45 cents by 9 September, the day the carefully constructed 30 June 1998 annual result came out. FAI reported an $8.6 million pre-tax profit and a $4.76 million loss after tax.

Clearly the market was unimpressed by this apparently miraculous recovery: the share price actually slipped back half a cent on 9 September to 45c.

Adler preferred to look towards the sunlit uplands, telling the press on 9 September 1998 that if it had not been for a $6.5 million tax bill, the company would have made a small net profit. The tax came, he said, as a consequence of FAI selling its aged care unit called Premier Care to the Moran Health Care group for $68 million, which was well over book value.

Talking round the fact that there was no dividend payable, Adler told the *Australian Financial Review* that 'It will be disappointing to our shareholders, but our dividend was never a great percentage. Most people buy FAI for the capital growth rather than the dividend.' That's one way of putting it. The annual dividend had effectively dived by two-thirds from 1.5c a share in 1996–97 to half a cent in the previous half year to December 1997, with nothing on offer for the half just ended.

Rodney Adler has been accused of many things but has never been accused of lacking chutzpah. His stock was at its lowest level in the share market for five years and was down by almost 40 per cent in 1998 alone. He said he believed that on fundamentals the stock should be higher, but admitted the company had not been 'a great performer' in recent years. 'Am I concerned? No,' he said, using his pet style of asking himself a rhetorical question.

'Am I working hard to try to improve that? Yes. All the measures that we take are to improve the performance of the company and we hope that the share price will follow the performance.'

It was vintage Rodney Adler. A fact or two, a red herring, a smile and a wild general prediction that there would be jam tomorrow.

It certainly got Ray Williams in.

As previously shown, Adler had dragged his coat very successfully past Williams. During September 1998 the two men had a number of meetings about a possible bid by HIH for FAI, although neither troubled to tell their board about what was going on until the bid was almost public knowledge.

Ray Williams did a neat pitch to his directors, even if he did not give them any time to consider the deal. He devised a list of five benefits that HIH would obtain from what he called Project Vitamin: putting HIH up another level in the insurance industry; achieving substantial savings, particularly in the information technology area; making HIH the biggest gross premium earner in Australian general insurance; taking HIH into the direct market such as car and house insurance; and making HIH the biggest professional indemnity and public liability insurer in Hong Kong.

Rodney Adler did not allow Williams to do any due diligence analysis of FAI even though he said Williams asked at least twice. The answer was always 'No', but since Williams had spent the first half of 1998 doing his damnedest to prevent trade buyers from doing due diligence on HIH, he was in no position to baulk at Adler doing the same. Adler had explained that HIH was a competitor to FAI in domestic insurance in Australia and there was no merit in giving away sensitive information.

Williams tamely accepted the verdict and got down to brass tacks with Adler on the mechanics of how the deal was actually going to happen. Aside from price, which in Williams' eyes was 50c per FAI share, and in Adler's eyes was $1 a share, there was a lot of painful detail on a number of subjects. First, HIH could not pay cash for all of FAI. Second, Rodney Adler wanted cash for all of his family's 30 per cent stake. That was a complication in itself since the Corporations Act forbids a bidder from offering one shareholder a better deal per share than any other shareholder.

Third, Ray Williams wanted the bid to be conditional on 90 per cent acceptance, meaning that he did not want any minority shareholders left after the deal was wrapped up. In Australia, if a bidder gets to 90 per cent of a company they are allowed to mop up the rest by compulsory purchase, so 90 per cent is the best outcome they need to hope for.

Adler did an awesome job of pretending not to be desperate to sell but he did show his cards by saying he wanted a 50.1 per cent acceptance hurdle rather than 90 per cent. Ninety and 50.1 are the two opposite ends of the spectrum in that business, 50 being the 'oh, all right' level at which control passes to the bidder, but lots of small shareholders are left and the target company, in this case FAI, stays listed.

Adler always had a painfully dynastic perception of FAI, to the aural detriment of many of his employees and other such people who could not easily get away. And if he could not control all of it, he was off.

By 17 September a number of buyers around the world began to show a strong interest in buying FAI shares.

A subsequent investigation by the Australian Stock Exchange revealed that on Thursday, 17 September Rene Rivkin bought just over 900,000 FAI shares at about 47c each.

On 16 September trading in FAI shares in Australia tripled in volume, with buy orders coming from Zurich and the US as well as locally.

On Tuesday, 22 September, the day before the bid, Adler hosted a lunch in the FAI boardroom attended by Rivkin and a number of leading lights in the Australian Labor Party including Bob McMullan, John Faulkner and Gary Gray. Although he liked to call himself a 'blue blue chip' Liberal, Adler maintained good relations with the ALP and although FAI was a bigger contributor to the Liberals than to the ALP, his office was still worth a visit.

(In 2001 he burned his bridges with the Liberal Party in spectacular fashion by using a new website he had called 'The Rocket' to describe Prime Minister John Howard as being 'politically dead'. Aside from the fact that he earned the instant enmity of the senior echelons of the Liberal Party, who at the time of writing were settling happily into their third consecutive term of office, he seems to have adhered a bit too literally to the old adage 'never forgive a favour'. It was John Howard's decision, back in 1978 when he was federal Treasurer, to give FAI a licence to operate as a general insurer, thus pulling it out of the mud.)

There is no suggestion that the ALP people heard or said anything untoward — they were after all looking for a contribution, not a conspiracy — and they had to leave early.

But after they left the looming bid by HIH was an open topic of conversation. Rivkin told the diners that he had been 'supporting the stock in Europe over the weekend'.

That remark could be taken a number of ways, not all of them nefarious. It was for instance a reminder that FAI was riding a knife edge and, even if there was a bid just round the corner from HIH, the stock needed all the friends it could get.

At that point there was a very strong reason for Adler telling his friends to buy the stock. Not only would there be a nice trade for them in buying at 50c and selling out in a few days for 75c, but their buying gave Adler a much needed hand to put a floor under the stock, as Rivkin had unashamedly stated. It's hypothetical now but with the FAI stock price moving up from 45c to perhaps 55c, it might give Adler the chance to force Ray Williams' bidding hand up towards the $1 a share which in a moment of financial euphoria he had told Williams that FAI was worth.

Jeffrey Pokross, Rodney Adler's man on the spot in New York, certainly put his shoulder to the wheel. Evidence from his trial in the 'mob on Wall Street' case shows that although he started buying FAI shares on 30 April 1998, he did not go into the stock in a big way until September. For instance, he bought 3000 American Depositary Receipts in FAI, or the equivalent of 30,000 FAI shares, on 21 September, two days before HIH made its bid for FAI. His uncle Harvey Pokross also appears to have caught the FAI bug at the same time, buying in on a smaller scale.

The share price of FAI jumped in Australia from 52c to 75c in the space of a few hours on Wednesday, 23 September 1998 in Australia, having climbed up from around 44c in the preceding week. The surveillance department of the Australian Stock Exchange compiled a report of share trading in FAI in the week preceding, including Rivkin's acquisition on 17 September, but a subsequent inquiry by the Australian Securities and Investments Commission (ASIC) did not conclude any wrongdoing.

Pokross had told the New York court that he had had no inside information from Rodney Adler about FAI, which is an improbable claim for a man who was hired to 'get behind' FAI by Rodney Adler.

His evidence in New York was all about what happened after HIH started bidding on 23 September in Australia. He told the court that Adler had called him on 23 or 24 or 25 September and put a proposal to him that appears to have shocked him. 'He wanted to figure out if I can assist him in secretly parking stock in the US so he can get some money and drive the price up in Australia to attract a higher takeover bid than apparently he was getting.' He said he declined to that because it was illegal. Even mobsters have values, it would appear.

Rodney Adler's evidence differed, but more in the interpretation of what might have been a fairly cryptic conversation. Adler told the commission he had received a call from Pokross after HIH started bidding and that he asked Pokross to, 'you know, maintain his interest in the company [FAI] and buy stock, that may be positive for the stock and it may help flush out another bidder'.

That old conversational stopgap 'you know' could have meant a number of things, since Pokross and Adler knew a few things that the rest of the world did not.

Pokross in fact informed his FBI handlers of most of what was going on, although he appears to have succumbed to the trader's disease in buying stock for himself. There is no record of him telling the FBI about the mysterious urge that overtook him and his Uncle Harvey on 21 September. They bought FAI shares via Crabbe Capital, an organisation that shares an address with DMN Capital at 5 Hanover Square in New York. And even mobsters from Fraud Central, the nickname given to DMN Capital, know right from wrong.

He said he told Adler that 'parking' stock on the New York Stock Exchange was very difficult due to market surveillance, and that he thought that was not such a bright idea. But, he continued mysteriously, 'plans could always be formulated'.

And meanwhile he and his Uncle Harvey began selling FAI shares on 30 September, which at 75c Australian a share was a profit of more than 50 per cent in a week.

In the New York court he was asked if he had told the US government (the FBI) that he had already bought shares in FAI and that he had already made a profit of about $US100,000.

Pokross: 'Not in that e-mail, no.'

Counsel: 'Did you ever tell them that?'

Pokross: 'I don't recall.' Pokross subsequently explained that it took him about six months to make $US100,000 trading FAI.

The first official rumblings of the bid came on 22 September, when Adler summoned Turnbull from Melbourne for an urgent meeting about an imminent bid. He had written to Turnbull earlier that day noting clearly that 'I am conscious of the possibility of FAI receiving a bid this week', but his main aim in that letter was to point out that he did not want it to look as though there was a connection between the 'engagement letter' that Turnbull had sent Adler, seeking an official signature and a mandate, and the HIH bid.

Although there has been much debate about what Turnbull and Goldman Sachs did for Adler in 1998, it was Adler alone who lined Ray

Williams up to buy FAI. Hiring Turnbull and Goldman Sachs officially on 24 September to advise FAI what to do about the HIH bid not only looked logical, but it was a reflection of the reality that Goldman Sachs had no role in Adler's very successful fishing expedition in early September.

Turnbull came into talks on the evening of Tuesday, 22 September because Adler had a long way to go before he had Williams where he wanted him. Adler wanted a 'pre-bid agreement' from Williams that he could have cash for all his shares.

John Atanaskovic, a Sydney corporate lawyer and partner of Tony Hartnell, formerly the chairman of ASIC, was advising HIH and his view was that any such agreement would be illegal. Section 698 of the Corporations Act states that every shareholder in a target company should be given equal treatment.

Atanaskovic said that there could be a problem as HIH wanted to offer shares and cash and: 'The Adler family cannot get consideration which is better than or more valuable than the consideration offered to the general body of FAI shareholders.'

Adler was far from amused, despite the fact that FAI was only hanging on by its fingernails, and he hoed into Atanaskovic for failing to find a way round that particular fact.

'Do you recall saying some very disparaging things to Mr Atanaskovic about his qualities as a lawyer?' Norman O'Bryan, SC, asked Adler on 20 June 2002.

'Yes, I don't think I was overly polite to him,' said Adler. He dismissed Atanaskovic's line by saying 'Everyone argues with John, that is nothing new really.'

So by the end of 22 September, there was no bid on the table, Rodney had crossed swords with HIH's very experienced lawyer, Adler and Williams could not agree on whether the bid would be conditional on 50 or 90 per cent acceptance, and the pre-bid agreement had gone west.

The HIH board, meanwhile, had finally been brought in on the bid secret by Ray Williams the day before the bid began. On the afternoon of 22 September he asked company secretary Fred Lo to convene a meeting of directors for 6.30 p.m. that evening. The resulting meeting was more noticeable for who wasn't there than who was.

Terry Cassidy, Ray Williams' long-time cohort, was in Vladivostok in eastern Russia seeing a possible client, so he will never be blamed for the

FAI acquisition. Short of being in Ulan Bator or Timbuktu, he could scarcely have been further from the action. Randolph Wein could not be contacted either, since he was in Hong Kong running HIH Asia. 'Gorgeous George' Sturesteps was in the US and Michael Payne was in London. They were told after the event.

(Cassidy's reaction on hearing the news was to offer to resign, since he knew all too well what FAI's reputation was like in the market. Once again Ray Williams' relentless reliance on loyalty prevailed and he was able to talk Cassidy out of resigning, to Cassidy's eternal regret.)

Bob Stitt, QC, a Sydney-based director, could only attend by telephone so was almost certainly unable to see the two relevant documents: a financial model devised by Société Générale Australia's Colin Richardson and an assessment of FAI's assets (such as they were) by finance director Dominic Fodera.

Only one non-executive director, Sydney lawyer Neville Head, attended in person, with Fodera and the man driving the deal, Ray Williams. Chairman Geoff Cohen, Charles Abbott, and Alex Gorrie all hooked up by video from Melbourne, and there is no certainty that they got both or even one of the documents to look at when they sat down at 6.25 p.m. to discuss the bid.

Even the ultra-cautious company secretary Fred Lo said he didn't have a copy of Richardson's document until the next day.

Richardson, who told the Royal Commission that his role in the takeover was 'purely executionary', produced his model which specifically mentions a 75c a share bid price, although it also postulated a range of 61c to 77c. It also said that 'the expected synergy benefits need to be of the order of $25 million pre-tax', which is not the same as saying they would be. They weren't, largely because FAI's and HIH's back office systems were so far apart that a lot of expensive rectification work got in the way.

As everyone now knows, it was the bid from Cloud-Cuckoo-Land. Richardson had done a fair amount of work previously on FAI for Williams but had done almost nothing in 1998 and had always told him previously that it needed further examination. The judge noted in his report that he was not sure what Richardson's 'purely executionary' comment meant. 'If it means no more than ensuring that all of the paperwork was in order, then the amount of fees levied in respect of the transaction seems difficult to justify', he wrote. Jeff Simpson, the HIH accountant who left in 1999, said that SG Hambros' fee was $5.4 million. Although Malcolm Turnbull and Goldman Sachs had had access to five years of optimistic FAI forecasts and had walked away from investing only weeks before, Williams and Richardson had nothing more than FAI's artificially inflated results and a set of Macquarie Bank analyst forecasts to work off.

If Ray Williams had been a weather forecaster, at this point he was sitting in his room with all his data systems broken down, with a window open and a licked finger to identify wind direction. Richardson admitted to the Royal Commission that Williams wanted to do the deal, and that effectively was that.

The meeting itself to decide on the FAI purchase couldn't have been simpler. Fred Lo, who later wrote the minutes, said it was mainly about getting a commitment from Rodney Adler regarding his 30 per cent parcel of shares, without breaking the law. Lo summarised John Atanaskovic's contribution as 'You can do whatever you like as long as you comply with the law.' The law states that you cannot offer any shareholder a special deal four months or less before a takeover offer. Lo stated that nobody expressed any opposition to the proposal. The meeting ended at 8.30 p.m.

Project Vitamin might have been the tonic Williams wanted to administer to his bleeding HIH, but it was going to be as useful in the long term as a revolver aimed squarely at his foot.

Atanaskovic and Turnbull had a brief conversation that night, according to Atanaskovic, at which Turnbull expressed the view that it might be possible for Adler to be paid cash for all his shares and still satisfy the law. Atanaskovic says that in response he mentioned two court cases that suggested he could not, and there the conversation ended.

By 23 September there was still no agreement on whether Rodney Adler was going to get cash for his 30 per cent stake. There was also the fact that in Australia one insurance company is only allowed to buy 15 per cent of another before it has to seek approval from the federal Treasurer to go any further.

First up was a meeting at 9.00 a.m. in the HIH office between Williams and Fodera, their lawyers John Atanaskovic and Mark Pistilli, and Colin Richardson. They wanted to get a legitimate agreement from Rodney Adler that would allow them to get certain access to his stake. Adler met Malcolm Turnbull five minutes later in his office to discuss how best to get cash for his stake.

The groups got together at 10.00 a.m. in the FAI office, with Turnbull being introduced as Adler's adviser despite the fact that nothing had been signed. Turnbull went in to bat for Adler with his usual relentless verve.

Atanaskovic remembers that Turnbull conceded that HIH 'couldn't do any better' on the issue of getting Adler cash for all his shares. In other words, he was going to have to get the same deal as other shareholders in response to HIH's planned mix of shares and cash. The big stumbling block was the 50.1 per cent acceptance level sought by Adler, against the 90 per cent level sought by HIH. HIH understandably wanted to be able to pull out of the deal if anyone at all got in their way, such as for instance a spoiling player getting an eleven per cent stake and hanging out for a higher price.

(That idea was straight from the Larry Adler school of 1980s greenmailing, which just goes to show you should never let sentiment get in the way of borrowing a good idea.)

Rodney Adler wanted a deal that would guarantee him as much cash as possible for as many of his shares as possible, so the lower the bidder's 'get-out' conditions were, the happier he would be. As lawyer Mark Pistilli put it in a later note, 'Adler indicated that he had a reasonably pressing need for cash personally.'

Most people would see in a comment like that an air of desperation, but Rodney Adler throws everything he can at a deal. Despite his shaky negotiating ground he pressed on.

At around 11.15 a.m. negotiations had stalled on the acceptance level issue, which Adler described as a 'deal breaker'.

'I informed Ray Williams that I intended to place a large line of stock, approximately 15 per cent of the company, on the market and I told him I was going to inform all the other parties who were interested,' said Adler in a file note he wrote after the event.

'Over the next hour I rang Frank O'Halloran from QBE, John Hatton from Liberty Mutual (the Boston-based company that had recently tried in vain to buy Winterthur's 51 per cent stake in HIH) and Finley Middleton from CNA.'

He said he 'advised them that I was placing a line on the market capable of being bid for'. That was when he called up Michael Crowley at ABN Amro, as was mentioned in the Prologue.

Rodney Adler was the man in the middle, calling round the world and telling everyone there was a deal brewing. There was copious use of the vertical pronoun, I, and to the unpractised eye it all looked like a wheeler-dealer's auction developing. In fact it was nothing of the sort. Rodney Adler the poker player was still sitting on his pair of threes and not one of those other insurers he had called was a serious chance.

Liberty had been looking at FAI, had staff in Sydney and hoped to have a valuation of FAI in Boston by the next day, but at that pace there really only was one serious bidder left: Ray Williams. And what was really happening was that Adler was playing with paper and matches under Williams' chair in the hope that if he offered the first 45 million shares of his stock, Williams would grab it, spurred by the realisation that Adler had been tickling up all the potential buyers he knew.

Crowley's unusual sales technique, which he carried out under close instruction from Adler, was to 'be vocal and loud in placing the stock on the market so that everyone had an opportunity to bid'.

Both Adler and Williams knew two vital numbers, even if the rest of the world took a while to cotton on to what happened between 2.11 p.m. and 2.12 p.m. At 2.11 p.m. Crowley placed 35 million shares on the market to sell at 75c, well above the current market. Ray Williams' broker, JB Were, had been told by Williams that Adler might suddenly offer a big line of FAI shares and when it came on for sale at the exact price Williams was prepared to bid, Were took the lot.

Within two minutes Crowley had asked Adler for the other 10,000 shares to sell and they too were snapped up. By 3.00 p.m. Ray Williams was calling Adler and saying he was the buyer of the 15 per cent stake.

'It was at this stage that I learned he was the acquirer of the shares,' wrote Adler, with what almost sounds like surprise in his tone. Even a man with a lousy hand can sometimes win if he plays those cards carefully. He had quite legitimately been paid cash for 15 per cent of the company, or half his stake, because no bid had yet been made. That was imminent but the share trade and subsequent bid were made under completely different terms.

By 3.50 p.m. Williams was in Adler's office and telling him about the bid he was going to make for FAI.

And by that time Adler had told his board what was going on. At 3.48 p.m. his company secretary, Rob Baulderstone, sent out a vintage piece of Adler prose which said that Williams was about to come and see him 'to discuss a full bid for the company'.

'I will keep you informed of events as they unfold,' he said, before reminding them why they were still coming stone last in the information chain.

'It should also be noted that I still own approximately 16 per cent of the company and therefore still occupy the position as the single largest shareholder.'

He could afford to be smug. He had Williams exactly where he wanted him and he had even got Williams to pay his asking price without a murmur.

Mark Pistilli, John Atanaskovic's sidekick, noted that his boss had suggested HIH apply a discount of 'about 10 per cent or more' in bidding for the first parcel of Rodney Adler's shares. In Pistilli's words the discount would be 'to compensate for the fact that the offer to Adler would be unconditional and perhaps all-cash' compared to the conditions that would be bound to apply to a formal takeover offer. The suggestion was ignored, making Adler richer by about $3 million.

CHAPTER 13

PAY DAY

WILLIAMS AND HIH put a formal bid on the table for FAI that offered one
HIH share for every three FAI shares, or one HIH share and $2.25 cash
for every six FAI shares. With the HIH price closing on 23 September at
$2.29, the scrip bid valued each FAI share at 76.3c. The bid was
unconditional, which is exactly what Adler had wanted.

By this time Williams was supposed to be the main player in the game,
with Adler merely planning a well-financed exit. But the usual roles
stayed reversed. It was Adler who dictated terms and Williams who
started something he was going to have to get used to, paying too much
for anything to do with Adler.

Adler hopped into the share market the following day as a seller of FAI
and got 76c in cash for a parcel of more than a million of his family's
shares, exploiting the fact that some arbitrageur who was clearly on the
outside of the deal was paying up in the hope of a higher bid.

The Australian Corporations Act forbids a bidder from paying more
for stock on-market than they are offering as part of a takeover, but
nothing stops a vendor from getting the best price they can from a third
party.

The price of HIH, meanwhile, dropped 17c, or 7.4 per cent, on the
day following the bid, to close at $2.12. Not every holder of HIH stock
was as keen on FAI as Ray Williams was. Not long after the bid Rodney
Adler was asked if he was off to the Bahamas with the $80 million that

rough calculations suggested he was worth after the sale of FAI. His wife Lyndi beside him reportedly looked very enthusiastic about the idea. 'I'm going to be a billionaire,' he replied, making it clear that FAI was just the first step in a stellar investing career.

He never got closer to that goal than $80 million, but he personally got so much money out of HIH in late 1998 and early 1999 that you might think he was using HIH as a testing ground for his billionaire strategy.

Before he accepted finally for the rest of his FAI shares on 11 January 1999, Adler obtained from Ray Williams a series of financial and verbal promises that would set him up with a $3.8 million 'severance' payout closely followed by a $40,000 a month consulting fee at HIH, and a board seat at HIH.

Not surprisingly, the investigators at the HIH Royal Commission were concerned that Adler had screwed a better deal out of Williams as the price for accepting the bid, but that was not how Williams saw it at all.

Giving evidence in August, Williams bristled at any suggestion that the two were related. That would have been a breach of Section 698 of the Corporations Act, the same one that caused all the anxiety between John Atanaskovic and Rodney Adler on the day before HIH's bid was made. 'I wouldn't have been a party to anything like that,' said Williams. 'There was absolutely no connection whatsoever. That never entered my mind,' he said.

The $40,000 a month consulting role had no formal duties attached to it, apart from the fact that Rodney Adler was also put on the investment committee at HIH. That was a disastrous appointment, which ended up leading to the Pacific Eagle Equities mess in July 2000. 'It ranks somewhere between putting Dracula in charge of the blood bank and putting the lunatics in charge of the asylum,' said one battle-scarred HIH veteran. Wayne Martin mused out loud to the commission 'whether in fact the major activity that Mr Adler engaged himself in was the solicitation of HIH's funds for ventures in which he had a personal interest and which invariably proved to be disastrous for HIH'.

But there was one job that even Ray Williams was not giving away. Although he offered Adler a board seat at HIH (without consulting any of his fellow HIH directors, by the way), he told Adler he could not be deputy chief executive of HIH when Adler asked him before the bid even began. 'That wasn't possible . . . that couldn't happen . . . I didn't think that Mr Adler would fit into that team,' he explained to Wayne Martin.

Section 698 says clearly that you cannot offer any one shareholder in a company a greater benefit in a takeover than any other, and despite legal advice to the contrary by Sydney lawyers Minter Ellison, Ray Williams agreed to pay Adler more than $4 million in severance on 7 December 1998, four days before he accepted the takeover offer for his remaining 15 per cent of FAI, on 11 December. That took HIH almost to 50 per cent of FAI, effectively sealing the takeover's success.

Pressed by Martin, Ray Williams maintained his denial of any connection between the two events. Martin asked Williams if he had asked his corporate adviser, Colin Richardson, to look at this issue 'urgently', as he had written on a fax, because the bid would not be successful if Rodney Adler did not accept it. 'Mr Martin, there was absolutely no connection between the agreement to pay Mr Adler these amounts — this amount under his contract. After all it was FAI that was going to pay it, not HIH,' he said, perhaps forgetting that by then HIH was going to end up footing all of FAI's bills.

Martin pressed on a short time later. 'I am obliged to put to you that in fact those arrangements were entered into by you with Mr Adler as the price for his acceptance into the bid.'

'Oh, Mr Martin, that's so totally wrong. Completely wrong, there is absolutely no connection with it whatsoever. I wouldn't have been a party to anything like that,' Willams replied.

As with so many events surrounding HIH at that time, even if there was no malevolent intention, it looked absolutely terrible. Rodney Adler accepted the consultancy deal on 7 December 1998 and then on 11 December accepted the takeover bid from HIH for the second half of his holding (still around 15 per cent of the stock). He also recommended the HIH bid to FAI shareholders. Ray Williams conceded to the commission that until Adler had accepted the bid, acceptances had been 'at a very low level' and that afterwards, the level rose dramatically.

When his turn in the box came, Rodney Adler also denied that there was a connection between the consultancy and the acceptance. He also noted that the consultancy and the $3.7 million payout he got from FAI were totally separate, although by the time the deal was signed FAI was a subsidiary of HIH.

He said that if he had not accepted the consultancy with HIH, 'I would have just got that termination payment and sailed into the sunset' and that he could then have accepted a consultancy 'from any company in Australia'.

That was Rodney Adler's chutzpah striking again.

As if that was not a cosy enough deal, in March 1999 Adler's private company charged a UK company, Gross Hill Properties, some £36,000 'for services rendered in connection with discussions with HIH'. He was representing the UK company. He told the Royal Commission that he had no recollection of how he had calculated the fee and he was unsure whether he had disclosed it to HIH. 'But I'm pretty sure I didn't get paid,' he added. The judge noted several times that Adler had a flawed understanding of what a conflict of interest was. 'The fact that he was not paid had no bearing on his duty to avoid circumstances in which his personal interests were in conflict with his duty to HIH,' the report stated. The judge did not, however, make a negative finding against Adler on that issue.

Why was Rodney Adler getting such a comfortable deal out of HIH? He had no defined duties, he was effectively being simultaneously paid by FAI and HIH, and as every day went by in 1999 it was becoming apparent to HIH management that they had been sold a company that was in much worse shape than they had allowed themselves to believe.

Lyndon B. Johnson, the 36th president of the USA, was once asked why he kept the alleged transvestite and certainly paranoid J. Edgar Hoover on as the head of the Federal Bureau of Investigation. 'It's probably better to have that fellow inside the tent pissing out, than outside the tent pissing in,' he explained.

You could construct a good argument that Ray Williams took the same view of Adler, although he was an optimist. By mid–2000 Rodney Adler was passing very destabilising confidential board information to the press and agitating for Williams' job, so obviously everyone at HIH knew where the information was coming from. To revisit the Hoover analogy, Adler's shoes were getting very damp.

And why was Williams offering Adler a directorship? For a hard man, Williams had a soft spot a yard wide and it sometimes terrified his staff. 'About twenty of us got a briefing from Ray the day after the bid for FAI was announced,' remembered another HIH executive. 'He started out by telling us that the merger would make HIH number one, two or three in most insurance categories in Australia, and his briefing was all upbeat and positive.

'Then he adopted a strange sentimental monotone and started to tell us about old Mrs Bobby Adler, Larry's widow, and Rodney and how it was going to be a partnership rather than a takeover and some of us started to exchange glances.'

It was a takeover because HIH was bigger than FAI and, as Williams found out later, FAI was falling to pieces.

'A takeover is usually the perfect moment to clear out all the old management in the target company and go through the accounts to write down anything at all you think is overvalued,' said the former executive.

'And here we were listening to Ray waxing lyrical about the biggest player in the whole FAI structure.'

But if Williams was upbeat about having Adler on board, his enthusiasm was a molehill beside Adler's mountain of self-belief. Adler's letter to Williams on 2 December 1998, before he sold the second half of his holding in FAI, is a prize example: 'I am assuming four months at a cost of say $40,000 a month. Obviously if more time is required I will be more than willing to extend the arrangement,' he said.

'When are directors' meetings scheduled for next calendar year and what are the director's fees you are suggesting for me? On Thursday, after you have had time to digest these and other questions, let's try to finalise the situation for both our benefits,' he concluded with a flourish.

It was one of the last times he was to sign a letter 'Rodney S. Adler' since he was made a Member of the Order of Australia (AM) in the New Year Honours of 1999. From then on the title went everywhere with him, even on the many occasions when he got notes back signed 'Regards, Ray'.

The word 'benefit' was a surprising choice of words considering that the Corporations Act uses the same word to describe what it specifically proscribes in Section 698. And benefits they were, in spades.

There was 17.77 months of pay in lieu of notice, worth $1.18 million, plus three times his $800,000 a year FAI salary as severance pay — that's $2.4 million. The numbers were calculated by FAI's lawyers, Clayton Utz. HIH asked its lawyers Minter Ellison to check on whether it could pay Adler out in lieu of notice. Minter noted a problem with the law and suggested that FAI could terminate his contract and let him sue for damages which would then be paid. 'That was a most inappropriate suggestion for a solicitor to make to a client,' the judge's report noted.

The whole reason that most severance packages are put together is that the recipients have no new job on the horizon, whereas Rodney Adler was stepping nimbly from one cracked and melting ice-floe to a much bigger one, on a promise of $480,000 a year. And Williams authorised a $3.8 million payment to Adler anyway.

Williams said that the $40,000 a month proposal subsequently 'fell in a hole', but it jumped out again in some style. It didn't start until April of 1999, after being ratified by the board, but the proposal ended up like one of those standing orders that gets paid out of a bank account because somehow no one gets round to asking why it is being paid.

It lasted until December 2000, nineteen months or $760,000 later.

And what did HIH get for its money? That depends on whom you talk to. Ray said he was getting expertise on all those awkward long-term assets like the St Moritz Hotel and Oceanic Coal in the Hunter Valley.

Rodney was not only getting a non-executive directorship with attendant fees, and his $40,000 a month, but he was also on the investment committee at HIH. Rodney believed it was getting the benefit of his expertise but in fact the FAI acquisition gave the investment department at HIH a monumental headache.

Normally, when one asset-managing insurer takes over another asset-managing insurer the two portfolios are quietly merged and any odd-shaped investments sold off.

FAI was almost nothing but odd-shaped investments. Aside from all the old Alan Bond assets, each of which had a story a mile long to go with it, there were myriad small technology stocks and joint ventures, plus FAI's holding in Home Security International, which was to end up costing HIH some $83 million by the time HIH sold out a half share for $1.25 million on 8 December 2000 to Brad Cooper, the man who started it all.

There was also a big portfolio of shares in One.Tel, the telephone service reseller which Rodney Adler had helped to found and whose shares were on what looked like a solid climb.

Adler was no fan of the fixed-interest investments that HIH had, safe and solid and returning perhaps 8 per cent per year. 'A monkey could do that. It takes talent to create a One.Tel,' is how former HIH executive Bill Howard remembered Adler talking at that time. Others remembered Adler joking in Investment Committee meetings, muttering 'not more FFI!' That stood for Fucking Fixed Interest.

The year 1999 was the high noon of the fortunes of One.Tel Ltd, a telephone service reseller that Adler had founded in 1995 with former

Cranbrook schoolmate Jodee Rich and Rich's friend Brad Keeling. Rich had had a spectacular share market failure in the 1980s with Imagineering Ltd, a computer company, but had the same degree of self-belief as Adler and, most usefully of all, the same network of friends.

The key to the company, once it listed in November 1997, was that the friends controlled almost all of the stock and anyone who wanted 'in' had to pay up.

The company was floated at $2 a share in that month, valuing it at $208 million, even though only $1 million was actually raised on the market. Even though there were a lot of sceptics among professional investors who remembered Imagineering's collapse in 1991 and winced, the founders pressed all the right buttons by having major names among the founders.

James Packer had put in $250,000 of his own money as a foundation investor, getting 5 per cent of the stock after other founders were asked to cut back; Adler put FAI in for $950,000, or 17 per cent; Optus $1.5 million, or 28 per cent; while Rich and Keeling had just over 50 per cent. There was only about $4 million in cash in the company to start with, but the float lifted all the holders up nicely with the tide. FAI's holding was already worth more than $51 million.

In that environment it was just a question of maintaining the excitement among investors and, by a dazzling campaign of telling them only the good news and concealing the bad as much as possible, the company's young and apparently savvy promoters made it a 'must have' in the year leading up to the technology boom, which took off in late 1999.

In December 1998 FAI sold 16 million One.Tel shares to the Packer family company Consolidated Press Holdings for around $2.68 each, or $43 million altogether, a whacking return on the 'entry' price of less than one million dollars for the whole 25.4 million shareholding.

By February 1999 the Murdoch family was in too, brought in by the friendship between heirs James Packer and Lachlan Murdoch. News Ltd and PBL agreed to put up $430 million with a promise to put a further $280 million in later, in exchange for 40 per cent of the shares. This was real money, although $106 million of it went to existing One.Tel shareholders as a 'return of capital', with Rich and Keeling getting $62 million between them.

The share price was racing ahead, jumping from $9.30 to $13.55 in the two days preceding the announcement of the big cash injection in

February. The Australian stock exchange was unable to prove there had been any insider trading, but it was that sort of stock.

And FAI's holding in One.Tel, meanwhile, was being taken over by HIH. Rodney Adler had a foot in every camp. He jumped straight from FAI to HIH and was also a director of One.Tel. There was almost no overlap between insurance and phone service reselling but the conflict he had between his duty to shareholders of both companies was to loom very large once the One.Tel price rose to a level that HIH's investment department could not ignore.

By December 1998, when HIH was in the process of taking FAI over, HIH investment manager John Ballhausen was handed all this, but without an insider's road map.

He knew nothing much about One.Tel but he did know that HIH's exposure to One.Tel was absurdly out of kilter with the rest of HIH's share portfolio. Aside from any dispassionate but accurate considerations about One.Tel being a highly volatile and speculative stock, the 43 million shares that HIH acquired via FAI (post a ten-for-one share split on 13 April 1999 that multiplied FAI's remaining 4.3 million shares by ten times) were worth a startling $101 million. That was the biggest single equity asset that HIH had, ahead of conventional blue chips like bank shares, and Ballhausen had been softening up the investment committee with notes about HIH's 'investment exposure'.

On November 26 1999 the One.Tel price hit a record $2.84 (or $28.40 on a pre-split basis), making the stake worth $122 million. Ballhausen did what any normal fund manager would do in the circumstances and moved to sell the holding. The shares were in the books at $1.01 each, so any sale above about $2.03 would net HIH a dollar a share after sales expenses.

He put a few shares on the market to sell and immediately got a call from Mark Silbermann, One.Tel's finance director, who told him there was an agreement between One.Tel founders not to sell without the others' agreement. 'He asked me what I was doing and I told him,' remembers Ballhausen, older brother to the man who helped float HIH in 1992.

'He had his lawyer with him and he tried to infer there was a share issue coming in One.Tel and that I should expect a call from Merrill Lynch. That would have made me an insider, which made me very angry.'

Insiders are defined by law as people who know about a deal before it happens. They are greatly limited in buying and selling shares. A share issue puts more money into a company but dilutes its earnings per share, and is offered at a discount to the ruling share price, so it puts a double downward pressure on a company's share price. An insider selling out in advance of such an issue would be rightly seen as a profiteer.

Ballhausen said he sat tight for a couple of weeks but there was no call from Merrill. There was no share issue so Ballhausen was not an insider. Meanwhile, there was a move by One.Tel's founders to tear up the pre-emptive 'club' agreement, which would make Ballhausen's selling job much easier. He said that all the members of the club agreed to ditch the agreement except one, former FAI director Peter O'Connell. O'Connell had taken a parcel of shares in One.Tel at the start in lieu of payment for legal work but had sold them not long afterwards for a nice profit. Since then Jodee Rich had enjoyed ribbing him at every opportunity about the profit he missed out on by selling his shares, and according to Adler there may just have been a note of revenge in O'Connell's brief stalling. 'I think he'd had it with Jodee's humour and felt this was a chance to take a stand,' he told Ballhausen.

'Leave him to me,' said Rodney Adler, taking O'Connell out for a cup of coffee and some soothing words. That worked and the agreement was torn up by unanimous consent, leaving Ballhausen in the awkward position that he was about to cause great irritation to Adler, the man who had just helped him out. It was an unusual situation, unless Adler had some other plan in mind for the disposal of the shares. It was never revealed.

By 7 December the price of One.Tel shares had eased back to $2.48 but that was still a very comfortable margin. Ballhausen spoke to HIH Australia managing director Terry Cassidy and between them they decided that they would ask chief executive Ray Williams for permission to sell half the shares as soon as possible, to reduce HIH's exposure.

'We wanted to sell the lot, but decided to ask Ray for half as he was more likely to say yes,' he explained.

And what about telling Adler?

'We made the decision that we were going to keep Australia Square [the office of Adler Corporation] as far away from this one as possible,' said Ballhausen candidly. 'We knew Rodney wouldn't like it and might try something to stop it happening.'

They did not in fact need Adler's agreement and, in any company with strong adherence to corporate governance norms, he would have had to stand aside from any decision because of his conflict of interest between his directorships of HIH and One.Tel.

Ballhausen and Cassidy were just saving him the dilemma.

Unfortunately, Williams was on one of his many trips to the UK but eventually he agreed to the sale request on Friday, 10 December 1999, and agreed not to tell Adler. Williams might have been very impressed with One.Tel's performance but he also knew that a rising share price means nothing if you can't lock it in. And HIH was trying hard to restore investor confidence after reporting a loss of $39.8 million, its first ever, in the year to 30 June 1999. A booked profit of more than $10 million on the One.Tel shares was just what Williams wanted.

Ballhausen commissioned JB Were and Macquarie Bank to sell around 20 million shares on 10 December, which just happened to be the afternoon of Were's Melbourne office Christmas party.

The dealers were duly separated from their drinks and a ring-around of institutional clients shifted the shares, again at a discount.

Ballhausen let the price come down by around 15c to get 10 million shares away at $2.25 each, shifting another five million shares at $2.20 within the week. But before the second parcel went, the expected volcanic eruption from Mount Rodney hit the HIH office.

A furious note to Ballhausen from Adler, wryly headed 'Dear John' started 'Congratulations. You have helped the One.Tel price go down 15c today!' It was written in some haste on Friday, 10 December and sent on Monday, 13 December.

Office myth had it that the fax went on the HIH office noticeboard before Ballhausen had a chance to look at it, but he disagrees. 'I came in and everyone was smiling and laughing,' he said, before he found the note on his desk. The note was copied to Williams, finance director Dominic Fodera and, perhaps in case Ballhausen might be tempted to hide it, to Ballhausen's offsider, Ronni Chalmers.

It read: 'We have spoken about the process of selling a strategic parcel when the register is very tight and you have premeditatedly and secretly given the stock to various brokers which was very successfully highlighted and reported in the weekend press. Now the world knows that HIH is a seller.

'John, you may think it is really smart to act alone and your motherhood statement about "HIH's investment exposure" is correct but not relevant. However I have experience in selling strategic stakes and you clearly have none.

'HIH's half yearly result closes in a matter of weeks. Obviously the 10c to 15c additional price per share is not material to you but to the rest of the shareholders it is actually of importance. Why would you have to do something in the last couple of weeks of the calendar year? Why would you have to do something in isolation without working with the management of One.Tel? Why you would do it in the manner that has put offside the Murdochs, the Packers and the board of One.Tel is beyond my understanding.

'Whether you sell out successfully or not, the issue is this has been handled atrociously,' he thundered, before signing off with his recently acquired flourish, Rodney S. Adler, AM.

Ballhausen said afterwards that he should have sent off a smart reply but he wisely stayed silent. Why should he pick a fight when he had won?

Reading between the lines of Adler's note, he was furious that he had lost face with the Murdoch and Packer camps, because he had almost certainly been telling them that HIH was a 'locked in' shareholder. It was not, and his supposed control of the shares had vanished in a puff of dust.

Ballhausen and Cassidy's decision to sell the shares turned out to be a godsend for HIH, which was starting to unravel markedly on the liabilities side. They had sold after the peak of One.Tel but moved the balance of HIH's holding off the books at just under $2 each in February 2000. One.Tel shares were never to break up through $2 again and by April 2000 fell through $1.50.

HIH was able to announce a profit of $18.4 million for the year ended 30 June 2000, mostly thanks to a $12.4 million fillip provided by the One.Tel sale.

Most transactions involving Adler and HIH all seemed to go one way — his — but those block trades were a shining exception. By the time Adler sold five million of his own shares in November 2000 the price was down to 50c and his alliance with the Packer family was on the rocks.

Adler resigned from the One.Tel board on 12 April 2001. He sold six million more of his own shares in May 2001 for just over 20c each. Administrators were appointed to the company on 30 May 2001, ten weeks after HIH had collapsed. Rodney Adler's career as the man who could turn promises and optimism into riches had come to a final and almost universally painful halt.

CHAPTER 14

MORE DESPERATE DEALS

AS A PAIR of wide boys whose sole focus at HIH seemed to be the cash side of the business, Rodney Adler and his friend Brad Cooper carved a shocking swathe through the cosy, non-confrontational culture of HIH in 1999 and 2000.

While One.Tel was still a success story in 1999, there were times when Adler could do no wrong with Ray Williams. This was despite the fact that FAI turned out to be possibly the worst investment HIH had ever made, among a pantheon of shockers. Just in management time alone, FAI completely dominated management's thinking at a time when HIH should have been looking hard at its own problems rather than worrying about the business it had just bought. In the words of one auditor from Andersen, dead bodies kept falling out of the FAI cupboard.

For all that, Williams started demanding One.Tel-like performance from HIH's investment department.

Any value-driven fund manager will remember about the technology boom of late 1999 and early 2000 that it was a difficult time to be old-fashioned. No matter how much they believed the technology boom would turn into a bust, every day that they avoided technology stocks was another day when their funds fell behind market benchmarks. Tiddler stocks were jumping from 20c to 50c in a day and, no matter how often a manager said the stocks were going to finish worthless, sitting on the sidelines was not really an option. Other fund managers with an equally sceptical view could make a quick 'in and out' trade and finish well ahead.

And meanwhile, Brad Cooper seemed to be everywhere. Not only was he walking in and out of the HIH office as if he was one of the staff, but he seemed to be a part-owner of a lot of stocks in the FAI portfolio. There was often an unwritten 'profit sharing' arrangement that had been entered into where FAI seemed to be taking the risk and Cooper seemed to have an interest in any profit made. 'You can't sell that' became a new and irritating mantra around HIH's investment department as staffers discovered in many cases that FAI had purchased some line of stock but that Cooper was to have a 40 per cent interest in the upside.

More of that later.

Rodney Adler joined the board of HIH on 16 April 1999 and it was not a happy encounter. HIH's board was made up mainly of lawyers and accountants — a common enough phenomenon in Australia — but although Adler is an accountant, he knew he had a much better understanding of insurance than they did. He also saw himself as an entrepreneur.

Until Rodney Adler appeared on the HIH board, Ray Williams was the only person there who fitted that description, so they should have formed a natural bond.

To Adler, the non-executive directors at HIH were dozy drones who had no practical understanding of how to run an insurance company, and as for the investment side, that was somewhere he could really make a difference.

To them, he was a noisy upstart who had not allowed HIH to do due diligence on FAI and who now spent his time tormenting them for paying too much for it. They were probably both right, but having two opposing camps in an uninformed board is not a situation conducive to running a successful company.

The real scandal was how little the HIH directors had been told, or had chosen to ask, about the big-picture decisions taken at HIH in their name. Not only were they almost complete bystanders at Ray Williams' quixotic charge at the FAI windmill, but they had almost no idea about the real nature of HIH's reserves. This was because they were never shown actuary David Slee's reports and they never asked for them.

Aside from chairman Geoff Cohen, who will forever carry the tag 'totally ineffective' cast upon him by Wayne Martin in January 2003, the other non-executive directors were people who at first glance seemed independent-minded corporate veterans, but they did not bring much actuarial understanding to the table. There were three lawyers: Bob Stitt, QC, a veteran 'blood and bone' specialist who had had a long and prosperous relationship with CE Heath in workers' compensation cases; Neville Head, a former senior partner at Clayton Utz who did in fact resign in August 1999 over unhappiness at the board's lack of input; and Charles Abbott, a former partner at Blake Dawson Waldron whom Hawthorn Football Club tragics remember as a centreman in the club's first ever premiership-winning side in 1961.

Abbott had resigned as a partner of Blakes in 1990 after some awkwardness relating to the collapsed Trustee Executor Agency, although he was never charged. He failed to disclose to the HIH board that he had thereafter made an arrangement with Blakes which would pay him 10 per cent of any legal work he could push their way. Other than them, everyone else was either an HIH executive (Williams, Sturesteps, Cassidy and Fodera), or Rodney Adler.

Former HIH auditor Justin Gardener joined the board on 2 December 1998, within two weeks of his retirement from Arthur Andersen, so he cannot be described as independent. The most experienced insurance hand outside of Adler was Randolph Wein, who headed HIH's Asian operations at that time, out of Hong Kong. He had spent twenty years in the insurance industry, the last eight of them at Winterthur, but he was not based in Australia. The most knowledgeable director of all was Michael Payne in London, but by that time he had had his crisis and had been 'kicked upstairs' to chair the UK operation on 9 July 1998.

When the HIH Royal Commission resumed on 14 January 2003 and Wayne Martin, QC, summed up his colleagues' 'case for the prosecution', he did not mince his words. Apart from noting the board's failure to get to grips with reserving, he said the board had 'no apparent awareness of the gross self-indulgence of senior executives which was occurring under their noses or even of the sordid saga pertaining to Home Security International and Mr [Brad] Cooper.'

The full extent of the FAI disaster had not yet been revealed to the HIH directors but they got a few clues in the 30 June 1999 result when the company recorded its first ever loss.

It reported a net loss of $21.2 million for the eighteen-month period from 1 January 1998 to 30 June 1999, an odd-looking number for an odd-looking period. For reasons that were never properly explained, HIH moved its financial year from a December to a June year-end. While older companies tend to use December and newer style companies use June, it is a fact that moving the date could confuse more gullible investors. The only justifiable reason was to bring HIH's accounts into line with FAI's, even though HIH was much bigger.

Not only did HIH have to 'fess up to a real live loss, thanks to a $50.1 million writedown on the sale of FAI's Oceanic Coal operation in the Hunter Valley, but HIH had to mark around $160 million to its goodwill account to cover 'prior year deterioration' in FAI's books. And that was only the beginnning. It was becoming apparent that asset values had been consistently overstated while liabilities had gone precisely the other way.

But Rodney Adler, the man who had brought all those overvalued assets and understated liabilities into HIH, appeared entirely unfazed by the developing cash disaster, seeing the problem as HIH's rather than his own. Rodney rode into HIH boots and all.

He wrote letters. Dozens of them, verbose, opinionated, often careless with apostrophes and invariably dotted with the vertical pronoun. He wrote them to Ray Williams, mostly, and copied them to other members of the board.

On 6 September 1999, Adler wrote the following letter to Ray Williams:

'Dear Mr Williams,' he typed, leaving out his trademark handwritten slash he liked to use to replace the formal title with 'Ray', 'As a non-executive director, a consultant to HIH, a major shareholder, a past chief executive for ten years of the company that you acquired, I would like to inform you about my fears and concerns regarding HIH ... even though you had to increase the reserves quite substantially for the insurance business conducted by FAI, as a pure takeover due to the success of the sale of several non-insurance assets, One.Tel in particular, the takeover must be considered a success from HIH's perspective. Saying that, that is the only successful statement I can currently make,' he wrote.

'Ray, HIH is in turmoil. It is not a question of profitability, it is a question of survival. Leaving aside the raw fundamentals which are net assets of just shy of 70c [the HIH share price at that time was diving unerringly towards $1.50 for the first time] therefore HIH is already trading at two and a half times book value, a solvency margin that does not allow for further growth and an investment strategy which is not only so conservative that it does not maximise the opportunities that currently exist in the market. The company has no vision nor any real structure that will successfully lend itself to the 21st century.'

His analysis was flawed in terms of investment strategy, for instance, never mind the fact that his sentences were far too long. But at the time he was saying things that the shareholders were definitely not hearing. 'You remember the $2 billion of reserves that HIH said they had? Well, it's just not there,' said Adler to one insurance contact shortly after joining the board.

He achieved a lot of impact by leaking information to Mark Westfield at *The Australian* from mid-2000, with shareholders at least. Regulator APRA and the board of HIH failed to act on them, however, simply because they distrusted Adler.

The claims in the articles were the same as the complaints that Adler had been making to Williams and copying to his fellow directors. In case there was any further uncertainty about where the material was coming from, there were also clear suggestions in the press that Ray Williams should retire and 'the name this columnist is hearing is Rodney Adler's' to succeed him. We now know where that suggestion was coming from: Adler.

The HIH board, meanwhile, merely closed ranks and avoided discussing contentious issues with Adler. And Ray Williams subconsciously switched Adler from the tray marked 'Allies' to the bin marked 'Enemies'.

They were only being human.

Adler's blast to Williams, copied to the other HIH directors, about how HIH had made a 'complete failure' of taking over FAI must have rankled. After saying he believed that HIH took over FAI for its intellectual capital, he noted that HIH had lost 'just about every senior employee of FAI that could have helped build the combined group'.

What he did not say, or chose not to notice, was that there was a huge cultural clash between the two groups of executives. There always is in any takeover and it is standard practice for the executives in the smaller company to make for the exit first. While Rodney saw his executive cadre as vigorous, inventive and entrepreneurial, the HIH executives regarded the newcomers as overbearing, slapdash and infinitely more interested in the investment side than the insurance side.

The FAI executives were always going to leave, given the fact that their company was hugely under-reserved and that almost every single inquiry that HIH management made of them was going to result in a robust exchange of views. But instead of starting with a clean sheet, Ray Williams and Dominic Fodera did two things that were to end up making things worse rather than better.

First, they decided to book any lack of value in the FAI acquisition as a positive addition to HIH's goodwill account in the balance sheet, rather than 'biting the bullet' and writing down the profit and loss account. It was legal, but created a monster in terms of intangible assets. As they found out more about the woes in FAI they gradually added to the goodwill account until by 2000 they were carrying over $400 million on the *asset* side of the balance sheet from that $300 million acquisition. In other words, they had bought a company that they valued at minus $100 million but were still carrying it as a $400 million asset.

Justice Neville Owen said his knowledge of accounting was still based on 'credits on the door side, debits on the window side', but he understood clearly what had happened. He suggested to Ray Williams on 15 August 2002 that goodwill was 'like a jewellery box that you put on the table and put things into and take things out of when you want to adorn financial statements'.

Williams merely protested that the goodwill adjustments all related to the acquisition of FAI, even though they took at least a year to be booked. 'If you look at FAI, as problems emerged ... with the under-reserving and hiding of information, those items were regarded as being pre-acquisition amounts and were booked to goodwill,' he told the judge.

Wayne Martin, QC, counsel assisting, then asked Williams on what basis HIH was able to assume that HIH would be able to earn back the $275 million that it had just added to the goodwill account. A company can only carry goodwill in its balance sheet if it is very confident of earning that money back in the future as a result of the deal.

Williams got rid of that ball with commendable speed. 'Certainly our financial people would have gone into that in detail, led by Dominic Fodera and, of course, naturally discussed and cleared and signed off by Arthur Andersen.'

The second disastrous move was to take out a reinsurance contract in June 1999 with Hannover Re to fix up the HIH balance sheet, in exactly the same way that FAI had done.

Two deals that HIH did with Hannover Re, effectively executed by Dominic Fodera in August 1999, allowed HIH to lift its operating profit from $10 million to $102 million in the year to June 1999. Not only that, but they allowed it to turn a looming loss of $45 million for the following year (to 30 June 2000) into a profit of $61.9 million.

The background to the deals was eerily similar to FAI's adventures with General Cologne Re and National Indemnity. Once again, Hannover Re was not actually taking much of a risk at all.

Richard White, SC, the counsel assisting with a better grasp of detail at HIH than anyone else alive, said that Hannover ended up taking a fee of $3.3 million plus annual premiums over seven years to arrange a deal whereby HIH could claim $400 million in immediate reinsurance 'recoveries'.

The deal looked on the face of it as if it would lose Hannover around $50 million in its first year, something that excited the surprise of Andersen auditor Jonathan Pye, but he appears to have been fobbed off with a story about how for every bad piece of business, reinsurers tended to hope they would get a good one.

That is a telescoped version of what happened. For reasons that by now are starting to look familiar, Hannover wasn't actually taking a risk and was never going to lose $50 million at any time, let alone the first year.

What Pye never got to see was an agreement by HIH to set up a letter of credit arrangement (LOC) whereby HIH would set up and run a $200 million fund out of which claims could be made. The clincher for Hannover was that the fund was supposed to return 8 per cent a year compound for seven years until it hit $450 million, and if it didn't, HIH would make up the difference. The LOC was signed by Ray Williams and Dominic Fodera.

In other words, HIH was free to make a claim on the reinsurance policy but if it did, it would have to make it up in the fund. Hannover's risk was so small as to make it laughable to suggest it was real 'reinsurance'.

It was another disguised loan, and like FAI's reinsurance with National Indemnity in 1998 it was retrospective. HIH signed the papers in August 1999 to cover the year to June 1999, since it only had to announce its results thereafter.

And it went right to the top of HIH. Unlike Daniel Wilkie and Tim Mainprize at FAI, who never got their boss Rodney Adler's signature on anything of consequence, Dominic Fodera had a boss who was not afraid to lend a hand.

Richard White, SC, said that Ray Williams asked Hannover Re to eliminate from the reinsurance documents any cross-references between the reinsurance deal and the letter of credit arrangement.

Henning Ludolphs, one of the two Hannover Re executives to make the trip to Australia to talk to the Royal Commission, admitted that HIH's auditors (including Pye) were not shown a side letter sent on 19 August 1999 by Hannover Re to Dominic Fodera stating that the insurance cover would not be activated in the way in which the policy documents suggested. Under the deal, HIH agreed it would make no claim on the fund until 1 October 2009. HIH's contributions were to start out with a deposit of $200 million to get the fund going, followed by further annual deposits of $11 million each. HIH guaranteed the shortfall for exactly the same period, which was eleven years.

In other words, Hannover Re was protected in two ways. First, HIH had to make good any claims it made, and second, there wouldn't be any claims until so far into the future that it would scarcely matter.

Jeff Simpson, the HIH executive who left in August 1999 because he was not happy with the Hannover deals, kicked a rip in a carefully painted canvas on 14 March 2002 when he told the commission: 'I think the objective was to get them [the contracts] past the auditors and, if they approved it, as reinsurance.'

It is worth noting that HIH used a subsidiary called Underwriting and Agency Services (UAS) as the vehicle for one of the more controversial Hannover transactions and that Henning Ludolphs wrote an e-mail to a colleague in German on 17 August 1999 to explain that 'Dominic' wanted to use UAS 'due to there being fewer board members' involved.

Dominic Fodera's explanation on 23 August 2002 was that UAS was used because it was scheduled to have a meeting on 5 August 1999, whereas the main board of HIH was not scheduled to meet until 25 August and time was pressing. Richard White, who is not quite as cynical as some of his colleagues, still found it in himself to point out that when HIH took over FAI in 1998 an HIH board meeting had been arranged at half a day's notice.

Dominic Fodera did admit it was an 'oversight' that the HIH directors were not told about the $450 million Hannover transaction. Nor, he admitted, did he remember telling the auditors about it. 'It wasn't my responsibility to give them all the information, that's why we have a financial services division,' he said in evidence on 23 August.

Ray Gosling, HIH's reinsurance manager, admitted in evidence that the Hannover deal should have been booked by HIH as a liability rather than an asset. Certainly no one at HIH remembered to tell regulator APRA about it. Like school children confronted with a broken classroom window, no one ever did end up owning up to the deed. Gosling said that his recollection was that Dominic Fodera was going to tell APRA about it. Gosling spoke to Fodera after HIH collapsed and said that Fodera told him 'something has fallen through the crack in the floorboards'. About $450 million, if you wanted to be cynical.

Fodera's evidence was that 'I only found out through the Royal Commission that it appeared that it hadn't been approved by APRA.'

It is interesting that just as General Cologne Re named its financial reinsurance division 'Alternative Solutions', Hannover went the same way by calling its division 'Advanced Solutions'.

What makes all the Hannover Re transactions look so ridiculous and inexcusable on the part of HIH is that they were in many ways a carbon copy of FAI's reinsurance deals the year before. Which makes it all the more odd that when Ray Williams came to give evidence, he said that when HIH bought FAI, the HIH management knew nothing about the FAI reinsurance contracts. He said he had relied on the Andersen sign-off of the FAI 30 June 1998 accounts and the PricewaterhouseCoopers work on FAI's CPID reserves, although both turned out to be fatally flawed.

Williams said he also relied on what he believed was a 'nod and a wink' from FAI's English auditor, Alan Davies, who also happened to be HIH's auditor at that time, that there were no nasty surprises in the FAI accounts. That might have been a logical thing to do if it had worked, but Davies was what even his colleagues called an 'old-fashioned auditor' with a ferocious sense of client confidentiality.

Williams thought that Dominic Fodera had got a quiet reassurance from Davies before HIH made the bid but Fodera never got anything more than a simple statement from Davies that the FAI accounts were not qualified, something he could have found out from public documents. Indeed Davies was so traditional in his guardianship of FAI's secrets that even after HIH had obtained control of FAI, he still did not reveal anything about FAI that was not publicly available. Given what we now know about the mess FAI was in, Davies can be forgiven his outburst of professional discretion.

Davies, meanwhile, blew the doors off Ray Williams' 'we trusted our advisers' defence by telling the Royal Commission in October 2002 that Williams and Fodera had 'known all about' the FAI reinsurance contracts before Williams made the bid. That would help explain the fact that in November 1998 Williams effectively banned FAI's chief operating officer, Daniel Wilkie, from finding a reinsurer who would manage the whole run-off of FAIs' troublesome CPID 'minefield' portfolio. The judge concluded that although Williams and Fodera thought they knew all about the contracts, in fact they did not.

If the cynics thought Williams was desperate in bidding for FAI and his confidants saw him behave as though he had shrugged off a burden, the insurance industry was somewhere in between. 'Ray desperately wanted access to FAI's cash flow,' said one reinsurer who was offered FAI's long-tail business and declined it. Any reinsurer who offered to tidy up the CPID mess was going to keep a firm grip on as much of FAI's revenue as it possibly could.

As Rodney Adler has never tired of telling anyone since the collapse of HIH, FAI had a good business. It had a major brand name in Australia, at least among retail policyholders, and it was a good fit with the long-tail style of insurance that HIH specialised in: public liability, professional indemnity and workers' compensation.

Williams was always a 'bigger is better' man. Throw in the nice element of revenge he got in taking over a company that had tried to take his over twice in the early 1990s, and the elimination of a competitor, and you can see some rational motivation.

There were supposed to be around $30 million a year of synergy benefits but that never happened.

But it takes two sides to do a wonky deal. One of the deals that most typifies HIH's reckless and often desperate behaviour in 1998 was the very poorly explained issue of $176 million worth of convertible preference shares that HIH made in early 1999 to help pay for the acquisition of FAI.

The catch was that the French bank Société Générale was not actually raising $176 million at all, as it appeared, but it was actually raising $141 million and HIH was putting up $35 million of its own money as a deposit. There was a matching pair of $35 million investments, apparently devised by HIH finance director Dominic Fodera, in which HIH put up $35 million and Société Générale then reinvested it in HIH. A common financial transaction, it was called a 'total return swap'. And like a lot of swaps, it offered joy to both sides and confusion to outsiders.

The episode was one of the few to cause discomfort at the Royal Commission for Colin Richardson, who was heavily involved in the transaction. (He worked at that time for Société Générale Hambros although in 2000 he moved to Deutsche Bank, where he played a crucial role in arranging the Allianz deal that removed HIH's main business and associated cash flow at a time when it desperately needed the latter.)

It became clear that the French bank had understandably decided that it needed some security in the deal, but the $35 million 'pound of flesh' that it extracted from HIH was never explained to investors. The prospectus put out by Société Générale made no reference to the fact that the French bank only looked as though it was taking $35 million of risk, when it was taking no risk at all. The supposed 'anchor tenant' in this financial development was not actually a tenant at all, but like anchor tenants in big property developments it brought a lot of investors along all the same.

Wayne Martin, QC, ever the terrier, went for Richardson over that on 5 August. 'Would you not agree that the reader might draw considerable comfort from the proposition that a prudent organisation like Société Générale has committed to contributing $35 million of its own funds to the issue?' he asked.

'They might draw that conclusion,' replied Richardson without emphasis.

What the total return swap did for HIH was two things. First, it allowed HIH to get Société Générale in on the deal in the first place. And second, it allowed HIH to claim $35 million in assets on its balance sheet that it should not have claimed.

Leigh Brown, the Minter Ellison legal partner who was to have a painful experience in 2000 over HIH's disastrous Pacific Eagle Equities foray, was also involved in the transaction. On 2 October he told Richard White, SC, counsel assisting the commission, that although the presence of Société Générale as an investor would attract others, 'I do not recall having that thought at the time.'

The judge's report stated that although Brown had said there should have been expert witnesses summoned to discuss whether the swap needed to have been disclosed, he (the judge) believed it was a straightforward issue. 'Brown should have given consideration to the board's need to be fully informed about the impact of the swap on HIH's disclosure obligations in the prospectus,' he wrote.

The judge recommended no less than six separate sets of charges against Dominic Fodera over the Hannover Re contract, five of them potentially criminal. All were made on the basis that the deal was not genuine reinsurance but was accounted for as such, and that the board of HIH and its auditors were deceived. He made two recommendations against Williams on a similar basis, one relating to sending a report by Fodera to the HIH board which contained misleading information. The judge found that Williams 'failed to take reasonable steps to ensure that the information given to the board was not false'.

Both Fodera and Williams got a possible criminal referral over the media release that HIH put out on 25 August 1999 after lining up the Hannover transaction. In it Williams started by talking about strengthening FAI's reserve arrangements — something he was going to spend a lot of time doing — and then he moved on to talk about Hannover. 'Going forward, we have also taken decisive action, through the purchase of whole of account insurance protection, in order to protect our business from claims development uncertainties,' he wrote.

The judge noted that the media release did not disclose that the reinsurance protection would be fully funded by HIH.

He stopped short of making any negative findings against the Hannover executives but he was damning of the fact that they made minimal attempts to have the deal accounted for properly by HIH — which it was not.

'Although I have not found that Hannover's representatives documented the transaction to assist HIH in misleading its auditors, nonetheless I am of the view that reinsurers in Hannover's position should have been scrupulous in ensuring that contractual documents purporting to record the reinsurance transaction did so accurately and completely,' he said. 'That was not done.'

HISTORY DOES NASTY things not only to memories but also to investments. When HIH collapsed in March 2001 Société Générale was able to keep the $35 million that HIH had put up in the deal, to make up for what had been $35 million worth of convertible notes. The other institutions and individual investors who held the notes did not have that luxury: they merely lost all their money.

There were two other elements of the share issue which reflect badly on Colin Richardson and Société Générale. One is that Société Générale got a fee of more than $3 million for arranging the deal even though it was taking no risk at all. Historically speaking, that is HIH's bad planning as much as Société Générale's smart planning, and it is not illegal. But for its work, Société Générale should have got a fee closer to $1 million, or less.

The other element is more ominous: the issue was structured to create that most dangerous of share market beasts, the exploding convertible. Exploding convertible shares are so named because they are designed to be converted in the future into ordinary shares on a dollar-value basis, in this case $5 worth of HIH ordinary shares, rather than the more conventional 'fixed proportion' system. Usually, convertible shares carry the carrot of being converted on a 'one for one' basis at the far end of their lives. If the ordinary shares have gone up in price, the conversion is attractive but it should not greatly dilute the number of shares on issue. What happened in this case was that Société Générale created a sure-fire way of diluting the company's capital if the share price fell sharply — which it did. The only reason that did not happen was that the 35 million convertibles were not in existence for long enough to reach the first conversion date in June 2001. There were only two limits imposed on the 'explosion', and they were both in the prospectus, so someone must have at least seen it coming. One was that 25 cents was the minimum value that would be imputed to HIH shares, which is about the price they were trading at when they were finally suspended in February 2001 at management's request. The other was that no more than 620 million new ordinary shares were to be issued by the company to converting shareholders. Considering that there were only 472 million ordinary HIH shares on issue in June 2000, that would have left the convertible shareholders acquiring 56 per cent of the company.

CHAPTER 15

THAT MAN BRAD

OF ALL THE people who might figure in a book about an insurance company, Bradley David Cooper is almost certainly the least likely. Not only was this former motivational speaker and burglar alarm salesman the biggest risk taker in a risk-averse business, but he knew least about insurance and, having left school at thirteen, had the least formal education of anybody involved in the whole sorry tale.

Cooper got into Ray Williams' life two years before HIH collapsed and would not let go, but he was only doing what he had already done with Adler and FAI. By the time HIH collapsed Cooper had not only extracted some $14 million from HIH in settlement of myriad complex non-core deals, but he had also taken up immense amounts of FAI's and then HIH management's time that would have been better spent running insurance companies.

Wayne Martin, counsel assisting the Royal Commission, calculated that at the time of HIH's takeover of FAI in late 1998, FAI had lent Cooper's company, Home Security International, $50 million and HIH was to lend a further $21 million. His colleague Robert Beech-Jones worked out that HIH had lost about $36 million on the share market value of HSI, which peaked just before HIH took over FAI, and poured a further $35 million into HSI until throwing in the towel in December 2000 and allowing Cooper to buy control of HSI back from HIH for a modest $1.25 million.

Cooper enters the story via his burglar alarm business, which he persuaded Rodney Adler to help finance in 1990 after he started it in Newcastle in 1988.

Adler had always seen himself as something of a 'business angel' for small players with big ideas, and Cooper was certainly one of those. Adler advertised on behalf of FAI in 1990 looking for projects in which to invest venture capital. Cooper had been broke at least once before but at thirty-one had a reservoir of self-belief that almost rivalled Adler's.

A fascinating interview recorded between the two men as part of 'Brad Cooper's Mentor Club' in late 1999 demonstrates how Adler was always receiving business proposals but dismissed around nine out of ten of them, often for their sheer illiteracy. 'My idea, your money,' Adler scoffed about them, adding 'that's not a joint venture, that's charity.' A strange view for a man who had actually advertised for proposals, and for all his front, he gave in to Cooper.

Folklore says that Cooper could not get an audience with Adler so arranged to book a seat beside Adler on a flight from Sydney to Melbourne to get an hour of his time, but Cooper says it was simpler than that. He said he wrote out a business plan and waited outside Adler's office in Sydney's St Leonards at around 5.30 a.m. for several mornings until the arriving mogul took pity on him. 'Good morning, Mr Adler, I'd like you to have a look at this,' he remembers saying, and passed half a dozen pages through the car window. To judge by some of Cooper's later messages that ended up in full view of the Royal Commission, most notably one from August 2000 in which he proposed a 'Round Rodney' financial transaction to avoid what he called 'Amagedon', he is a much better public speaker than writer. But Adler backed him initially with $600,000 from FAI to create FAI Home Security, taking that up in short order to something like $4 million.

They were a Tweedledum and Tweedledee pair with enough common traits to make them dangerous, and enough differences to make it near-certain that their relationship would blow up eventually.

Adler supported what became Home Security International through its early years as a venture capitalist, both via FAI and personally. Indeed the two crossed over. Paul McGeough of the *Sydney Morning Herald* wrote that after the first investment funds ran out in about 1990, Cooper asked Adler for more help from FAI but was turned down. Cooper was walking out of the door when Adler said, 'FAI can't help you, but I can.'

McGeough relates that when Cooper got back to his office nearby he found a blank cheque signed by Adler, which Cooper filled out for $113,000.

HSI did not make the alarms: that was done by a company called Ness Security in Sydney's Seven Hills run by technician Nazareno 'Naz' Circosta. Ness stood for New Electronic Security Systems, and in about 1990 Circosta had devised a residential alarm system that did not need a control panel. Cooper, who saw the product at an exhibition in Queensland, was the super-salesman who predicted explosive growth for alarm sales, and after a few false starts he got it.

Initially, the costs chewed up most of the revenue but Cooper really got the business moving by setting up a network of independent distributors who bought the alarms wholesale and then retailed them to householders. His skills as a public speaker, where he specialises in getting ordinary people motivated to do extraordinary things, helped greatly. (In one speech on seizing opportunities he admitted that he kissed his alarm clock every day after it woke him, a habit he has almost certainly shaken off but it is an image that will linger in the public's imagination.)

None of this made much difference to FAI in the early years but the ownership of Ness became a key issue in 1995 after Circosta approached Cooper for money. Circosta, who still makes the alarms in Sydney after a decade of upheavals, was having trouble financing a management buyout after the major shareholder, the UK-based BTR plc group, declared Ness to be 'non-core'.

Since FAI Home Security was the biggest customer, it made sense. There are several levels of financing in a management buyout, and Catalyst — a noted Sydney venture capital group — were all ready to take a hefty 'mezzanine' stake despite having reservations about Cooper. But instead, Cooper produced a group of investors who were either anonymous or had ties to Rodney Adler, and the deal was done that way.

Dorigad, an investment company run by James Packer and his friend Theo Onisforou, picked up 19.2 per cent and later sold out for a modest profit to Paul Brown, Adler's old schoolmate. Circosta kept 25 per cent and Brown took 51.8 per cent. The whole deal was small beer, being worth around $2 million, but the profits that flowed from it were immense.

Ness subsequently became a major financial football being kicked around, most particularly between Brown, FAI and HIH, at prices which made Brown very rich and helped Cooper significantly at times of major financial stress. FAI started out as the benevolent uncle paying the bills but after HIH took it over in late 1998, HIH ended up writing the cheques and ended up blowing over $80 million on this sometimes profitable but always entirely irrelevant business. All this at a time when HIH management should have been working full-time on boosting reserves and keeping their main business afloat.

Although HSI's sales took off in the early 1990s, selling as many as 5000 systems a month or 60,000 a year by 1996, it was not all plain sailing. In 1995 the company had a run-in with the assistant commissioner for police in New Zealand, Ian Holyoake, over its high-pressure sales tactics, and it sued the Consumers Institute of NZ the following year for $NZ1.8 million. In Australia, meanwhile, there was an unflattering story by Channel Nine's 'A Current Affair' which alleged among other things that burglars had been stealing the alarms. A class action by disgruntled buyers followed, which took a payment of more than $1 million to settle. HIH paid for that too.

The basic kit consisted of a smoke detector, a loud alarm, a fire blanket and an extinguisher, retailed at around $2200 and was valued, according to some who had seen it, at around $500 wholesale. Prime prospects were single mothers in Sydney's western suburbs who were offered hire purchase terms at credit card rates of interest, i.e. more than 20 per cent. That was offered by FAI Finance Corporation, which FAI had founded for that purpose, in a startling rerun of Larry Adler's first car yard in Sydney's Parramatta Road. Anyone can sell a widget but the profit's in the finance.

The cynics, who were legion, suggested that sales were helped along by mysterious 'softening up' visits by unidentified men banging dustbin lids around the streets of an area on the day before the salesmen were due to make their first pitch.

None of this sounds like the preamble to a successful float and listing in the United States, but that is exactly what happened for Home Security International in 1997, with spectacular benefits both for FAI and Cooper.

The stock was issued on the American Stock Exchange at $US6.50 but came on at $US10.50, capitalising the company at $US55 million. The issue raised $US27.5 million for the vendors, who were selling down 53 per cent. Cooper had sold his last shares to FAI before 1997 for some $8.1 million so was no longer a holder. FAI made $US23.5 million from the float, allowing it to book a $39 million investment gain in the year to

30 June 1997. That alone was enough to allow FAI to declare a small profit for that year, as opposed to the insurance underwriting losses it suffered all the way through the 1990s, while still leaving it with a 47 per cent stake in HSI. FAI had also taken a $US5.8 million dividend out of HSI, causing Adler to say in 1998 that HSI had been a 'fabulous investment' for FAI. He said that FAI's investment in HSI and FAI Finance Corporation had climbed from $600,000 to $60 million, 'more than half of which has been taken out in cash profits'.

This was how Rodney Adler liked things to be. Cooper, meanwhile, bought back a 5 per cent stake for $US2.5 million. He only stumped up $US125,000 and had to borrow the balance.

It was an inspired result for FAI considering that the HSI prospectus had had to concede that it 'has been the subject of isolated news articles accusing its sales agents of high pressure sales practices focusing on customers' fears ... and for charging above-market rates to consumers who cannot afford the product'.

That did nothing to stop Cooper, the man who began it all, from paying himself at the rate of $US700,000 a year plus 10 per cent of annual net profit.

Cooper had done FAI a favour in January 1998 when HSI paid FAI $US7.4 million to buy half of FAI Finance from FAI, using $4.4 million of finance supplied by FAI. That deal was included in FAI's 31 December 1997 accounts to get the company's result to a pre-tax profit of $3.17 million despite the company having lost almost exactly $60 million in the six months, half on investments and half on insurance. Because not only did FAI book most of the $US7.4 million as profit but the insurer was then able to revalue the other half of FAI Finance that it still held in its books, at a much higher level.

In other words, FAI and HSI were doing a deal at less than arm's length which allowed FAI to book a 'double whammy' on the upside at a time when it needed all the help it could get.

The underlying uncertainty over Cooper, HSI and Ness surfaced in FAI in mid–1998, when Cooper tried to persuade the FAI board to buy out the 75 per cent of Ness that the self-effacing Monaco resident Paul Brown now owned, for $20 million. Given that Brown had laid out an estimated $780,000 for the stake, his net profit for a three-year investment he had never seen was around $19 million. Three members of the board objected: chairman John Landerer, Geoff Hill and Ted Harris.

Peter O'Connell, who supported the deal, noted drily that any mention of Cooper to the FAI board 'did stimulate a fairly instant reaction'.

He said that Landerer was 'not a big fan' and that Ted Harris, elder statesman of the board, 'had a very significant prejudice in regard to the management style and persona of Mr Brad Cooper'. Harris had said briskly of another Cooper deal that 'frankly, all this is starting to insult my intelligence'.

One of the directors later confided that 'the trouble with Rodney is that if he ever gets the chance to choose between doing business with honest businessmen and with spivs, he will choose the spiv every time'.

Landerer sent a cynical fax to Brown congratulating him on the profit (around $19 million) he had made on Ness but the deal went ahead, as previously described.

By the middle of 1998 FAI's stake of 2.15 million shares in HSI was a big part of FAI's liquid assets. Most of FAI's holdings were in illiquid real estate assets the company had acquired from Alan Bond and which had signally failed to add any value to FAI in ten years. The HSI stake, meanwhile, was actually listed on a share market so its price moved up and down. And Rodney Adler knew several useful people in the US.

Among a colourful cast of characters in this story, Jeffrey Pokross still stands out. A New York Jewish banker with cast-iron links to the Mafia, he is the only character in the farce of whom no photograph can be found. He is under FBI protection in a witness protection program.

Pokross is a household name in New York over a case known colloquially as 'The Mob on Wall Street', in which he wore a wire on behalf of the FBI. New York's *Village Voice* stated he ran his business under the tutelage of the head of the Bonanno crime family, Bobby 'Little Robert' Lino. His evidence allowed detectives to arrest more than ninety people in 2000, most of whom have since been convicted. The cases relate to a scheme to divert union superannuation funds into stocks that criminal brokers were promoting.

The pension funds belonged to Police and Fire Brigade unions, for instance, whose trustee committees included serving officers. The scam exploited those officers by appealing to their personal greed in a way which, on paper at least, seemed good for all insiders in the deal. The joy of the scheme was that the trustees could 'front run' big orders in stocks being peddled by DMN Capital, which had close links to the Bonanno crime family. To 'front run' means buying a stock ahead of a big order that is bound to push the stock price up.

The pension funds did indeed buy the stocks, putting the trustees well ahead, and careful ramping by the brokers at DMN would push the price further ahead thereafter. For a while at least both the funds and the manipulators enjoyed significantly enhanced returns until the normal business laws of gravity intervened and pulled the high flyers back to earth. 'Pump and Dump' is the name used in the US to describe such schemes, since they depend on finding a hapless buyer at the far end before gravity kicks in. Inevitably, there were a few upsets and one broker involved, Frank Persico, is understood to have fired a gun into a computer at one point.

Rodney Adler was referred to Pokross in 1997 by Jim Bettner, who worked for Canadian stockbroker Yorkton Securities in Vancouver. Bettner was also described in evidence as corrupt but Yorkton is a serious Toronto-based stockbroking operation with an international reputation.

Where the lights should have been flashing for Rodney Adler about Bettner, and Adler has no excuse, is that the Vancouver Stock Exchange (now carefully renamed the Pacific Stock Exchange) was in the 1980s and 1990s the playground of some seriously unscrupulous stock promoters.

On 9 June 2002 Channel Nine's Sydney-based 'Sunday' program ran a major segment on Pokross, thanks to some vigorous investigation by Walkley award-winning reporter Ross Coulthart. The Australian defamation law regime is often a hard one for reporters and it is not usually easy to describe a person as having confirmed links to the Mafia, but in Pokross's case, Coulthart could and did.

He had obtained a transcript of Pokross's evidence to the New York court which included this memorable exchange: 'Mr Pokross, have you ever had a job that did not involve lying or cheating or stealing? Have you ever had such a job?'

'Not since college,' he replied. Pokross appears to have done a deal with the FBI in 1996, about a year before Rodney Adler swam into his ken.

Pokross had described himself as 'the mobbed-up corrupt investment banker' so had clearly come to terms with what he was really about. Manhattan District Attorney Mary Jo White said that from 1998 until June 2000, when the Bonanno family operated DMN Capital, it was 'the investment bank to the crooked and corrupt' and 'fraud central' for racketeering.

Rodney Adler's reaction to the television report was less than amused, and he released a statement just after the program went out which stated: 'Mr Adler from time to time used the services of Mr Jeffrey Pokross as a broker specialising in small listed companies in the United States. During his dealings, Mr Adler had no knowledge of Mr Pokross' criminal links or behaviour.'

After a complaint that the program had not contacted him for comment, he went on to say that 'Mr Adler specifically states all his dealings with Mr Pokross were in the normal course of business and did not involve any illegal conduct.'

For all that, there is a hefty congruence between what Rodney Adler appears to have wanted and what Pokross specialised in: pushing small stocks.

It is an odd contrast that in late 1997 Adler had begun a major association with Goldman Sachs, one of the best credentialled investment banks in the world, with a view to doing much grander things. Top of the list was converting FAI Insurances from a publicly listed company to private ownership, with the Adler family keeping control. Clearly the people at Goldman knew nothing of the Pokross connection since if they had, they would have dropped Adler and FAI like a hot rock.

Rodney Adler has almost certainly achieved the distinction of being the only person on earth whose two favourite brokers in New York were DMN Capital and Goldman Sachs.

What did Pokross do for Adler? There are two parts to that answer, one being what he and Adler approximately say he did and the other being what he may well have done. In the first category is Home Security International (HSI).

Adler told the Royal Commission that he gave Pokross a mandate to 'get behind' and support the price of shares in HSI. That description covers a multitude of activities, which are as legal as you want them to be. At its simplest, the process means being the broker of choice for anyone who wants research on the stock, and who might wish to buy a biggish line of shares. Over the years that has been standard operating practice for small companies in Australia and the US. That broker will tend to know who owns the stock and is more likely to be able to bring buyer and seller together without causing any ructions up or down in the stock price.

Less ethical and less legal is the practice of propping the share price or 'window dressing' it to make sure it looks stronger than it is. In modern computerised share markets that might mean checking the screens towards the close of trading to see if the price can be nudged up at the close to be square with, or ahead of, the day before. We do know that Pokross kept a very close eye on the share price.

Norman O'Bryan, counsel assisting the commission, asked Rodney Adler if Mr Pokross had been involved in a dramatic price 'spike' that the HSI share price enjoyed on 30 June 1998. The shares, which had been at $US10.75 on 26 June, jumped to $US12.70 on 28 June and closed the month at $13.88. 'Not specifically,' replied Adler.

FAI subsequently valued its 2.15 million HSI shares at the official 30 June 1998 price of $US13.75, giving its portfolio a much needed $12 million boost.

Pushed further by O'Bryan on what he and Pokross were doing with HSI, Adler added that as far as HSI was concerned, 'I would have done nothing different in June 1998 from what I would have done in April or May or January.' A sceptic would point out that he and Pokross might have been doing the same thing then too.

Further questioning of Adler at the Royal Commission in November revealed that in fact it was Steve Rabinovici, a director of HSI and a US resident, who called Adler three times on 29 June and 30 June 1998. Adler said he did not know that the Rabinovici family had caused the share price of HSI to lift by 10 per cent in the three days before 30 June from $US12.50 to $US13.88.

Adler told the commission on 10 October that Rabinovici 'never mentioned any purchase of significant quantities of stock' in HSI to him.

US records obtained by the Royal Commission show that Steve Rabinovici had bought 25,000 shares, his son Geoffrey had bought 13,000 shares and his daughter Barbara had bought 10,000 shares, accounting for almost three-quarters of the volume of HSI shares traded during those two days. They all sold the holdings within the next six weeks, accumulating a loss of around $US80,000 in doing so, since the price slipped back to $US9.85 by the end of July 1998.

But their buying had, like Cooper's deal on FAI Finance, done FAI a huge favour. The spike in the share price allowed FAI to claim an extra $12 million on the value of its holding of 2.15 million HSI shares. FAI declared a pre-tax profit of $8.6 million which would otherwise have been a loss, despite having arranged the $57 million worth of reinsurance recoveries that would produce guaranteed losses of at least $30 million for whoever owned FAI over the following five years. And to top that off, the HSI parcel was now sitting in the FAI books at a value of $US29.6 million or almost $50 million Australian at that time. Even though the Australian dollar subsequently sank sharply against the US dollar, the HSI share price was sinking even faster, so Ray Williams was going to have to keep HSI alive at all costs to justify the high valuation. Knowingly or not, the Rabinovici family's buying spree in late June 1998 had created a rod that was going to leave deep financial lacerations on Ray Williams' back.

And it didn't take long to cause pain. By the time HIH wrapped up the FAI takeover in 1999 HSI had been delisted from the main NASDAQ board because its price had fallen below $US2, in this case to $US1.85. It was left to languish on the Pink Pages, where low-priced stocks are traded on a 'by appointment' basis.

We also know that Pokross visited Sydney the month before all that happened, since the Royal Commission obtained his itinerary. Pokross and his wife stayed at the Hotel Nikko in Darling Harbour, were offered a trip to the Star City Casino and had dinner at the Wokpool restaurant. Pokross and his wife appear to have dined at Mezzaluna in Potts Point with Adler and his wife, Lyndi, who apparently gave Pokross the nickname 'Mr Pokemon'.

Pokross clearly made life as easy as he could for Adler to play the US market. On 19 August 1998 he opened a trading account for Drenmex, Adler's trading company, at a broking house called Robb, Peck McCooey in New York. 'Please be advised that this firm has been in business for 75 years and is the second largest specialist firm on the New York Stock Exchange next to Spear Leeds Kellogg.' For 'specialist' read 'small stock specialist'. Pokross was subsequently forced to concede that he 'may have' opened an account at the same broking house for his company Crabbe Capital on 10 September 1998, thirteen days before the HIH bid for FAI, and that he had borrowed money on margin to buy shares in FAI, as had his Uncle Harvey. And he forgot to tell the FBI.

But at least no trader forgets a favour.

In January 1998, the US National Association of Securities Dealers had issued a complaint that Pokross, among others, had been manipulating the price of a stock called Accessible Software. On 31 March 1999, Adler placed an order on behalf of FAI to buy 20,000 shares in Accessible Software on the US market. They were bought for $US12.06 each. By that stage FAI had been taken over by HIH but Adler was a non-executive director of HIH and was on the HIH investment committee, buying and selling shares on FAI's behalf.

The deal cost FAI $US241,000, but the shares failed to flourish and in March 2000 the software company was taken over at $US7.10 a share. The sale incurred a net loss for HIH, the beneficial owner, of just over $US99,000, offset by a small currency gain.

Again in 2000 Pokross tipped Adler into a stock called Medical Innovative Services. Pokross subsequently admitted manipulating the share price but there was some good news for his friends meantime. He said that Adler made an estimated $US700,000 trading the stock during 2000 while he himself made a mere $US454,000 trading the stock.

Other Adler connections to become involved were Sofisco, a company associated with FAI property manager Dr Frank Wolf who worked at one time with disgraced financier Spedley Securities, and Paul Brown. Brown's interests, which so often coincided with Adler's, took a $US1 million placement.

Pokross and Adler went from strength to strength.

'I don't know why he would need me, but Mr Adler would call me at 5 in the morning Australian time or 4 in the morning, which was the next day, and he would have a practice of calling me on his mobile phone to find out the state of the markets,' Pokross testified.

'If he wanted to execute a trade Mr Adler would ask me to patch him onto somebody so as not to interrupt the signal from his mobile phone on the beach in Australia,' he added.

The beach can only have been Bondi Beach, where Adler has long been an early morning fixture, with and without his personal trainer.

In April 1999 Adler was taken on by HIH Insurance as a 'consultant' at $40,000 a month, with a special brief to sort out assets such as the St Moritz Hotel, but there is no mention of the St Moritz in any Pokross evidence, nor of Adler doing anything at all for HIH. Drenmex was his own company and the only time it came into close contact with HIH was in June 2000 when Adler set up the $10 million Pacific Eagle Equities scheme to buy stock in HIH and to take a number of near-worthless technology stocks off his hands. Drenmex was the original vehicle to be used before Adler changed his mind and asked for the shares to be booked to a new company called Pacific Eagle Equities.

When HIH decided in October 1999 it had better increase its holding in HSI, who should get the order but Jeffrey Pokross. The vision of

Pokross doing legitimate business is fun to imagine, particularly as there is a note from the time signed by Rodney Adler, AM, and addressed to Ray Williams which states: 'I have had a phone call from a Mr Jeffrey Pokross,' using the indefinite article to create a bit of distance.

Crabbe Capital ended up being paid a $US104,000 spotter's fee by HIH for finding a line of 10 per cent of HSI or 580,000 shares to take its holding from around 37 to 47 per cent. The deal only cost $US1.1 million all up.

The 10 per cent line of stock was bought from a Milwaukee-based fund manager called Heartland that had long been close to Pokross, so it was probably the easiest $US104,000 the veteran mobster had earned. Nobody close to the case appears to know why the spotter's fee needed to be so big. The Pink Pages do at least offer an introduction service between buyer and seller. By 2000, Rodney Adler was on what Pokross boasted was his 'Rolodex of millionaires'.

Every stock promoter needs either a large group of small investors or a small group of big ones to get things moving fast. In one conversation that Pokross taped during 2000, he boasted to someone that 'when you go out with Adler, when you go out with Rodney, you're going out as an equal ... and here's a guy who you're not kissing his ass, because he's a fuckin' lunatic'. Maybe you had to be there to know what he was trying to say, but clearly he and Adler had a social relationship.

In another taped conversation Pokross boasted: 'I can find stuff anywhere from 500,000 up to about 10 million. When the deals get more than 3 or 4 million, I got to bring in the cavalry, OK? Rod, I need 3 million, I needed 4 million. OK, it's what I would generally do with you.'

Asked by his counsel, Gerald Lefcourt, if Rodney Adler was a person whom he could get money from when he needed it, he said 'Yes'. He also told the District Court in New York that he told clients that Adler had half a billion dollars of discretionary funds — other people's money that they trusted him with — to invest.

IS BRAD COOPER a street-wise genius or a bumbling buffoon? People who know and have worked with him say he is a bit of both.

His great skill, despite his lack of syntax, is to establish 'facts' by a mixture of talking, confusing people's recollections, extracting promises and drafting letters. 'Incremental persuasion' is one polite way to put it.

Take for instance a stock called Data Advantage Ltd, which FAI Insurance Ltd was allocated in 1998 because it used the stock's predecessor, the Credit Reference Association. FAI paid the subscription but, like a friend who sometimes uses your gym card or your car space, FAI Finance Corporation (FFC) made thousands of inquiries on the FAI account. The finance company FFC was half owned by Cooper's burglar alarm distributor, Home Security International, and spent thousands of hours on FAI's subscription checking the financial records of potential burglar alarm buyers. On the basis of its heavy use of the subscription, FFC put in a request to FAI Insurance to hand over some of its 217,000 share allocation.

FAI was taken over by HIH and the investment managers at HIH saw the request, laughed, and said no. FAI had paid the entire subscription to the Credit Reference Association and was the registered owner of it. They quickly saw what Cooper was about, although they were wary of the amount of support Cooper was getting from Rodney Adler. Although Adler had sold FAI to HIH he was not only a main board director of HIH but a member of HIH's influential investment committee.

Just to be on the safe side, someone at HIH got an opinion from Sydney law firm Watson Mangioni in 1999 which said the same thing as the investment managers had concluded: the FFC claim was groundless.

That, you might have thought, was that, but not for Brad Cooper.

At some date about eighteen months later he drafted a letter which ended up bearing the signature of Rodney Adler. It was backdated to 2 August 1999, addressed to Cooper and backed the FFC claim. He admitted to the Royal Commission it was his work. Wayne Martin, QC, pointed out some flaws in the letter, such as that Adler was addressed as chief executive of FAI Insurance when he had resigned months before, and the street address on the letterhead was wrong, but that was a mere bagatelle since Cooper freely agreed it was his letter.

The awesome touch is that Cooper then got a letter on 7 February 2001 from his lawyers, Browne & Co, which not only mentioned the 2 August letter — 'agreement was reached between yourself and Rodney Adler', it summarised — but it also said that Cooper's company was to get not 50 per cent of the share allocation, as had been asked for previously, but 80 per cent. That later climbed to 85 per cent.

It's also worth mentioning that the dodgy 2 August letter said the shares or proceeds should go not to FAI Finance Corp, which Cooper half controlled in 1999 and then sold, but Home Security International, which he ended up controlling totally after 8 December 2000.

So did Cooper retreat in shame, apologising for his outrageous claim and suggesting that HIH should forget it since he had taken HIH for so much money in the past?

No. He persuaded the HIH general manager finance, Bill Howard, who carelessly allowed Cooper to order a $118,000 BMW convertible on his behalf at that time without proper discussion about how the car was going to be paid for, that he (Cooper) had had the agreement of the HIH financial controller, Jock MacAdie, to pay him out $1 million, and could Howard please hurry up and pay?

Cooper wrote to Howard on 15 January 2001, while Howard was trying to keep HIH afloat, 'Without any delay if the amount of $1.5 [sic] is not settled immediately we will instruct our lawyers to take legal action to recover the shares, being the property on HSI and all damages.' Howard missed his opportunity to shut Cooper up with $1.50, or half the price of a beer. MacAdie denies he authorised Howard to pay and indeed even Cooper wrote to MacAdie on 14 February admitting that 'we may not agree on the exact amount'.

But an inescapable fact is that a few days later HSI was paid exactly one million dollars in settlement of the claim, based on an estimate of discounted value of how high the shares would have got if FAI Finance had been allowed to have them.

The judge was scathing about the Data Advantage affair, pointing out in his report that Cooper's claim had gone from being on behalf of FAI Finance Corporation, which was sold by HSI before the claim was pushed in 2001, to being a 'direct entitlement on behalf of HSI'. 'The claim was entirely without merit,' he concluded.

He also accepted counsel assisting's submission that Adler had signed the letter in January 2001 with the knowledge that it was backdated and that it was being used to bolster Cooper's claim that HSI had a direct entitlement to shares.

He said he found that Adler knew that the document was false and misleading and that Cooper could use it to prejudice the company of which Adler was a director. In Adler's case he named two possible breaches of the New South Wales Crimes Act and referred the matter to the director of Public Prosecutions and to ASIC. That particular Act carries heavy maximum penalties of five years' gaol for one possible breach, and ten for the other.

He recommended Cooper for a referral under the breach which carries the maximum penalty of five years, since he was not a director of the company being disadvantaged.

A further episode involved Cooper, Howard and Ray Williams in a situation where Cooper was pressing Howard for $1.2 million relating to his seminar business, Vision Publishing, and over which the judge believed Howard misled Williams. Howard paid Cooper in early December 2000 without Cooper having provided any seminars; Howard then told Williams in early January 2001 that the money was still outstanding, and Cooper was then paid again. There was an offsetting arrangement involving Cooper's Goodwill Group. (The Goodwill Group was behind a concept that Cooper started called National Kindness Week, which he said was to foster 'random acts of kindness'.)

Over the Vision Publishing and Goodwill Group affair, the judge referred Cooper and Howard for possible breaches of the section of the Crimes Act which carries the five year maximum sentences, adding in an ASIC referral for Howard.

THERE WERE ABOUT five more examples of similar financial achievements in HIH's dying weeks before it finally collapsed on 15 March 2001. In one case Cooper secured a payout of $65,000 for the loss of the logbook in his Ferrari even though it was not covered by the car's insurance policy. It was not the claims department but Howard who authorised the payment.

Brad Cooper is many things, but bumbler is only one of them. As one former colleague put it, 'he has an almost mystical ability to get money out of people'.

CHAPTER 16

EVERY MAN FOR HIMSELF

HSI WAS YET another complete disaster for HIH, representing a drain on the insurer's hard-pressed funds from the moment it came into Ray Williams' orbit in early 1999. There is no evidence that he paid any attention to it in 1998 in his rushed bid for FAI, and it is a shining example of one of the many time bombs that he acquired in his desperate push to get access to FAI's cash flow. In his report the judge said HSI was 'a case study' that reflects on Williams' management approach. 'It puts in question Williams' ability to adopt a strategy and execute it, to make judgments about individuals and to act accordingly. It also gives an insight into the way he approached transactions conferring private benefits of the type I have discussed. HSI tested Williams and he was found wanting.'

He had nothing to do with HSI's purchase of Ness, which all happened before the bid, but he bailed HSI out twice in the following two years to the tune of at least $30 million before allowing Brad Cooper to buy almost half of HSI back for $1.25 million in December 2000.

Cooper didn't even pay that in cash. He agreed to buy the 47 per cent stake with payment in two years' time, putting up only $250,000 by way of a deposit; on the same day that he arranged for HIH to send an HIH cheque for $250,000 to his beloved Collingwood Football Club, in the week preceding a board election at the club. And he admitted to the HIH Royal Commission that the $1.25 million price was 'a figure plucked out of the air'.

Cooper was a vice-president of the club, on the ticket of club president Eddie McGuire. McGuire is a street-wise former newspaper copyboy who is jokingly dubbed 'Eddie Everywhere' for his myriad interests in Melbourne, which include calling AFL football matches for Channel Nine, even those involving Collingwood. McGuire had very presciently persuaded Cooper to join the Collingwood board in 1998 in order to bring money from Cooper's Sydney contacts down to the Melbourne-based club. As an old Melbourne boy with a lifelong allegiance to Collingwood, now rubbing shoulders with some of the richest people in Sydney, Cooper looked at first glance like a logical choice.

Wayne Martin, QC, said that the payment appeared to secure the re-election of Cooper as a director of Collingwood, shoring up support for McGuire as president. It went through on 11 December 2000, just before the McGuire ticket won by a 500-vote landslide, although there had been a spirited attempt to make it appear that the deal had been done a lot earlier.

Bill Howard, general manager finance at HIH, said a letter existed which said that the deal was arranged in May or June 2000 but that Cooper had actually written it only a few days before the club's election. Howard conceded that he had been accommodating to Cooper but that 'I just gave in to the incessant battering' of the man.

The episode turned out to be embarrassing for the club and Cooper resigned from the Collingwood board in early 2002, although McGuire shrugged the affair off with his usual nonchalance. Asked afterwards if he counted Cooper as a friend, he replied: 'I know plenty of people.'

One of Brad Cooper's greatest skills is getting money out of people, to the extent that back in 1996 and 1997 he was running seminars on the subject, not to mention keeping some impressive gate receipts. Sharing a podium with advertising man Siimon Reynolds and marketing spruiker Bob Pritchard, he ran the 'Winning Edge' series around Australia. His topic was 'how to get customers literally queueing up to do business with you' and 'no-fail tips for power negotiating to help you win the deal every time'.

'Brad will demonstrate to you that when times are tough and you lose everything, you CAN still get through it all ... AND WIN,' his flyers said. They explained that Cooper had taken his company from 'Zero to $100 million turnover per annum ... zero to more than 750 staff and ... zero to more than 70 outlets globally'.

Clearly Ray Williams didn't attend them, since Cooper subsequently tied Williams in knots by sticking carefully to his own notes called '15 tips for power negotiation'.

Most were logical hints like taking your lawyer or accountant with you to meetings to make you look more authoritative, but some were canny such as 'know the other party's needs', 'make time your friend' and 'don't burn your bridges'. One of the best was 'build scarcity into your proposal' but there was a brain-acher also there which said 'ask for more than you expect to get'.

That latter tip contains the sort of twisted logic that would have sent the traditionalist Williams half mad.

'This will lift the perceived value of your offer and give you more room to move,' Cooper explained in his 'Winning Edge' subscriber's pack, concluding that 'the other party will think they have had a small win'. No explanation about what you do if you are not the one writing the cheque.

One of the hardest things on earth to do is to have an argument with someone who is not logical, and Cooper clearly has moments of being on another planet.

He certainly impressed Sydney radio host Alan Jones, who was very briefly a director of related company, FAI Home Security Holdings Pty Ltd, and who gave Cooper a generous but carefully worded accolade to go with the seminars. 'Brad Cooper is one of those people for whom nothing is impossible. He generates drive, energy, ideas, application, evaluation and achievement in a way that sweeps others up with him. His record to date is extraordinary. In my view, it's but a pale imitation of what lies ahead.'

Cooper had no difficulty in persuading Nazareno Circosta to sell out the remaining 25 per cent of Ness for $4 million in 1999, paying him with a raft of HSI shares which ended up worthless anyway. It was a much less generous deal than the $20 million in cash that Paul Brown got for three-quarters of the business the year before.

In November 1998 Cooper tried to buy FAI out of HSI because he was concerned that once HIH bought FAI, it might not be so keen as FAI had been to support his burglar alarm selling operations. He should not have worried. HIH still came to the rescue with its fat chequebook anyway.

The first of many awkward surprises for the new owner, HIH, was when Arthur Andersen quit as auditor of HSI two months into the bid. It takes a fair amount to make an auditor say 'no more', as the audit of FAI in 1998 showed, but Alan Davies of Andersen didn't mince words. He said that HSI's corporate governance was 'abysmal'. He told Adler, who told Cooper, that HSI owed Andersen around $180,000 in fees and that Andersen was prepared to waive some $40,000 of the fees 'in order to resolve the situation'. Which was a discount for cash.

So much for HSI's booming international business. Davies told Adler that 'board approval is lacking for many major transactions, in particular the recent nursing home investment'. He was referring to an investment in Victoria that HSI and some of its executives went into as a 'June 30' tax-driven scheme. What was a burglar alarm vendor doing buying a nursing home? No one really knew, although at least the deal was designed to make people money, which is the opposite of the fate that awaited HIH in propping up HSI.

Davies, who enjoyed his reputation as a curmudgeonly but accurate auditor, said there were too many related party transactions occurring and too many non-HSI matters being handled by executives of HSI. In case Adler still failed to get the message, Davies wrote: 'There is not a proper division between Brad Cooper personal and Brad Cooper, the chief executive.'

Cooper's explanation of the occasional confusion between personal and corporate business was that in the case of the nursing home investment, 'others chose to go into it because the recommendation seemed very prudent'. Cooper was a walking conflict of interests but he had learned from some of the best in the business. Larry Adler had taught his son Rodney all he knew, and Cooper had clearly picked a lot of it up along the way.

Adler may have taken Davies' scathing message on board but there is no evidence it got anywhere near the person who was going to have to carry the can for all this — Ray Williams.

Williams' problems with HSI took a while to get going, but they came with a vengeance. April 2000 was the deadline for Paul Brown to get the balance of his payment for selling three-quarters of Ness to HSI, but there was nothing like enough money in HSI to pay Brown the $US8.3 million that was still owed, particularly with the Australian dollar sliding. Doing business in greenbacks was losing its appeal for Cooper.

On 11 April 2000, HIH rode to the rescue of HSI by buying half of FAI Finance Corporation for what may have been $25.5 million — certainly a great deal more than it was worth. While Ray Williams had already proved that he was a champion at overpaying for other people's dud assets, this was the beginning of a subtle new variation on that system.

Now he was doing deals in which he *knew* he was overpaying for the assets. Deals were happening not because they were good for the buyer, but because they would stop the vendor from collapsing. The only reason they were happening was that the buyer (HIH) also happened to have shares in the cash-strapped vendor, HSI.

That half of FAI Finance Corporation had changed hands in January 1998 for $US7.4 million, at which point HSI shares were worth around $US11 each. By the time HSI flipped the asset on to HIH in a deal that was clearly designed to get HSI out of a financial jam, the price of HSI shares had crashed to $US1.25, or less than a tenth of what HIH had paid for them. Sales had gone into a downward spiral and existing clients were complaining. You would have thought that the finance company selling the alarms, FAI Finance Corporation, would therefore see a fall in its value, but instead it jumped sharply.

HIH recorded the purchase of half of FAI Finance at $25.5 million in its books, although HSI filed statements to the Security and Exchange Commission (SEC) in the US that the purchase price was actually $US8.1 million and that a further $US4.4 million was an extension of a previous loan made by HIH to HSI in January 1988. Not that it made a lot of difference to HIH: it was still down $US12.5 million on the deal, which by then tallied almost exactly with the $A25.5 million number in its books.

At a guess, the deal should have been worth closer to $US2 million or $A4 million, since the deal brought greater financial worries to HIH about HSI's liabilities in the US.

Under creditors' statutes in the US, if HSI went into liquidation, HIH would be liable for consumer claims because FAI Finance Corp had been a linked credit provider for the sale of the burglar alarms.

HIH never did get its money back.

But if that looked a crook deal, it was just a warm-up for the deal in which Cooper sold half of Ness to HIH for $17.5 million in September 2000, the last month in which Williams was in charge of HIH. He resigned on 13 October.

August 2000 saw an avalanche of thinly disguised pleas by HSI for money, mostly sent by Rodney Adler, since Williams had broken the habit of a lifetime and in December 1999 told Cooper pretty much what he thought of him.

On 30 December 1999, after Cooper had kept Williams sitting waiting in the HIH office for hours, Williams wrote to him: 'Brad, I have tried to contact you by phone without success. This constant humbugging is to me without precedent. For my part, I have acted in good faith to support HSI in its most precarious financial position. I am totally exasperated by your behaviour.'

History does not reveal which particular enormity Williams was referring to, but he had a smorgasbord of odd demands to choose from, any one of which would have sufficed. And Cooper did not even need to do all the demanding, since he still had Rodney Adler onside.

On 10 August Adler wrote to Williams to say that HSI had 'spiralling sales going down' and that the company's situation was 'dire'. Cooper had noted not long before that sales were down by 30 per cent overall and 700 per cent in New Zealand, a dramatic claim considering that if your sales are down 100 per cent, they are zero.

Adler played his strongest card against Williams early, warning that a collapse of HSI would cost HIH 'in the order of $50–$60 million'. This reflected the fact that although HIH had written down its HSI holding to $A3 a share, that was still markedly more than the shares were worth.

Adler had been made a director of HSI back in December 1999 and subsequently became chairman but told Williams he would take over as caretaker chief executive of the company if 'HIH provides the financial support in order to change the financial "smell" of HSI', he said. 'The consequence of HSI's collapse would I think be more burdensome than putting in another $5 million.'

Five days later he made it look as though others might put money in too. He told Williams that HSI needed another $2.5 million and that a restructure of HSI was imminent. He suggested that Paul Brown should 'place $AUD1m of additional equity in the company when we raise equity ... this is planned to be done as soon as possible'. It never did. All the talk of offshore benefactors was just talk.

The HSI auditors, meanwhile, played into Adler's hands by noting in the audit of HSI's 30 June 2000 results that there was 'substantial uncertainty about the company's ability to continue as a going concern'. They said that if more money was not put into the company before 30 September, they would modify the company's accounts to a 'non-going concern' basis. That would have been the death knell of the company, since it was carrying a number of intangible assets on its books that would disappear in a puff of dust in that case. As it was, the auditors, Andersen, quit at the end of 2000.

Adler then sent Williams another demand but, like a fisherman casting a fly in front of a trout, left just enough optimism in there to keep Williams' hopes up. On 16 September he wrote to Williams to say that HSI owed HIH $16 million and that it had external debt of $1.2 million and creditors of $1.5 million.

'We believe that sales will be in a positive cash flow position by March [2001] but we will probably sustain $500,000 losses per month until that date, therefore, we need $3 million minimum to meet these requirements.'

Sign here, please.

On 18 September 2000 Adler and Cooper went to see Williams but on Adler's advice, Cooper stayed in the foyer of Williams' office at HIH and left Adler to do the talking. This was despite the fact that Adler had been a director of HIH for more than a year. So he should absolutely not have been soliciting money from one company that he directed, HIH, on behalf of another company he also directed, HSI. That is a classic example of a conflict of interest and directors who find themselves in such a situation are obliged by law to stand aside from any such negotiations.

A document dated 27 September and signed by Adler and Williams saw HIH promise to buy half of Ness from HSI for $17.5 million, plus, plus, plus. Not only was HIH buying something it did not really want for a price that was higher even than Brown had been paid, but it offered to provide HSI with a further $2.5 million loan before 30 June 2001. As well, HIH effectively promised to settle HSI's class action against all those angry buyers of the inadequate and overpriced alarm systems. The main part of the deal was that HSI would repay loans to HIH to the value of $13 million.

The price for buying half of Ness was twice what another buyer had offered to pay just weeks earlier, and a valuation by Deloitte's at the request of the HIH Royal Commission in late 2001 placed a fair market price for that share of somewhere between $6.4 million and $7.6 million. Deloitte revealed that while HSI controlled Ness, it had taken $14 million out of Ness in the two years to 30 June 2000. At that time Cooper was CEO of HSI.

(In early 2002, after HIH had collapsed, Naz Circosta bought back HIH's 49 per cent stake in Ness for $1 million. The other 51 per cent controlling stake still belongs to Brad Cooper, although he sold the phone lines and customer base of the security business to the UK-based Chubb Security group. Chubb is understood to be happy with the deal, which netted a huge customer list and about 30,000 monitoring lines for around $6 million.)

If all the nonsense about HSI seemed to Ray Williams like a bad dream, at least Cooper and Adler were trying to make him feel as though he was doing something useful for them. But shortly after HIH had done the $17.5 million deal, Adler wrote shamelessly to Williams to ask him to fall on his sword as chief executive of HIH and to give him the top job.

This was after Mark Westfield had been publishing the copious material leaked to him by Adler about what was wrong at HIH, which incidentally caused Adler to complain to Williams that there was a 'mole' inside HIH. There certainly was.

And now Adler wrote: 'I find myself in a very awkward position. I have been and continue to be inundated by institutions, and more particularly individuals, ringing me and suggesting to me that they place their proxy at my discretion to vote at the annual meeting, the sole purpose of which is for me to assume either the chairman or chief executive role.'

Adler went on to say that if Williams had not been so 'fair, so open and so honourable' then he 'probably would have moved a long time ago against' him. For a palace plotter, Rodney Adler owed more of his technique to the Marx brothers than Lucrezia Borgia.

It turned out that it wasn't the institutions and individuals that had been canvassing Adler, but the other way round.

Adler even put a request for money into the letter that asked Ray Williams to step down, asking for a further $2 million for a company called Business Thinking Systems, which will be described later. Needless to say, it was not a success.

Justice Owen made one of his strongest recommendations against Ray Williams and Rodney Adler over the Ness deal, even though neither Williams nor HIH obtained any benefit whatsoever.

He referred Williams and Adler for a possible breach of section 184(1) of the Corporations Law, which makes it an offence for a company director to use their position dishonestly or recklessly 'with the intention of directly or indirectly gaining an advantage for themselves, or someone else, or causing detriment to the corporation'.

It carries a possible five-year gaol sentence.

He also swept aside a submission from Adler that he could not have breached those provisions because he was only a director of HIH Insurance and the transaction had been done by subsidiary insurer HIH Casualty and General. The judge said that did not matter since the relevant sections of that law focus on a person making 'use' of their position, and that during the negotiations Adler used his position as a director of HIH.

What is amazing in this story is why on earth Ray Williams let Rodney Adler so far into the HIH camp in the first place. By September 2000 HIH had well and truly realised that the FAI acquisition had been a can of worms, a giant reserving headache that was on its way to a $400 million writedown, more than it had cost. Wayne Martin told the commission in July 2002 that FAI and one of the two other insurers in the HIH group were probably statutorily insolvent by June 1999. Even the strongest, HIH Casualty and General, was probably insolvent as well because of commitments it had made to support the acquisition of the Cotesworth underwriting operation at Lloyd's in London.

Why hadn't Rodney Adler been unceremoniously thrown off the board? Cynics suggested after the collapse that there had to be a 'goat photograph', something that compelled Ray Williams to keep Adler onside. There was of course no goat and no photograph. Adler was certainly behaving like a man who knew he wasn't popular, but who did not expect to be ousted.

When Ray Williams resigned on 12 October 2000 after the Pacific Eagle Equities fiasco, HIH chairman Geoff Cohen suggested to him that maybe Adler should resign too. It was a logical suggestion, since Pacific Eagle Equities was entirely Adler's idea.

Adler declined to fall on his sword, noting to Cohen that he was a young man with a long corporate future in front of him, and he stayed.

Not long afterwards Adler found he had a very strong reason to stay: HIH was planning possible legal action against FAI for misrepresentation of its condition when HIH bought it. It was going to be much harder for HIH to sue a fellow director than an ex-director and he dug in.

Rodney Adler has always been a keen sender of faxes. He sent a record twenty-two to other HIH directors between October 2000 and March

2001, including at least one complaint about the 'mole' in the HIH board who had been leaking to the press. But he really hit the 'send' button on 11 December once reports had come out that HIH was considering legal action.

He fired off no less than five faxes to HIH chairman Geoff Cohen on that day alone, including one which Cohen later described as a 'veiled threat'. Adler went on the front foot, asking out loud why FAI directors and shareholders accepted HIH shares in the takeover when HIH had unrevealed problems of its own.

This was a nice touch, since the FAI shareholders who had accepted HIH shares had actually had the chance of raising real money from selling them. HIH shares were above $2.00 each when the takeover was being settled, even if they subsequently skidded to $1.50 in January 2000 and $1 by July of that year.

Cohen testified in September 2002 that Adler was 'probably almost a desperate man at this stage', which suggests that Rodney Adler must be in the 'when the going gets tough' school of desperate men.

'There has been a campaign to denigrate and slur me and FAI,' he told Cohen. 'I have, this last week, kept my original directors at bay because they, too, are now interested to know why we accepted [HIH shares] on the basis of your financial statements at the time and with the knowledge I have as a director of HIH, proving a problem in those accounts is snack easy.'

In other words: if you sue me, I will sue you.

In fact, the HIH investigation of possible action dragged on so long that HIH collapsed before it could get the action organised.

Followers of the 'goat photograph' theory focus on what may have been one last, crazy move by Ray Williams to anoint Rodney Adler as his successor in late October 2000. Geoffrey Cohen's witness statement had it that after Williams had quit as chief executive on 13 October, Williams had told him 'on a number of occasions that, in his opinion, Rodney Adler was the best man for the role' of succeeding him.

Even if there was no goat and no photograph, Williams had been absurdly loyal to the man who had been trying so hard to knife him. And even if Williams had promised Rodney Adler his job if he ever left, you would have thought that the FAI disaster would have caused Williams to say to Adler 'all bets are off' some time in 1999, never mind late 2000.

Then there was the strange business of Williams thinking it was the other directors of HIH who were supporting Adler. Williams stated in evidence to the commission that after Adler joined the HIH board, he himself had concluded that FAI was a 'contaminant and pollutant' that had dragged down HIH, and that affected his view of Adler. But, he said, Adler had enjoyed the support of the other HIH board members. This was the 'I thought he was a friend of yours' theory.

No other board members chose to support that statement and most made it clear that they were not fans, particularly once the leaks started in mid–2000.

In February 2001, Adler showed his gratitude to Williams one last time, by allegedly threatening to 'come after' fellow director Charles Abbott if Abbott continued to hold up Williams' $3 million retirement payout. Abbot had written to former Blake Dawson Waldron colleague David Williamson explaining what he said had happened at a board meeting of HIH. He wrote that Adler had said 'words to the effect that "if you are responsible for delaying payment of the allowance to Mr Williams" then he [Adler] and Williams would come after' him.

'You had better be clean and have no skeletons because we will attack you and bring you down if you don't back off,' he quoted Adler as having said to him. As it happened, the board ratified the payment to Williams but because the company collapsed, he was never paid.

All the material about threats was very strange, and quite unproved. But what made it even more strange was that in late November 2000, just about two months previously, Mark Westfield had written about a 'likely $10 million payout outrage' due to Williams at the forthcoming annual meeting on 15 December 2000. Adler had also written to Cohen just before the meeting asking that HIH directors 'be circulated with information on exactly what Mr Williams will be receiving when he departs from HIH'.

There is no certainty that Westfield had been prompted by Adler to write what he did — back then, the prospect of a $10 million payout could have horrified any number of insiders — but it certainly hammered Williams' chances of a prosperous exit.

CERTAINLY, AN OTHERWISE dilatory HIH board acted with surprising thoroughness once it was decided in early 2001 that Adler had to go. The whole Pacific Eagle Equities affair had blown wide open, with auditor John Buttle telling Cohen just before Christmas 2000 that 'either you inform the regulator or I will' and that the atmosphere within what was left of the HIH board was clearly anti-Adler. All the executive directors had resigned in October, in deference to a push by the corporate governance lobby to have a majority of non-executive directors on boards.

The HIH board finally succeeded in persuading Adler to resign at a board meeting on 26 February 2001, after organising that the Australian Shareholders' Association requisition an extraordinary shareholders' meeting to oust him from the board for leaking confidential information. Cohen had formally asked him to quit on 7 February.

Ironically, Adler told the commission that he resigned because the board was not supplying him with information, which was true. He did not explain that the board had stopped telling him things because he kept leaking them. At the time he had said it was 'time to move on', which was unarguably correct.

At the time when Adler's ousting took place — and incidentally HIH remains one of the few large companies in Australia where a director has ever been forced out by the threat of a requisitioned meeting — it required the support of one hundred shareholders or the owners of 5 per cent of the stock to requisition such a meeting. Most of the shares were supplied by Darren De Bortoli, a Riverina vigneron whose family had bought up millions of HIH shares in the sliding market of 2000 on the incorrect premise that the shares were oversold. De Bortoli, grandson of the group's founder, was able to put up just over 23 million shares or 4.71 per cent of the stock, but the balance was provided by none other than George Sturesteps, Ray Williams' first ever employee from 1968.

Sturesteps had had as many as 6.2 million shares in 1998, although he had been selling down since then. Sturesteps was left with 2.6 million shares when the company collapsed, one of the biggest single holders of the stock. At least he had struck a blow for his old mate Ray on the way down.

Given that both the HIH board and the Australian Shareholders' Association have been accused in their time of being rest homes for supine geriatrics, Adler is clearly a person who is skilled in mobilising forces against him.

A FASCINATING FOOTNOTE to these struggles that included all three of Williams, Adler and Cooper was the bizarre episode of August 1999 in which Cooper made around $36,000 by short-selling HIH shares on what he said was Rodney Adler's recommendation, at a time when HIH announced its first ever loss.

What made the episode particularly odd was that it caused Cooper to visit Ray Williams twice and burst into tears at least once, and bad-mouth Adler for what Cooper saw as duplicity.

There are at least two versions of what happened, Cooper's and Adler's, but they coincide on enough detail to suggest there was a spectacular attempt to get Cooper into Williams' good books.

It began with what according to Cooper was a recommendation by Adler to Cooper to 'short' HIH shares. Shorting consists of selling shares you do not own and buying them 'back' shortly afterwards at what should hopefully be a lower price. The best time to do such a trade is when a company is about to announce bad news, such as HIH did on 25 August 1999, when it declared its first ever loss of $21.1 million for the first six months of the calendar year. (The company had actually been making significant losses for years, as was pointed out at length by the Royal Commission, but until that time had managed to cover over the losses by understating reserves.)

Cooper said in evidence that he was a novice at short selling, but if so, he had beginner's luck. He also said he had not known about the result coming out but whatever he did or did not know, he sold the better part of 1 million shares in HIH at $1.65 on 21 August and bought them back at $1.61 on 26 August, the day after HIH had announced the loss.

There is nothing very unusual in such a trade except the knotty question of how much inside knowledge Cooper had. He said himself that he had inside knowledge from Adler that the shares were a 'sell', although he said Adler had not told him why. 'Mr Adler tipped me that it would be a very good stock to short. He felt the company was in a, some form of mismanagement and it wasn't being managed well,' Cooper testified on 14 October.

By 21 August Adler should have had the board papers which revealed the loss, although Adler said that in that instance, it may not have been the case.

What is unusual is the letter that Cooper wrote to Ray Williams on 26 August, in which he said he had bought a million dollars' worth of HIH shares, that he planned to buy another $500,000 worth the next day, and that 'It looks like the day wasn't so bad after all.'

Williams was also sent the contract notes for the purchases, which only an expert would spot as the second leg of a short sale. They carried the suffix 's/a' for short account, in much smaller letters than the traditional 'We Have Bought' that appears on any 'buy' contract note. The clear intention of the note was to get the thoroughly dubious Ray Williams onside, although in his initial evidence on 23 July Cooper said he could not remember why he had written the note about the day not being so bad after all. 'I don't know what I was referring to,' he said.

By October he took a clearer line, saying that he had spoken to Williams after faxing him the note. 'A very dejected Mr Williams thanked me very much and was very grateful and acknowledged how helpful I had been on that day by buying those shares,' he said.

Cooper said that about a week after that he had sought a face-to-face meeting with Adler over the episode. He said that Adler had told him it was good for Mr Williams and good for HIH. 'In my mind I had, from what I could see, been part of something that was clearly not good for HIH and I believed that it was deceptive and that I kicked HIH in the guts when they were down and that the conversation I had had with Mr Williams was misleading,' Cooper told the Royal Commission.

He said that Adler told him he had done a great deal. He paraphrased Adler as having said 'You have gone and bought about $1 million shares. You've sent a buy note, you've sent a letter and now Ray is indebted to you for life, you've done a good thing.'

'He thinks you've helped him … when he was down and you know, he is a loyal person, he will like you more,' he quoted Adler as saying. 'He doesn't have a great deal of time for you, your company has caused him a lot of distress and now you've come and flown the flag, type of thing, and not only will he never know … you've made money. You haven't been overly greedy, I have tipped you a good stock. I've actually done a bit with someone else [he was still quoting Adler] … and that's a perfect situation, by the way if you want to ring and ask him for lunch he will say, which restaurant?'

Cooper said that his parting words to Adler were: 'Rodney, if you believe that is a good transaction for all, you and I have an enormously different view on the way life is.'

Cooper then said he had gone to see Ray Williams in his office in September or October 2000, more than a year later, where he said he broke down in tears because, as he put it, 'I needed to clear my own conscience.'

HSI was having one of its many financial crises and Cooper rang Williams in an agitated state, asking to see him urgently. Williams' evidence, in which he described both Adler and Cooper as 'very difficult individuals' to deal with, stated that Cooper had come to his office and had criticised Adler for 'using people' and that Adler had not honoured his obligations to him (Cooper) about a shareholding Cooper believed HIH was due to buy him in Home Security International. Because he had started the company and had sold down his stake in HSI, he had persuaded HIH to buy him more stock on his behalf. When he and Ray Williams came to a final 'divorce' in January 2001, he allowed HIH to renege on that in exchange for HIH forgiving a $1.3 million loan from FAI to a shelf company called Hemsway Investments for which Cooper had stood guarantor.

That was a classic Cooper move. He had done a deal with Rodney Adler whereby FAI would swap debt for equity in Hemsway, a company which for tax reasons was based in New Zealand, although there was nothing about the swap in the documentation. The Hemsway loan went straight to the Cooper company Vision Publishing. HIH clearly inherited the deal with reluctance, so much so that it preferred writing off the loan to Cooper's offer of free shares in Vision Publishing. Cooper's masterstroke was to parlay HIH's supposed promise to buy him stock in HSI into a deal that got him out of repaying a $1.3 million loan which he had been legally bound to pay. It took until February 2003 for the liquidators of HIH and FAI to pursue Cooper for the money, a very early representative of a plethora of cases the liquidators are likely to bring.

One can thus appreciate that Cooper was, as Williams put it, hard to deal with. Several followers of the Royal Commission believe that by then Ray Williams was at the 'aargh' stage of the relationship, ready to strangle this man who combined a clumsy manner with an old-time quack-cure peddler's ability to get money out of people. And here was Cooper, meanwhile, sobbing in Williams' office.

'He said that Rodney Adler had set out to use me, he referred to the PEE [Pacific Eagle Equities] Trust matter. He said that Rodney Adler had fed information to the press. He then started crying and said he had misled me when he phoned me in August 1999 after the announcement of our results when he told me that he was buying shares in HIH.

'He said that far from buying the shares to show support for HIH, he had done so at the request of Rodney Adler.'

Cooper said in evidence that he had then gone to see Rodney Adler 'and had a conversation with Mr Adler and said I would like to cancel all my relationships with him, that I think I had been very loyal for seven or eight years and I had worked around the clock and I realised he was not the man or anywhere near the man I thought he was and he was manipulative, cunning, deceptive and had taken advantage of me'.

Cooper then confessed that he knew the HIH 'short' was insider trading, thus implicating Adler in it too. 'I also would like to put on the record that I was aware that when he tipped me the stock that I was to make a profit,' he said, 'and let's not plead naivety here. Where I was well aware of the profit side of things, but I was very against the deception of the way it was done because I did not know he had a motive on the 18th or the 20th [of August 1999] which was to play out on the 26th.

'So I told him that I felt he had set me up and what he had was ... not a tip but it was a strategy for him to make himself look better in front of Mr Williams.'

This was a new Brad Cooper. Lawyer and journalist Richard Ackland had a beautiful description of the traditional Cooper, published in July 2002: 'Bursting out of his three-button suit, his yellow-tipped hair aglow, his face like a shining spud, Cooper gives this columnist the impression of being the very model of a modern business grasper.'

Ackland was spot on, but there is also Cooper the emotional man. Cooper is a bubbling volcano of heartfelt feelings, quick to spring a tear and put a quaver in his voice, which is why he is such a good public speaker. Even if he can almost 'cry to order', he is emphatically a man who wears his heart on his sleeve.

In case Cooper had not quite made his point to Williams, Cooper called him again in May 2002 and asked to see him. By then Williams had retreated to his extensive compound at Lake Macquarie, north of Sydney, so Williams said he should come up there. 'A meeting was arranged for a Tuesday which he failed to keep,' said Williams. 'He subsequently phoned to say that he had slept in and wanted to come later that afternoon. I said it wasn't convenient and eventually he came the following Friday. He sat down with me for about fifteen minutes and told me it was "cleansing of the soul" time.

'He said that "one comes to the point in life where one has to reassess the situation",' Williams remembered.

Williams noted that Cooper not only dropped Adler in the frame, but also Bill Howard, who had been a senior accountant at HIH. Cooper told him that Bill Howard had fed information to Rodney Adler, 'which I took to be confidential information relating to HIH's accounts'.

By that time Howard and Williams had clearly come to a fork in the road, since it was Howard's testimony in the Pacific Eagle Equities case in August 2001 which had counted against Williams.

Howard had testified that he had asked Ray Williams to make sure all the correct internal procedures had been followed when HIH put $10 million into Pacific Eagle Equities. Williams said Howard had not asked him. It was certainly very clear that the correct procedures were not followed because the $10 million investment was never ratified by the company's investment committee.

Considering all the antagonism between Cooper and Adler, it took a long time before they chose to stop collaborating. Adler was a key supporter of HSI all the way through until he resigned from HSI and was a supporter of Brad Cooper's various financial adventures until HIH collapsed in March 2001.

But when they fell out, they fell out in style.

They had two meetings on consecutive Sundays in early October 2002, at which the two had very different agendas.

If you believe Cooper, he wanted to get a payment of $1.8 million out of Adler to settle a business deal, and Adler wanted him to say that the 'short' scheme was not Adler's idea.

Adler's version was that Cooper was trying to extort money out of him in exchange for changing his evidence. Since there were no witnesses and neither man chose to wear a recording device, we will never know exactly what happened, but the allegations flying around were sensational. If Cooper was correct about Adler's attempts to get him to change his evidence, this could have serious ramifications for Adler because interfering with a Royal Commission witness is a dire offence. The attempt at extortion, as alleged by Adler, would put Cooper in similar hot water.

What was clear was that despite their previous differences, the two men were keen enough to meet at 6.30 on not one but two consecutive Sunday mornings, while most sane people are still asleep.

It was never easy working out exactly what was said. Rodney Adler's SC, David Hammerschlag, asked Cooper whether he (Cooper) had wanted to talk about HIH. 'I'm just trying to think, Mr Hammerschlag. Mr Adler initiated the meeting and I suspect he wanted to talk about HIH.'

'Mr Cooper, did you want to talk about HIH?'

'Mr Hammerschlag, I don't think you heard me.'

Hammerschlag, known to one and all as 'The Hammer', suggested to Justice Neville Owen that the witness was deliberately avoiding giving answers to questions: the judge preferred to put it that 'I think Mr Cooper has a particular way of expressing himself.'

The first meeting was in the Duxton Hotel, opposite Milsons Point Station, for two hours and the second was at Rydge's Hotel in North Sydney.

Hammerschlag suggested that Cooper had a 'desperate need for money' to which Cooper retorted that he had just won $240,000 from a bet on the Sydney Roosters winning the NRL Grand Final. No evidence was produced, or asked for, about the bet.

Cooper conceded that he had sent a letter of demand to Adler over the alleged $1.825 million debt, which related to a half share in the Phoenix Leisure Group Pty Ltd, a ski and camping equipment importer that Cooper had financed Adler into some years previously. The letter's final deadline for payment of $500,000 was 9.30 a.m. on Monday 14 October, the exact time when Cooper was to resume giving evidence. It was not paid. To complicate matters, Cooper said that Adler had offered him $500,000 via an inflated property deal, but that he had refused. It was that sort of evidence.

'Mr Adler, if I could use the words, tried to word me up,' said Cooper, to which Hammerschlag retorted: 'I want to suggest to you that the suggestion that anybody could successfully word you up is an absurd one.'

Which might have been a compliment of sorts.

Where the evidence got very interesting was over what Adler may have said while Cooper gave him a lift back over the Sydney Harbour Bridge in his BMW X5 four-wheel-drive after the second meeting on 13 October. The judge suppressed two pages of evidence, the only two in more than 19,000 pages of transcript taken by the Royal Commission. Because of the fact that a non-publication order was made by the judge, this book will have to leave alone the topic of what was said. But you can be sure it was not polite, and that the unlikely relationship between the two men was now well and truly over.

The Royal Commission chose not to pursue two issues when the counsel assisting summed up its evidence in January 2003: one, the 'short selling' issue; and two, the Sunday morning hotel meetings. In a magnificent piece of understatement, the counsel assisting the commission said 'the evidence was controversial and contradictory'.

He added that 'On the current state of the evidence, it is not appropriate for the commission to attempt to make definitive findings of fact as to what actually occurred or what contraventions of the law might actually have occurred.' That would have put Brad, Ray and Rodney in a sort of three-cornered contest that effectively came down to deciding who was telling whoppers. The Sunday morning meetings were simpler, with only two versions to wrestle with.

But even if these conflicting statements constituted a noisy blind alley in the investigations of the Royal Commission, they shone some fascinating light on the behaviour and attitudes of all three men.

CHAPTER 17

'KEEPING THE LIE ALIVE'

WHEN COMPANIES COLLAPSE, all those frivolous corporate expenses, lavish dinners and first-class air travel have a nasty habit of reappearing in the wreckage and drawing attention to themselves. The counsel assisting the HIH Royal Commission certainly did not pull many punches when it came to highlighting some of the more obvious examples of big-noting that seemed to have occurred in 1999 and 2000 at the same time as HIH was beginning to keel over.

Ray Williams opened his testimony in August 2002 with a stirring speech saying 'I may have been foolish and perhaps at times gullible but I never acted dishonestly.' He went on to say, 'I did not lie, I did not deceive and I did not seek, nor did I receive, any improper benefits.' Those protestations notwithstanding, Wayne Martin chose to start his questioning about the connection between Williams' honorary doctorate from Monash University, awarded in 2000, and the donation of $2.2 million of HIH's funds not long before. Indeed, the company gave $5.6 million to charity in that year, while at the same time it was beginning to have trouble paying out on claims.

Mr Williams' barrister, Robert Richter, described the questions as 'at best a cheap shot and at worst an attempt to besmirch my client's reputation' but the judge countered that he was 'intensely interested' in the culture of HIH. What the judge wanted to know was how a hard-driving man like Williams who had a strong low church Anglican upbringing and a ferocious sense of loyalty could get things so fantastically out of proportion in the last two or three years of HIH's existence.

Public irritation at his excessive expenditure did not take long to show itself. Michael West, an experienced knockabout journalist on *The Australian* who was writing the column 'Margin Call', accidentally touched a nerve when he wrote a spoof column about Ray Williams having bought a first-class air ticket for his briefcase, and how the briefcase was described on the ticket. 'Casey Williams AM' was how he pretended Williams had described it. Unfortunately, he wrote the vital phrase 'just kidding' at the top of the next item in the column, rather than at the foot of the spoof item. A huge number of people 'clipped' the spoof item alone and passed it around on the Internet. One version appeared under the heading 'It's a shame capital punishment has been abolished'. Several of the counsel assisting received e-mails from friends asking them whereabouts in the Royal Commission transcript it was and one or two began to assume they had dropped off or failed to notice. West himself had several people send him the cutting with notes such as 'Have you seen this?'

West conceded ruefully that he had never had such a reaction to anything he had written, before or since. He had created an urban myth, and like all such stories there was a touch of plausibility about it. For a start, Williams had been one of both Qantas and British Airways' best customers, flying out of Australia an average of three times a month for years. People who had flown with him said he always went easy on the food and drink, but he did indeed often have a spare seat beside him. They concluded that, as a prized client, he would get allocated a seat beside the empty one wherever possible. His favourite seat was 3K, in first class of course. Even in 2003 he was spotted in the Qantas Chairman's Lounge, so his reputation in airline circles has well outlasted his corporate clout.

One story had it that in the early 1990s, not long after CE Heath listed, he had heard a report that someone was planning a bid for parent company CE Heath plc and he had been unable to contact Peter Presland, the relevant UK executive, to check the rumour. He jumped on a plane to London and, on arrival, found his trip had been completely unnecessary. Presland was able to assure him that there was no bid, and he returned almost immediately to Australia. It happened at a weekend and, while his staff were taking it easy, Williams was bouncing back and forth too fast to get jet lag. 'It was a bit of a macho thing,' remembered one executive. 'You jumped on a plane and did whatever you needed to do then came back as soon as possible.' He noted that by the time of HIH's worst excesses, Williams was flying to a lot of 'meet and greet' functions that were of marginal importance. His wife Rita racked up $38,165 in travel expenses in 2000 on those trips, according to credit card records.

Another story was that Williams accumulated so many frequent flyer points with Qantas and British Airways that they began to give him gardening equipment for his Dural property — there was even a ride-on lawn mower — since he was never going to be able to redeem the points. He was alleged at one stage to be the biggest spending client for one of those airlines, worldwide.

Lycurgus of Sparta once wrote: 'When falls on man the anger of the gods, first from his mind they banish understanding.' Henry Wadsworth Longfellow refined that into: 'Those whom the gods would destroy, they first make mad.' At first glance you might not think that Ray Williams had much to do with classical tragedy, but there is one underlying plot line in every classical tragedy that goes like this: the hero is invariably a strong man with an innate belief in himself who goes from wise to foolish because of hubris, the tragic flaw, the pride that comes before a fall; he then commits some cathartic act that brings about his own destruction. Put Ray Williams in a toga and you can see his purchase of FAI was the cathartic act.

If you can't cast Ray Williams as a villain it's not hard to nail him for a fool, and a proud one at that. His strengths were inseparable from his weaknesses. He could be accurately described as single-minded, strong, generous and loyal, but then again he could just as well be criticised for being narrow-minded, autocratic, lavish and clannish. He had always been something of a paradox in his dealings with the press, too. While he was giving evidence at the Royal Commission in August 2002, the television cameras followed him back and forth as he crossed George Street in Sydney between the commission office and the Westin Hotel opposite. He carefully avoided making any comment but on one occasion he re-crossed the street for the cameras, without even being asked to do so.

One of the early allegations levelled against him involved huge generosity with HIH's money. Fred Holland, an old friend from London, was badly hit in 1993 by Lloyd's 1990 disaster and found himself being asked for more than £200,000 to cover losses. He wrote to Williams to explain his situation and Williams lent him almost $500,000 Australian unsecured, and interest free. As Wayne Martin pointed out to him, leaving that loan running for seven years deprived the HIH shareholders of some $300,000 in interest. Williams' explanation was that Holland had been chairman of CE Heath in London, the company whose Australian arm eventually became HIH, and Holland had been a 'very strong supporter' of the company. He again admitted that he hadn't consulted the board about the loan because he believed it was within his authority to make it. This is where generosity becomes folly.

When one considers that at one stage in 2000 Ray Williams ordered a $1600 box of cigars from Alfred Dunhill in London's West End for his old friend Holland, using HIH's money, it is not too difficult to grasp the intensity of shareholder anger. What Ray Williams saw was an old friend of the company who deserved a present; what the deprived policyholders and shareholders saw was callous prodigality. It should be noted that when Williams handed over the cigars he had not even asked for the money back and, when he was finally put under pressure to get it repaid, he stated that the original principal would be repaid. Shortly thereafter a number of entries appeared in HIH's books to infer that it had. But there remains some doubt as to whether it really was repaid at all. The judge referred the affair to ASIC for possible civil prosecution.

That was a prime example of Williams lavishing money on a person outside the company, but there were hundreds of painful stories about extravagance with staff. Stuart Korchinski, a young Canadian who moved up in HIH from internal auditor to general manager level, became notorious among HIH staff for the generous treatment he enjoyed. In May 2000 Williams gave him $17,000 worth of air tickets for him and his family to go to Canada after his father died, convincing the sceptics that Korchinski was an anointed successor to someone. At a subsequent management 'love in' in North Queensland, HIH managers were surprised to see a helicopter land on a pontoon beside the boat they were aboard out on the Barrier Reef. They were even more surprised when Ray Williams and Korchinski climbed into it and flew back to Cairns, leaving everyone else to get home the slow way. But plans changed when Korchinski's job was transferred across to the Allianz group in 2001. His payout was increased from $835,000 to $910,000 thanks to a note sent by Ray Williams to company secretary Fred Lo on 29 December 2000, even though Williams had resigned as chief executive. Korchinski was also allowed to buy his ten-year-old company car — a Saab convertible — for $1000, a deal that you could not even get close to in the real world.

It was around that time that Williams put a $700 tip on top of a $3162.50 bill at the Nautilus Restaurant in Port Douglas but that seems to have been standard fare. In that year he added a $600 tip to a $2018 bill at Forty One in Sydney, and $700 on top of a $2197.50 bill at the Pier Restaurant. While his wife Rita was spending that $38,165 on travel in 2000, he spent $157,796 on air travel and it was not at the back of the plane.

When Williams was being given a bumpy ride over his generosity with the company's money towards Monash University and other charitable causes, his barrister Robert Richter pointed out that the donations were ratified by HIH's board. Wayne Martin countered that the board was only asked to ratify the donations after they were made, and then they were given a single-line item in the accounts to tick off. If HIH paid, Williams got the benefit. The Ray Williams Mass Spectrometry Unit at the University of New South Wales benefited from a $1.9 million donation from HIH, with nothing from Williams. He did donate personally to other charities at a rate of about one dollar for five company dollars but the citation for his Order of Australia, awarded in 1998, specifically lists the $1.9 million donation by HIH.

What does that say? Presumably, that Ray Williams ran CE Heath Australia Ltd and then HIH as though they were his own operations. He seemed oblivious to the fact that a listed company has a board and shareholders who need to be told what is happening to their money.

One element of Williams' patriarchy was his insistence on staff training, a great idea in moderation but in which he, not unexpectedly, ended up going overboard.

Staff aged twenty-one found themselves being sent off to Port Stephens, north of Sydney, for a week at a time, with Williams and Fodera making lightning *deus ex machina* visits by seaplane. The induction courses, run at the rate of about twelve a year, took staff away from junior jobs. Terry Cassidy in particular, who ran the Australian operations, used to despair of the disruption. But far worse were the two 'world tour' extravaganzas which took groups of fifteen senior staff away for weeks at a time, first in 1998 and then in 2000. The 1998 trip was particularly memorable since everyone who attended was dressed in a made-to-measure blue blazer and beige trousers. The big excursions appear to have been, in best HIH tradition, all male affairs.

First stop was London, where HIH ended up losing about $1.7 billion, then it was on to California where the company only lost about $600 million. It was like a tour of the battlefields, except they were not being told they had lost.

Then the group flew to relatively unscathed territory on the east coast of the US, which took in a trip to Harvard. 'We got off the bus for long enough to get a lecture, although no one seems to remember what it was about,' said a veteran. But he had been to Harvard.

'Corporate governance' is a term that has had some bad press, since it is much misunderstood. It got a bad name in the late 1990s as being some sort of politically correct, new puritanism that was a 'must have' in any corporate annual report. Good corporate governance is all about running a company honestly and transparently. It's a bit like democracy: it might not be the most efficient form of government — that is usually conceded to be benevolent dictatorship — but it beats tyranny hands down. Good governance is just democracy applied to the business world, with concepts like independence and accountability playing a major role. Good corporate governance, for instance, is having a chief executive who does not just say he is answerable to the board, but genuinely is. The chairman should also be able to hire and fire the chief executive. Good governance is about making sure the company does not just have an audit committee, but it has one that works. Not only should it be a subset of the main board, not including the chief executive, but the company's internal auditors should be able to report directly to it and not to the chief executive.

In his evidence to the commission Greg Waters, the HIH internal auditor, revealed that he was sufficiently bothered about Ray Williams' decision to count money earmarked for policyholder dividends of Great States Insurance in the US as 'reserves' that he sent a report direct to the company's chairman, Geoffrey Cohen, rather than the audit committee. Not that it helped much in the long run. After Neville Head resigned from the HIH board, his place on the audit committee was taken by Cohen. That broke almost every rule of corporate governance, since the chairman of the audit committee is not meant to chair the company. This one did.

Another critical element of good corporate governance is having independent minds on the board. Ask ten experts what that means and you will get fifteen replies, but the consensus is that well-run companies should have a majority of independent directors. HIH's board was unfortunately a rest home for old partners in Arthur Andersen, to a degree which caused major heartburn as long ago as 1995 at Winterthur, the Swiss insurer which bought a 51 per cent stake in HIH in that year.

Willi Schürpf, one of the Winterthur nominees on the HIH board, noted in his statement to the commission that Winterthur was concerned about keeping Andersen on as the company's auditor when there were so many ex-Andersen partners on the board, particularly once Dominic Fodera joined in 1995. 'There was a real risk that Arthur Andersen's position and independence may be, or may be seen to be, compromised,' he wrote. It was.

There were some brave attempts by Andersen auditors to get round Ray Williams and to explain to the bemused non-executive directors what was really going on, but they made little difference and one of the auditors, Alan Davies, was effectively moved off the HIH audit for his efforts.

Davies wanted to show them that although the company declared a loss of $73 million in 1998, the real result was closer to a $230 million loss. The difference was some $157 million worth of upward adjustments that he and his colleagues had in fact ratified.

For instance, HIH had taken $50 million straight out of the prudential margins of its US operations. Alan Davies did not like what was happening, even if much of the reclassification of assets was legitimate under the existing rules, so he and colleague Jonathan Pye made a presentation on 25 February 1999.

The document showed that while the company's recorded 'core underwriting loss' went from $27 million in 1996 to $73 million in 1998, the real underlying loss trend was $50 million in 1996 growing to about $230 million in 1998. They never did find out if the message got through.

Meanwhile, actuary David Slee's role was another shining example of a consultant who does not actually get the chance to consult. He was described to veteran Canadian regulator John Palmer as 'the definitive compliant actuary', a definition Palmer repeated in his report to APRA.

Justice Neville Owen asked director Robert Stitt, QC, how much discussion there was on the board or on the audit committee 'about the assumptions on which the actuaries' figures were based and the auditors' review of the actuaries' work was based'. Stitt had to reply: 'I don't recall there ever being any discussion about assumptions, methodology or process of reasoning.'

Just one of those assumptions that Slee was told to use was that the cost of handling future claims would be 2 per cent of reserves. Ms Estelle Pearson, an actuary with Deloitte Trowbridge who came as the last witness to the Royal Commission in late November 2002, said that more realistic assumptions were for between 5 and 6 per cent for long-tail claims and between 4 and 8 per cent for short-tail claims. Since by 30 June 1999 HIH was setting aside $3.69 billion in undiscounted reserves, it appears that Slee was underestimating the cost of handling future claims by around $110 million.

It should also be noted that his numbers used a predicted cost of 1.49 per cent, which was even more dangerous.

And the only people that Slee was reporting to, in calculating the biggest item in HIH's balance sheet, were Ray Williams and Dominic Fodera. If there was ever an argument between actuary and management as to how much reserves to set aside, it was Williams and Fodera who invariably won.

Dominic Fodera told the Royal Commission he had *not* ordered Slee to change his calculations to suit the desires of management, but a memo Slee wrote to him on about 10 August 1999 said he was finding it difficult to 'update' his reserves to reflect management's estimates.

'I hold little chance of a significant reduction in some of those areas,' Slee wrote to Fodera. 'Even if we manage to mine out of the as-yet-unfinished numbers a further $50 million, it seems that it may be calling on too much to ask to certify a ... level below $2900 million,' he said. He was talking about what he thought was the right discounted equivalent of the $3.69 billion number, although Fodera wanted to get to a number below that, such as $2.649 billion.

The accounts of HIH at 30 June 2000 showed that the company had a surplus of assets over liabilities of $940 million, being the difference between assets of $8.3 billion and liabilities of $7.4 billion.

Slee was discussing the new rules that APRA had just brought in a week before on 1 July 2002 demanding higher levels of reserving and compelling actuaries to 'blow the whistle' on problems. He said that if the new rules had been in existence in 1999, he would have had to 'blow the whistle' on HIH's reserves as at 30 September of that year. Why? 'Because they just weren't there,' he said.

Fodera conceded that in early 1999 HIH had booked reserves which were 'at the very low end of actuaries' and auditors' tolerable limits'. To alarm the actuary sounds like standard practice, but alarming the auditors at the same time was something new. HIH was seriously sick and getting sicker.

Jeff Simpson had calculated (conservatively, as it turned out) that when HIH was taking over FAI, the two companies between them had a hole in their reserves of $265 million. But because like everyone else at HIH he was still coming to grips with FAI, he estimated FAI's problem at $50 million. In fact it was closer to $200 million, as HIH discovered later in 1999, which put the hole at a figure more like $415 million.

But if that was bad, almost everything that happened at HIH to rectify the problems was worse.

The first thing that happened, and one of the most constructive, was that the two auditors, Alan Davies and Jon Pye, invited Neville Head and Justin Gardener to lunch in March 1999. Head is a lawyer but Gardener was another former Andersen man, a national audit partner who retired from Andersen in August 1998 and was invited to join the HIH board in the same month. He joined the board formally on 2 December 1998 and although the board was getting the mushroom treatment, he was a good point of contact as he had a good general understanding of insurance.

Davies and Pye told the two directors that if HIH's insurance underwriting results got any worse they would have a severe effect on profitability. In other words, every possible adjustment to make the results look better had been made, and any further losses would have to be recorded as what they were: losses.

The lunch should have been a good idea, since it was the only chance the auditors had to get two directors (and audit committee members) on their own for a serious talk.

Unfortunately, Ray Williams hit the roof.

It was the first recorded instance in the seven years of HIH's listed life where Ray Williams was not fully briefed on what was going on. Williams saw his omission from the meeting as leaving him 'out of the loop', which was entirely true. That was the whole point. That did not shock Head, who knew all too well that there was a risk of backlash from the team-conscious Williams.

But when Williams said to him 'there appear to be people working against me', Head experienced what he called a change of view on Williams. He never used the word paranoid, but he clearly felt it.

Head subsequently presented a list of his concerns to chairman Geoffrey Cohen in May of that year, most particularly that he wanted to get the audit committee 'more involved in the process for determination of the financial results than they have in the past'. His proposals were not taken up and he resigned on 5 August 1999.

Justin Gardener fared little better. He too handed Williams a list of suggested changes to strategy in May 1999, particularly asking for more information for the board, and Williams handed it straight back to him saying that HIH's executive management had matters well in hand.

His evidence in September 2002 was very damning, saying that he found Williams 'arrogant, high-handed and ignorant' in doing that.

While Williams could have been excused for thinking lawyer Neville Head might not know much about insurance, he couldn't possibly believe that that applied to Gardener. Gardener had signed the HIH prospectus back in 1992 as investigating accountant.

Gardener said he was 'stunned' by Williams' action and that at the time he thought Williams' behaviour was related to his age (Williams was sixty-two) or that Williams felt the need to be respected. 'I began to think later that perhaps he was reacting in a way because he knew things that perhaps I didn't know and that he was perhaps worried about covering things up,' he said.

If Williams was being high-handed with his directors about being left out of the loop, he was close to feral with his auditors.

He made it clear he was 'annoyed' at Davies' actions and got Dominic Fodera to contact Chris Knoblanche, the managing partner of Andersen in Australia. If, as is meant to happen, an audit company is deadly serious about doing its job, then there would have been an internal meeting at Andersen between all the chiefs and Davies would have explained why he had had to go round Williams.

But instead, on 29 April 1999, Knoblanche was listening intently to Dominic Fodera tell him that his boss, Ray Williams, felt Davies was 'not bending over backwards to work through HIH's problems' and that Davies was too 'matter of fact' for Mr Williams. Williams had told Fodera he wanted someone more like Justin Gardener because he found that Gardener was 'more businesslike in thinking through problems and issues', a recommendation that Gardener has had trouble living down since.

But Fodera didn't have his heart in the role. He said he felt uncomfortable criticising his old colleague Alan Davies since he 'really didn't have any problem' with his performance.

On any logical measure, the Andersen people should have pointed out to Fodera that Davies was only doing his job, and tough luck if Williams found him inflexible. That is what auditors are for. They might even have pointed out that Andersen rated HIH as a 'high-risk' client. But instead, Knoblanche promised Williams that Davies would be replaced with someone more suitable.

Questioned in the Royal Commission, the normally confident Knoblanche had an awkward time explaining that the decision to replace Davies had nothing to do with the fact that the HIH audit was worth $2.4 million in fees to Andersen for the 1999 audit.

He admitted that he was not familiar with Australian auditing standard 202, which requires auditors to use 'professional scepticism' in dealing with their clients, and conceded that auditors at Andersen owed part of their in-house ratings to their ability to generate fees for Andersen for non-audit services. He said it never entered his head that such cross-selling might compromise the auditors' independence.

After Fodera's Byzantine meeting with Knoblanche on 29 April, where he was supposed to criticise Davies when he believed Davies had done the right thing, events moved fast.

Knoblanche arranged a meeting with Willliams at 9.00 a.m. on the following Monday, 3 May. Williams' evidence was that, without his even suggesting that Davies be replaced, Knoblanche had done so, although Knoblanche said he did not recall the subject coming up.

Whatever was said, Andersen effectively raised the white flag by 'rotating' Alan Davies, as the euphemism put it, off the HIH audit. The client's fanciful desire for a 'helpful' auditor had been briskly and subserviently addressed, even if there was not the slightest suggestion that Davies had done anything wrong. And in his evidence on 28 October Knoblanche admitted that 'it would be inappropriate for an audit client to veto [an auditor] and it would raise significant concerns as to the nature and the reasons for the veto.'

Everything seemed to have been back to front. Andersen had ticked off a result even though it had $157 million more of 'padding' in it than they wanted, their experienced man had explained this to two of the more conscientious members of the audit committee — as was his duty — and he was being marched off to the gallows.

The only consolation in that episode was that he ended up being replaced by John Buttle, who was the man who ended up blowing the whistle on the whole Pacific Eagle Equities mess.

IF HIH HAD problems with an autocratic chief executive and a board that wasn't even shown details of the company's reserves — or lack of reserves — FAI Insurance also had a fatal flaw. FAI also had independent directors and an audit committee chaired by a Sydney investment banker who was independent, Geoff Hill. But it had a chief executive whose family owned 30 per cent of the company. John Landerer, a Sydney lawyer, was chairman of FAI from shortly after Larry Adler's death in 1988 until HIH took over FAI in 1998. He was an old friend of Larry Adler's: it is said that Larry had so many complicated share deals arranged only by word of mouth that when Larry knew he was dying, he had to summon John Landerer to explain them all to him. Landerer had offered to act as temporary chairman of the company but, as often happens in situations where a regent has to oversee a young king in the making, his stay was extended.

On paper, Rodney was well equipped to run such an organisation. He had acquired a good 'business' education but, aside from the emphasis all chartered accounting firms put on the principle of audit independence, there was precious little formal training offered in business ethics. He gave journalist Anne Hyland a glimpse of his strengths and, inadvertently, his weaknesses in May 2001. 'I am arrogant,' he began. 'I'm very black and white. Either I like a person or I don't. Either I think they're very intelligent or I don't. I'm very staccato. I don't like procrastinators. I had a lot of responsibility thrust on my shoulders at a young age. I know the point I like to make.' He had been asked about himself, but after thirteen vertical pronouns in a few lines there was precious little evidence of genuine introspection.

If Larry had been able to retire and oversee Rodney's assumption of executive duties, that might have made some difference, but even then Larry was still Larry. Rodney overstated the value of FAI's assets and understated the value of its liabilities because that is exactly what his father had done. Rodney has two degrees, a network of school friends and a personal drive that is very unusual in inherited wealth, but there were gaps in Rodney's real education that were to make him more vulnerable to financial disaster than the man who empties your dustbin. At the time of publication of this book Rodney holds the record for the longest disqualification from serving as a director of a public company that has ever been handed out in Australia: twenty years. Rodney's problem is and was that he had ten years in which he never appeared to stuff things up. He always had his father to blame for most of what was wrong with FAI; even though Rodney is as likely as Larry to have ended up lending over $500 million to Alan Bond in early 1988.

That all happened on Larry's watch, and Rodney was able to paint an accurate and flattering picture of the young man who had a hard job forced upon him by his father's untimely death. He could not be completely frank about how crook FAI was, since a lot of its structural problems were caused by his father's entrepreneurial approach, plus there was the little matter of not frightening the shareholders, but he could point to the share market crash in 1987, Larry's death in 1988, and other events since as burdens he had to carry.

One of Rodney's most obvious shortcomings was his tendency to come all over grave and pompous at moments of change in FAI, as stockbroker Michael Crowley and others knew too well.

When he resigned from FAI on 19 January 1999, Adler sent what must stand as one of the most absurd messages that the ASX has ever received. Addressed to the companies manager at ASX, it began: 'Dear Sir, Farewell. My tenure as chief executive is nearly over. My life at FAI is at the same stanza in time.' He was aiming at Shakespeare but it came out more like McGonagall. It got worse, although there was a moment of clarity when he wrote: 'Can one distil ten years into a few words of advice (assuming anyone is interested)?' He finished it off with a paean to capitalism, saying that the invisible hand that regulates the economy is not the hand of politicians, journalists, bankers or even bureaucrats. Rather, 'The invisible hand is the notion of free enterprise and the purity of its endeavours for without it the world as we have come to know it would disappear into a sea of mis-allocated resources.'

Where Rodney developed impressive skills was in playing the investor networks like a violin during the technology boom that started in late 1999 and ended with a painful thud in April 2000. By networking with a number of big financial players in small stocks, Rodney Adler was able to lift the price of the stocks he was investing in. That made him popular among the circles in Sydney's eastern suburbs that he moved in, much more so than the people with whom he did business. Many say he paid his bills as late as possible, sometimes on the steps of the court, then said, 'No hard feelings, it's just the way we do business.' Those people have been enjoying what they now see as his comeuppance.

An interview he did in 1999 or 2000 with Brad Cooper gives an unsettling insight into Adler's view of how business is done. The interview was a part of 'Brad Cooper's Mentor Club', a scheme Cooper devised whereby successful people could pass on their secrets to entrepreneurs starting out. At one point Adler talked about the importance of 'Keeping the Lie Alive'. 'Now we have classic Adler,' exclaimed Cooper. 'You must keep the lie alive,' said Adler. 'By that I mean you can't walk into your supplier and say, by the way, I'm having a really rough time, would you mind giving me a little more credit.' Adler explained. 'Sure Rod, thanks for telling us,' he suggested sarcastically as the likely reaction. Adler then said it was important not to be caught up in your own propaganda. 'You can live the lie, you can deceive everyone, but don't deceive yourself,' he said, deadpan. 'If you believe in my philosophy of marketing it's going to be very hard for anyone to be totally truthful to anyone else,' he went on.

Because of all these attitudes and his behaviour, Rodney Adler has acquired the painful distinction of being one of the least popular figures in the Sydney business community. And over recent years there's been no lack of competition for that particular accolade. Comedian Vince Sorrenti told this joke at a business function in Sydney in late 2002. A gunman gets into a lift and finds himself face to face with Saddam Hussein, Osama bin Laden and Rodney Adler. His gun has only two bullets in it, so what does he do? He shoots Rodney Adler twice. That got a loud cheer.

CHAPTER 18

PACIFIC EAGLE EQUITIES

IF THERE WAS ever an episode which summed up HIH management's dysfunctional approach to its mounting problems in 2000, it was Rodney Adler's seamlessly successful campaign to get Ray Williams to sponsor Pacific Eagle Equities.

Despite the fact that Adler had by then been tormenting Williams and his fellow directors for more than a year about how they had paid too much for FAI, in mid–2000 Williams authorised Adler to set up a $10 million investment company using HIH's money. Adler duly spent the money on HIH shares, which is illegal, and on burned-out technology stocks from his own portfolio, at grossly inflated prices.

By this time, according to counsel assisting the HIH Royal Commission, HIH was insolvent. Justice Neville Owen declined to offer a view on that in his report, one of the biggest omissions in an otherwise very thorough document. HIH directors know that insolvent trading is one of the worst sins of which a company director can be accused. HIH had lost somewhere in the region of $1.7 billion in the UK and around $750 million in the US, it was heading for the biggest loss in its history, and here was senior management authorising a $10 million jaunt at the behest not of junior management, but of a non-executive director who was angling for the chief executive's job. It was as if a misfit bunch of winter holidaymakers had forgotten their differences for long enough to build a snowman, while above them an avalanche was careering off the peak to sweep them all away.

The Pacific Eagle Equities affair, as it became known, took on a life of
its own because it was 'done and dusted', in legal terms at least, in the
first half of 2002. At that time the HIH Royal Commission was barely out
of second gear, which caused it to restrict discussion to the issue of
whether there had been 'errors of corporate governance' in the episode. It
might have been easier if the commission had turned the question on its
head and tried to find any evidence at all of anyone trying to effect
corporate governance. The commission wouldn't have found much: for a
start, the HIH board and shareholders never got to even hear about the
affair until it was over and some $6.8 million of the money had effectively
disappeared. HIH's investment committee, of which Adler was a member,
was also left out of the loop.

It was investigated separately by regulator ASIC before the commission
even began sitting in late 2001, thanks mainly to the fact that ASIC was
presented with an A4 cardboard box that contained enough incriminating
documents to allow the case to stand alone. ASIC began a civil penalty
action, a special weapon in the ASIC armoury and one whose maximum
penalties stop short of gaol but can involve lengthy disqualification from
acting as directors, and includes provisions for heavy fines. Justice Neville
Owen's report uses those provisions as a back-up to its criminal referrals.
On 25 May 2001, when the action was launched, Adler was at the Mirage
resort at Port Douglas in north Queensland. It was an unfortunate
coincidence. Aside from the fact that Adler was photographed by the pool
in his Speedos, there were plenty of sceptics who remembered that the
resort with the illusory title was built by the late and unlamented
entrepreneur Christopher Skase.

When it came to Pacific Eagle Equities there was absolutely no doubt
that it was Adler doing the persuading: for a start, it was his sort of
project. While Ray Williams liked to see himself as a big-picture man, $10
million was just the sort of sum of money that Adler liked to play with,
particularly if it was somebody else's. Justice Santow of the New South
Wales Supreme Court, who heard the case, also concluded that it was
Adler doing the pushing, and disqualified him from acting as a company
director for twenty years. Williams was not found as culpable, but his
positive reaction to Adler's idea was to land him a ten-year suspension as a
director. At sixty-seven, that is as good as a life sentence. Both men have
appealed the decisions, which also included the imposition of hefty fines
and the demand for financial reparation totalling almost $7 million.

Dominic Fodera, HIH's finance director, was fined $5000 for letting all this happen.

But that was in 2002. Back in 2000, Ray Williams had become such a convert to Adler's enthusiasm for technology stocks that he was rhetorically asking his investment managers whether one of them would be 'another Rodney'. They wouldn't, because they did not want to be. They had spent the last year trying to sort out the mess of unlisted stocks and unwritten profit-sharing arrangements that characterised the FAI portfolio. There was also a big list of loans, many with no chance of being paid back, totalling at least $20 million.

To Williams, who was not concerning himself with such trivia, Adler was an investment dynamo who had been a key player in One.Tel, which by mid–2000 was beginning to slip but was still worth $3 billion.

HIH had been able to net some $42 million on that deal so to Ray Williams, Rodney was a genius. And Rodney knew how to get him in.

On 9 June 2000 he wrote to Williams to explain that Drenmex (an Adler company) would like to borrow $10 million from HIH 'for the purpose of venture capital and share trading'. What was in it for HIH?

'Drenmex would like absolute discretion to invest the funds as it sees fit but would report profits and/or losses on a quarterly basis,' Adler explained. 'The management of Drenmex suggests it would like to take 10% of profits to initially prove itself to HIH management with no management fee and only after HIH receives interest on its money at 10% per annum,' he continued.

In other words, there was lots of upside, a 10 per cent return and no fee payable. Williams, who had spent a lifetime building a reputation as a hard man to convince, fell straight for it. He did not dwell on the arithmetic, which was that HIH was putting up 98.8 per cent of the money unsecured while Pacific Eagle, of which Adler was the only director, was to get 10 per cent of the income.

The very same day Williams replied that the proposal was 'fair and reasonable since no management fees will be charged to HIH. I will therefore arrange for these funds to be transferred to you early next week.'

Note that there was nothing as vulgar as an investment target named.

Perhaps Williams assumed that Adler would be finding a whole new group of exciting stocks to buy into, a hard ask when the technology boom had burst about three months before and little pieces were still fluttering earthwards.

What Adler did was to place an order to buy 2 million shares in HIH on the morning of 15 July, at a time when the share price was threatening to drop down through $1 for the first time.

Meanwhile, HIH's lawyers Minter Ellison were still examining the investment structure, which involved a trust called the Australian Equity Unit Trust, to check whether it was legal for a new company called Pacific Eagle Equities to buy shares in HIH using HIH's money. PEE, as it was called, replaced Drenmex before the exercise began.

The answer was that it wasn't and even with the complex structure being devised it wasn't, although Minters partner Leigh Brown said it was. Companies have long been prevented from buying their own shares, except in the case of a formal 'buy-back', which is subject to all sorts of strict regulations.

Minters should never have become involved, since one of their partners, Margaret Taylor, had already been asked to give Rodney Adler advice about the project. Minters was therefore advising both sides of the deal, the borrower and the lender, and still managed to give incorrect advice. That was because Rodney Adler misled Brown about what he was actually doing. Imagine a conversation between two old men on a bench, one of whom does not want to explain and the other does not want to hear the full story, and you get the idea.

Questioned by the Royal Commission about the advice, Brown memorably noted that he had not asked certain questions because it was not his role to do so.

Tackled later in 2000 about the matter by HIH auditor John Buttle, Brown, according to Buttle's evidence, said that he knew that the affair stank 'to the high heaven' but that it was extremely difficult to prosecute a case of a company buying its own shares. Buttle's evidence was that he then said to Brown, 'Leigh, you haven't exactly covered yourself in glory in this affair', and Brown had hung up. Unfortunately this alleged conversation was never put to Brown in cross-examination.

PEE went on to spend $3.97 million on HIH shares in the latter two weeks of June 2000, causing the HIH share price to move up from about $1.02 to $1.07. The haste was almost indecent since the trust involved was not fully set up until at least a week after the first purchases were made.

The price rise was a boost to Adler's big holding in HIH and also a help to HIH.

But if there were major question marks over the ethics of propping up the HIH share price, it was a model of measured investment practice compared to what happened to another $4 million of the money.

Rodney Adler used that money to get himself out of a raft of worthless and near-worthless dot.com investments that he had been caught with when the technology boom collapsed three months earlier. The shares were sold by Adler's family company, Adler Corporation, and the price paid was exactly what Adler Corp had paid for them at the height of the boom.

Adler's counsel David Hammerschlag, SC, made the memorable statements that ASIC's claims against his client had 'nothing to do with the collapse of HIH', that it was a 'discrete little dispute' about an investment vehicle and a 'modest sum of money'.

It is true that $10 million is indeed small change compared with the $5.3 billion in premiums that HIH so conspicuously failed to collect, but it is a lot more than almost all of the policyholders' insurance claims against HIH that went unpaid when the company collapsed. Mr Hammerschlag's comment about its relevance to the collapse of HIH was correct in arithmetical terms, but in cultural terms PEE was relevant because it was a nonsense that would never have got off the drawing board in a properly run company.

The shares that Adler backed into Pacific Eagle Equities were almost all in cash-starved start-up situations that by mid–2000 were dying like plants without water.

There was a nominal $500,000 worth of shares in an on-line retailer called dstore, $820,000 worth of shares in something called Planet Soccer and $2.45 million worth of shares in Nomad Technology. None of the companies was listed and Nomad, for instance, had had its float pulled by Ord Minnett just prior to 15 June 2000. A note circulated to shareholders on 26 June stated that the delay in getting the company floated would leave the company with a cash deficit of $8.6 million at the end of the financial year in four days' time and that the company's auditors and directors 'require a minimum $3 million to be raised for working capital'.

It is clear that Adler had very much wanted 'out' of Nomad in June of 2000, since he asked an unofficial intermediary, Bradley Prout of BT Australia, at that time to find him a buyer. On 25 September Prout wrote to Nomad shareholders saying that possible buyer Leighton Holdings 'have now pulled out with little chance of any resumption of negotiations'.

So on 29 September Adler must have been very happy when Adler Corp sold half its holding in Nomad for $2.539 million or $1.40 per share, for which it had paid either 20c or 70c per share some time in about early 1999. Nomad failed to raise any more money and went into receivership on 18 January 2001.

PEE also lent $160,000 to morehuman pty ltd, a company associated with a property developer friend of Adler's called Ghassi Bayni, and $200,000 to a property company connected to Adler called Pacific Capital Partners which had a development under way at North Steyne in Manly.

By the time ASIC laid the charges it concluded that all the assets and loans except the last one were worthless, which put Adler in a clear conflict of interest because he did not tell HIH about how sick the investments were. Here he was, a director of a company that was relieving him of a big pile of unsaleable investments, and he was bypassing the board and shareholders by using this 'arm's length' company Pacific Eagle Equities to do the buying. Nor were the long-suffering staff of HIH's investment department being told what was going on.

That did not impress Justice Santow, but what impressed him even less was that once Ray Williams told Adler in September 2000 to wind up the company and sell the HIH shares, Adler sold big lines of his own shares in HIH at better prices before he sold PEE out of its by then thoroughly friendless shares in HIH.

Adler was getting around 65c a share for his personal holdings in HIH (which he had got from accepting the HIH takeover back in early 1999) but by the time the PEE holdings in HIH were finally sold off on 26 September, the price had sunk to 49c. For instance, Adler reported selling a parcel of 2.5 million of his own shares at an average 67c between 18 September and 20 September 2000. The stock's price dropped from $1 to 50c in ten days at that point and Pacific Eagle had lost $2.1 million trading HIH shares in just over two months.

As ASIC's counsel Robert Macfarlan, QC, pointed out in his final submission to Justice Santow, Adler had failed to show contrition or remorse for his conduct, and had made no full and frank disclosure to the court. His activities led to 'a high potential for improper conduct on his part to cause harm'.

In his judgment handed down on 14 March 2002 (almost exactly a year after HIH collapsed), Justice Santow noted that Adler's breaches of the law had been 'the most serious of all'. He said that Adler's 'true purpose' was shown by his selling his own shares in HIH before he sold

PEE's shares. 'His real purpose was to maximise the value of his own HIH holding even at the cost of (the Australian Equities Unit Trust, of which PEE was trustee) and HIH.'

Further, Justice Santow refuted a claim that Adler had made when PEE bought the HIH shares in the first place, when he said it was to make a quick profit on the resale of HIH shares. He also produced another reminder that Ray Williams was more than just a hapless victim in the affair, noting that Williams gave 'false and misleading' information to HIH's audit committee in October 2000 when he indicated that the PEE matter had been 'fixed, [and] that the trust had been brought to an end'. Justice Santow did, however, produce a familiar refrain on behalf of Ray Williams when he said that Williams 'did not profit in the way that Mr Adler and Adler Corporation profited'.

Later in the year Wayne Martin, QC, told the HIH Royal Commission that Williams 'doesn't appear to have derived any personal benefit from Adler's proposals' but he 'appears to have very readily acquiesced in proposals put to him by Mr Adler and Mr Cooper with apparently only the most perfunctory consideration of the benefits of those transactions from the perspective of HIH. He also appears on occasions to have approved transactions by signing and authorising them as chief executive officer at a time well after he had in fact resigned from that position.' Williams had resigned on 13 October 2000.

The whole nasty Pacific Eagle Equities mess took a while to become public, not least because of Ray Williams' misleading of his much-maligned HIH audit committee, and the fact that relevant documents had been parked in a box and ignored.

John Buttle, the Andersen partner who had been parachuted in to replace Alan Davies as leader of the HIH audit, was the prime mover in bringing it all to light. At an audit committee meeting on 12 September 2000 Buttle said to chairman Geoffrey Cohen: 'Not to put too fine a point on it, you tell ASIC or we will.'

It took Cohen until 22 December to actually do so, and that was after an awkward phone conversation with Buttle at which, in Buttle's words, Cohen became 'a little irate' and hung the phone up on him. This was the most emotional involvement Cohen appears to have shown in his many years of chairing HIH, and he was trying not to deal with the corporate regulator. Buttle had a bad bout of phones crashing in his ear that day, since it was that call that caused Leigh Brown to call him fifteen minutes later and acccording to Buttle make the reference to the issue stinking 'to the high heaven'. Brown also hung up on Buttle.

But if Andersen auditors came out of PEE looking like the good guys, a simultaneous problem with FAI's sagging solvency took a lot of the gloss off. Andersen auditors discovered after 30 June 2000 that FAI, by then a wholly owned subsidiary of HIH, was breaching its loan covenants and was at risk of being insolvent. They suggested an internal issue of $200 million in preference shares by FAI to HIH to resolve the solvency problem and keep FAI on the plus side of the ledger.

The catch was that it was going to be retrospective, particularly as the matter came up at a meeting on 12 October. Auditor Jonathan Pye, John Buttle's deputy, and footballer-turned-lawyer Charles Abbott, mentioned the idea at that meeting although a resolution to put it into effect never made the minutes, causing Wayne Martin, QC, to tell the Royal Commission in January 2002 that backdating the issue to 23 June would 'create a deception'.

Backdating the issue was in fact less controversial than the way it was recorded in the accounts. It was supposed to be added to the accounts as a 'post balance date event', but it was included in the accounts instead, making it harder to find. Dominic Fodera said he had been overseas on 23 June and that the first he knew of the document was when he was preparing for the Royal Commission.

Andersen was never going to look good about the June 2000 accounts, given how horribly wrong they turned out to be. They were a shocker. By June 2000 HIH was carrying $405 million of 'goodwill' on the asset side of its balance sheet, as the difference between what HIH had paid for FAI and what it really turned out to be worth. That was close to wishful thinking, in accounting terms, since any calculation of goodwill has to assume that it will all be earned back again in the future. It never was.

Goodwill was part of a whole raft of other intangible assets which collectively made up 117 per cent of shareholders' equity in mid–2000, according to Norman O'Bryan, SC, who was addressing the commission on 3 October 2002. Those intangible assets had grown from around 48 per cent in 1997, he said, and almost 90 per cent in 1999. He said that the goodwill component grew from 7.5 per cent of HIH's equity in 1997 to more than 50 per cent in 2000.

Almost every intangible asset would blow away in a puff of dust if the company ceased trading, and HIH's accounts were starting to look like a termite-ridden house that is held together by wallpaper, lead-based paint and old carpet.

And meanwhile, HIH's ability to meet its own internal budgets went the other way. 'In 1996 and 1997, figures for the budget and actual are not far apart,' Norman O'Bryan said. 'By 1998 and 1999 the actual net profit figure ... is very significantly lower than the budget figure. In 1998 it's less than 50 per cent of the budget figure. And in 1999, it's in fact $103 million below the budget figure of $45 million. It's minus $59 million,' he concluded with the finality that only someone who had not been a shareholder could say without wincing.

The company declared a 'profit' of $18.4 million for the 1999–2000 year, which included a loss for the second half of $21.8 million. Analysts and Justice Owen believed the real figure should have been a full-year loss of about $180 million, since the accounts included an *increase* in goodwill of $163 million relating to FAI.

A decidedly uneasy John Buttle of Andersen signed off the 30 June accounts of HIH on 16 October 2000, four days after Ray Williams announced he was planning to resign. Williams' status seemed to be still that of CEO until a successor could be named, which happened on 15 December, the day before HIH's last annual meeting.

HIH's balance sheet said that the company's total assets were $8.32 billion and its total liabilities $7.38 billion, leaving shareholders' equity of $940 million. Five months later the liquidators were to estimate that the company had a deficiency of $5.3 billion, which means that the 30 June numbers turned out to have been overstated by $6.24 billion.

So if those numbers were so bad, you might assume that in late 2000 HIH management was battling desperately to cut costs, eliminate all non-core businesses and focus totally on the main game, keeping the business alive.

In fact, the company's main businesses were sold to the Allianz group on 13 September 2000, in the deal described so accurately by Andersen London auditor Garth Hackshall as a 'hospital pass'.

Even the management of HIH conceded in the last annual report that the deal would effectively reduce HIH's retail annual premium by $300 million to $700 million. But it ran the spurious line that the company would get an 'upfront' payment of $200 million, when nothing of the sort actually happened. Because HIH's asset base had been seriously eroded and HIH had to put $500 million worth of assets into the joint venture, the $200 million had to go straight into the joint venture, of which Allianz incidentally controlled 51 per cent.

Hence Hackshall's comment to Jonathan Pye in early 2001 that the market in London was suggesting that Deutsche Bank should give back the fee it had charged HIH for the deal. (The fee was $5.4 million plus GST.) The other major last-minute deal, which earned a fee of $6.1 million, was the sale of HIH's workers' compensation business to rival insurer NRMA. That was concluded at 2.00 a.m. on 14 March, the day before HIH collapsed.

Deutsche was to bill HIH successfully for $10.8 million altogether for work done on four transactions, after Colin Richardson at Deutsche had inserted a clause in mandate agreements in November 2000 that guaranteed Deutsche would be paid by intercepting the proceeds of future transactions, rather than waiting for payment afterwards. Richardson said it reflected the 'commercial reality' that Deutsche had at that point been waiting to be paid for a previous deal.

The system certainly worked a treat, since Deutsche said that it had its final fee of $6.1 million ratified by Tony McGrath, the liquidator of HIH, ten days after the company collapsed. McGrath may have a different view.

Richardson took the line with the HIH Royal Commission that the collapse of the company came as a surprise to him. He said that it was only after he put in the bill for $6.1 million to HIH on 14 March, the day before the company collapsed, and had it ratified by chief executive Randolph Wein, that he learned that HIH was about to collapse. He said that he walked round to see finance manager Bill Howard and 'gathered the implication' from Howard that HIH 'would be going into liquidation' the next day.

And he evidently missed a clue despite learning on 4 March 2001 that there was a team from KPMG investigating HIH's accounts, including noted insolvency experts Alex Mcintosh and Tony McGrath, who were subsequently appointed joint liquidators.

On 29 October 2002 Justice Neville Owen broke into proceedings to ask Richardson, 'What did you think KPMG were doing?'

'Liaising with regulators,' replied Richardson, neatly echoing the official announcement put out to explain their presence.

(Richardson was not the only person to profess surprise at HIH's collapse. HIH director Charles Abbott maintained that he submitted his bill for $181,000 in expenses at 4.00 p.m. on 14 March and was only told about the imminent liquidation at 6.00 p.m. At the last hearing of the

HIH Royal Commission on 4 February 2003, a different picture emerged. Tony McGrath said that Abbott had been at a meeting at 10.00 a.m. that morning at which he [McGrath] had announced that he would recommend the next day that all of the HIH companies should be put in liquidation. He duly did exactly that. The judge noted McGrath's testimony and referred Abbott to ASIC. One of the alleged breaches, of section 184(1) of the Corporations Law, is classed as a criminal offence and carries a possible five-year gaol term. Abbott repaid all the money before the report came out.)

All of the last-minute money grabbing was spelt out in painful detail at the Royal Commission, but one issue not covered was the intriguing question of when Ray Williams concluded that the game was over.

What was not explored was that HIH's last lifeline disappeared in August 2000 when New South Wales Premier Bob Carr announced that workers' compensation insurance would not be privatised in his State. If insurance is something of a cargo cult for providers, and in certain circumstances it can be a real gravy train, privatisation of workers' comp would for HIH have been a new messiah stepping nimbly down from a cloud.

Some analysts believe that privatisation of New South Wales workers' comp could have given HIH as much as a 25 per cent share of about $2 billion of premium income a year, or $500 million. As a well-established player in that area dating from the time in the 1980s before the sector was nationalised, HIH would have almost automatically been granted that market share.

It was a shocking teaser for HIH because the proposal had been in and out of State government for a few years, based on the reasonable logic that the government should allow private insurers to shoulder its risk where they wanted to do so. In September 1999 Carr, a Labor premier with an intellectual reputation, said he planned to defer privatisation for a year and in August 2000 he merely set in concrete what he had previously proposed.

Carr did not know it but his decision meant that HIH had to say goodbye to some $500 million of annual revenue with a likely gap of eight years between premium and eventual payout, the ultimate free gift for an insurer.

Richard Grellman, a senior KPMG partner who was to distinguish himself in late 2000 by recommending that an official inspector should be appointed to HIH, had concluded in September 1997 that the New South Wales government should pass the risk onto private insurers. His more conservative estimation was that if the market was broken down by existing market share, HIH would come away with 8 per cent of a market that could be worth $1.6 billion a year in premium.

Ironically Rodney Adler liked the idea, a conclusion that current opinion would classify as the kiss of death. 'It's a very well-researched and sound document and it's positive for the industry,' he said, before noting as an afterthought that 'the industry does not intend to go into workers' compensation insurance unless it's profitable.'

The deal was meant to be in place by 1 July 1998. The fact that it wasn't is another possible reason for Ray Williams' resignation in October 2000.

Williams has never explained his resignation, and the reason he gave — age — has been shown by his subsequent good health to have been a bit hollow. A relentless early riser and gymnasium visitor even after the collapse of the company, Williams enjoys the health of a man closer to fifty than seventy.

'I'm sixty-four years of age,' he told reporters on 12 October 1998. 'One would look to retire at 65,' he said. 'Certainly, as we go into this process it's very important for the group to have management stability to manage this transition. I haven't decided exactly the date when I'm retiring.'

Any analysis of that statement shows it to be more full of holes than a good Swiss cheese. One point is that he was not going to get to 65 until 11 June 2001, a simple piece of arithmetic which has him blowing the 'age' whistle no less than eight months early. The other, bigger hole is his claim that it was important to maintain management stability. Although he was right, why then was he resigning with no successor in view?

HIH had to stagger through two months of appalling uncertainty, at one of the direst phases of its gradual disintegration, with no chief executive at all. As Wayne Martin, QC, put it on 15 July 2002, there was 'a veritable flood of cash pouring out of HIH during the last six months before the appointment of the provisional liquidators'.

Ray Williams' resignation was almost certainly caused by a mixture of embarrassment about Pacific Eagle Equities, and pressure from investors who forced Cohen to actually ask Williams for his resignation. The fact that the last possible lifeline of New South Wales workers' compensation had disappeared just weeks before, with an unknowing stroke of New South Wales Premier Bob Carr's pen, could well have pushed Williams over the edge.

CHAPTER 19

THE REGULATORS

HIH INSURANCE HAD started to come badly undone in 2000, by every measure, but it is disturbing to discover how little was actually done to investigate the company's woes at that time. The prime overseer of the insurance sector is APRA, the Australian Prudential Regulation Authority but, as Wayne Martin, QC, noted in his summary in January 2003, APRA 'missed every opportunity' to identify and rectify HIH's looming financial problems.

The prize example of that was the presentation put on by actuaries Peter McCarthy and Geoff Trahair at their professional actuaries' conference on 8 November 1999 at Sanctuary Cove in Queensland. The two men had worked together at FAI, although by then McCarthy was at Zurich Insurance and Trahair had moved on to HIH after the takeover in 1998.

With considerable courage the two men decided to blow the whistle as loudly as they could on what they saw as chronic under-reserving in the Australian general insurance industry. As barrister Simon White of the HIH Royal Commission put it in November 2002, the paper said that the industry 'may be under-reserved by up to $1 billion'.

Trahair in particular was taking quite a risk, since he was aiming fairly and squarely at his own employer. He and McCarthy singled out public liability insurance, the category in which HIH was the overwhelming market leader in Australia, as being the worst problem. They believed reserves in that category alone were short by between $500 million and $1 billion, which was between a quarter and a half of claims that were already outstanding. HIH had almost exactly half of the Australia PL market. They said that in Australia public liability premiums were 60 per cent underpriced and that the situation was 'frightening'. No wonder they referred to a survey done the year before by Ord Minnett and Deloitte Touche Tohmatsu entitled 'Not on the Rocks, but Close'.

Most of the graphs they produced were of the type that wriggle up and down for most of the way across the page then crash downwards at the right-hand end, the sort beloved of cartoonists.

But there was nothing very funny about what they were saying, and they were nervous in trying to be light-hearted about it. Sitting beside them on the podium and introducing them was Dr Jeffrey Carmichael, the chairman of APRA. Carmichael later testified to the commission that it was what he called 'a curious paper and not one that I've seen the likes of before'. He said that 'they were laughing and carrying on as though it was almost an industry joke'. They did their best, producing a list of ten pretend tips for insurers. The first was very telling: 'When all else fails, ask the government to privatise CTP [compulsory third party] or workers' comp.' The latter nearly happened in New South Wales, but Bob Carr decided against it. They also made a joke at their profession's expense by saying that 'There are three types of actuary — those who can count and those who can't'.

Carmichael said their presentation 'left me less than amused' but he took a copy of the paper, read it and passed it on to his staff to read. He had told the two presenters, whom he had introduced, that 'It's very concerning, what you had to say. I'm coming up to speed on general insurance.'

He subsequently told ABC television's 'Four Corners' that 'It certainly raised a concern with me. The paper came back into our system here. We were given reassurances that there was no immediate solvency problem and that it would be monitored.'

If Carmichael did know enough to do the sort of delegating of which any public servant would be proud, very clearly no one at APRA rang a bell. It has never been revealed who it was who was giving the assurances about HIH's solvency, but several of Carmichael's underlings had a pretty good idea of what was going on.

'You know which company they're talking about, don't you?' one insurance executive said to a senior APRA man as the delegates were having coffee afterwards. 'Yes, HIH,' the APRA man replied. The regulator did not actually start serious investigation of HIH until June of 2000, seven months later.

If APRA did nothing, other people did. About ten actuaries employed by Australia's biggest actuary, Trowbridge Consulting, were at the conference and several passed on their concerns to their boss, John Trowbridge, who is now head of general insurance at Suncorp-Metway in Brisbane. He in turn appears to have mentioned it to other members of a very high-level industry group called FSAC, the Financial Sector Advisory Council, which had direct links to Treasurer Peter Costello in Canberra, most likely in early 2000.

FSAC was created by the Treasurer at the same time as APRA was, in 1998, to report to him on how the implementation of the Wallis report was going. Stan Wallis, the former chief executive of Amcor Ltd, had recommended collapsing eleven different regulatory bodies into one, APRA. The idea was sound but the execution has since been shown to be little short of disastrous because of the disruption in staffing, training and corporate memory between the Insurance and Superannuation Commission and APRA that coincided almost exactly with HIH's takeover of FAI in late 1998. FAI's 30 June 1998 results, probably one of the least reliable sets of figures that came out until HIH's June 2000 numbers, were based on reinsurance deals done on almost exactly the dates when the ISC was being transformed uncomfortably into APRA.

FSAC was given a direct reporting line to Treasurer Costello and its members included people like National Australia Bank chief Don Argus, ASX Ltd chairman Maurice Newman, Mr Trowbridge, former Sydney Futures Exchange chief Les Hosking and AMP director Patricia Cross. FSAC is something of a Masonic body as far as releasing information is concerned, so it was never proved whether a warning was passed to the Treasurer himself.

But one member of the group was sufficiently annoyed by what had happened to tell this author that HIH's situation 'was discussed by FSAC at that time and highlighted to a number of senior people in Canberra'.

After that information was published by the *Australian Financial Review* on 17 January 2003, Shadow Treasurer Bob McMullan then revealed he had been told the same story early in 2002. He wrote a letter to Justice Neville Owen on 23 January, explaining that he had not taken it further because he had been told 'in confidence'. That ended up getting him something of a bucketing from the government benches for two reasons: one, that he had sat on information; and two, that it might not have been correct.

In early February 2003 the chairman of FSAC, Maurice Newman, wrote a letter to Treasurer Peter Costello that appeared to put a lid on the affair. 'I can confirm that to the best of my knowledge and belief, and after reviewing my own record, no advice or information was provided by FSAC to Treasury or the Treasurer ... on the performance and financial stability of HIH Ltd, before its collapse in March 2001,' he wrote.

That allowed Mr Costello to dump the bucket on McMullan, accusing him of 'not having the guts' to put his allegations to the Royal Commission during its 220 sitting days. All of which made people wonder why McMullan had stuck his neck out so far in the first place unless there was some substance in his statement to the judge.

The hard part in any pursuit of this issue is that any warning would almost certainly not have been written down. And since Treasury actually finances FSAC, it is a bit hopeful to imagine that a member of FSAC would be likely to announce that the organisation had quietly warned Treasury about HIH but that nothing was done.

But if that was a messy and unsatisfying business for almost everyone involved, it was a scale model of what happened to the other major whistleblower, former HIH accountant Jeff Simpson.

Simpson left HIH in August 1999 after becoming uneasy about the way HIH accounted for the Hannover Reinsurance contracts in that year. He was deputy chief general manager finance and in many ways Dominic Fodera's right-hand man. He was angry at Andersen's acquiescence with the idea that the $400 million-plus Hannover deal in 1999 was real reinsurance when there was a letter of credit arrangement that relieved Hannover of all the risk. The arrangement, devised by Fodera after a visit to Hannover, had the same effect as the side letters that FAI had signed with General Cologne Reinsurance the year before.

Simpson also knew that Andersen's tax department had been hired separately by HIH and had concluded that the premium payments to Hannover were not tax deductible because the policy was not real reinsurance. Unfortunately, the tax people at Andersen did not talk to the auditors at Andersen and the latter did not query the way the Hannover deal was accounted for as a disguised loan, allowing HIH to claim more than $92 million in reinsurance 'recovery' in the first year. HIH was able to report a profit of $102 million in the year to 30 June 1999, compared with the $10 million it would otherwise have been able to claim, and Simpson was to tell the commission that he thought the HIH numbers had been 'stretched to the limit' to get there. He believed that the only reason that Andersen was so indulgent toward HIH over the Hannover deal was because they had ticked off very similar arrangements for FAI the year before, since they audited both insurers.

After leaving HIH Simpson took a job with a health insurer but decided he really didn't like the industry at all, and approached APRA in June 2000 with a detailed 21-page document which made it clear he believed HIH was probably insolvent at that time.

He calculated that HIH's net assets had been exaggerated by between $750 million and $1.1 billion, which gave HIH a net asset value of between $42 million and minus $308 million. It turns out that he was being conservative.

He didn't get much of a reception at APRA. He was warned by the APRA officers he saw that he was leaving himself open to legal action, so they asked him to give them the document anonymously. He did that, but it turned out to be a valueless exercise because there is no evidence that they did anything constructive with it once they got it. Because they decided that he was a 'disgruntled ex-employee', they treated his very thorough document in the same way they treated Rodney Adler's leaks from the HIH board via Mark Westfield. Rather than investigating the claims, which would have brought HIH's dire position into the daylight and would have prevented thousands of policyholders from buying policies in 2000 that became worthless on 15 March 2001, they wrongly discounted the value of the information because they were suspicious of where it came from.

In both cases the information would have given them significant help.

Perhaps the real problem was unearthed when one APRA officer confessed to the commission that they did not have the expertise to follow up on Simpson's information.

No wonder Simpson gave up on APRA. He had had an equally bad experience in late 1999 when he went to the Institute of Chartered Accountants to try to raise awareness of what was happening at HIH. As a qualified chartered accountant himself it was a logical step, but he told the commission that the reaction he got from the people he spoke to was 'don't go there'. He was referred to the institute's voluntary counselling service, which provided him with an experience that would turn most people paranoid.

On 26 October 1999, he was referred to a telephone counsellor who was a qualified chartered accountant and they had a roundabout conversation in which Simpson said he avoided raising the name of the insurance company, or even that it was an insurance company he was talking about. It did not help that the person he was talking to was driving across the Sydney Harbour Bridge to the city and wanted to keep the conversation to a minimum.

Simpson subsequently discovered he had been talking to Geoff Barnum, chief executive of General and Cologne Reinsurance Australia. Barnum had been one of the main players in the first policy that FAI took out in 1998, right down to being at the meeting which convinced Martyn Scrivens of Andersen that the way FAI was going to account for the policy was all right.

Simpson was horrified, although it was an unfortunate coincidence, since Barnum was an anonymous volunteer. Barnum quickly put out a statement to that effect once the affair came to light at the commission. If the two men had been having a dialogue of the deaf, it was certainly another reason why Jeff Simpson was never able to make his concerns public until it was way too late.

He summed up a lot of his frustrations in a document he sent to the commission in early 2003, entitled ' Whistleblowing — You shouldn't have to be brave'. He noted that there are a huge number of cultural and legal impediments to whistleblowers that make such a course hazardous, summing up some of the difficulties as follows:

Deciding whether to whistleblow or not is one of the most gut-wrenching decisions we as humans can face in our lifetime. At some time in our lives a sizeable number of us will become aware in reasonable detail of a significant practice that could range from undesirable to illegal behaviour. Your mind will more than likely tell you that the consequences of whistleblowing on you personally could be quite disastrous. Your friends will at a minimum advise caution. Contact with whistleblower support groups will probably give you even more reasons to be concerned given the experiences they have been through. Reading of your organisation's instructions for whistleblowing will just reinforce your concerns. The initial contact with people you initiate the whistleblowing with may scare you into silence or further delay you in coming forward. All are a reflection of the community's attitude towards whistleblowers and the act of whistleblowing. Hence most people do not come forward.

Little wonder that Simpson, who is now an internal auditor at Wyong Shire Council, north of Sydney, let his campaign drop quietly. He also noted that the effects of whistleblowing include stress, guilt and self-doubt, career change, financial disaster, problems with family and friendships, legal expense, social ostracism and sometimes, in extreme cases, suicide.

Meanwhile, even if APRA had had a better look at what it was being told, it was also being lied to in many cases, or at best was getting the wrong end of the stick.

Craig Thorburn, who was the head of APRA's Diversified Institutions Division and who ended up being the scapegoat for a lot of APRA's shortcomings, had an interview with Geoff Trahair in April 2000 at which they discussed whether HIH's provisioning arrangements were adequate. (Thorburn, a former Australian Government actuary, now works for the World Bank in New York.) He said that Trahair told him that all of FAI's problems were fully covered by reinsurance, which would have reassured him, since the market was full of talk that they weren't. Trahair has emphatically denied that was what he said. Given that he had been 'blowing the whistle' just months before, it seems very unlikely that he was now trying to cover things up.

HIH's notorious 30 June 2000 accounts, released on 13 October of that year, included a $163 million addition to the goodwill account to cover deteriorations in FAI's position. That was all that was keeping the accounts alive by then, since the company reported a half-year profit of $40 million and a full-year profit of only $2 million more. The only reason HIH was able to declare a profit was for the perverse reason that FAI was in worse shape than anyone had imagined.

The big lift in goodwill in the accounts makes Thorburn's 'we were lied to' position less easy to maintain because he or his staff should have spotted that problem and didn't.

John Palmer, the urbane and very experienced Canadian regulator who is now deputy chairman of the Singapore Monetary Authority, wrote a report at APRA's request and made that particular point in his systematic demolition of APRA's performance.

The Palmer report was a masterstroke. By commissioning a report which was what Wayne Martin, QC, called 'impartial and thorough', APRA was able to draw the teeth of public criticism when its turn in the HIH Royal Commission witness box came. Since Palmer's report effectively said 'they blew it', it left little room for any of the usual critics of APRA to come to any more telling conclusions.

By October 2000 the bells were ringing all over the place.

Joe Hockey, the then Minister for Financial Services and Regulation whose career has never quite recovered from the HIH collapse on his watch, got a solid warning when he went to London in October 2000. Hockey went to Lloyd's famous 'Room' in its extravagant glass-covered office building in the City and while he was there, an Australian broker recognised Hockey and walked up to him. 'Joe, there's one company in this place that's picking up all the really dud business and it's HIH,' he said.

Unfortunately Hockey did the logical thing when he got home and asked APRA what was happening at HIH.

Craig Thorburn sent him a briefing note which said that 'HIH is a company under considerable stress', but added that 'HIH remains profitable and is taking action to cement its position'. At the Royal Commission he was unable to say how he had concluded that the company was profitable.

The goodwill-loaded 30 June 2000 result had come out in October, causing the HIH share price to sink to a miserable 55 cents, and the company never was able to produce a set of numbers for the six months to 31 December 2000. By the time HIH collapsed it was clear that the company was going to lose at least $800 million in the six-month period, or even $1 billion, but no result was ever published.

As with any major disaster, there were half a dozen circumstances that conspired to conceal HIH's dire situation from the regulators. One of the organisations that Jeff Simpson did warn and which acted on the warning was Westpac Bank, which in late 2000 had an exposure of about $300 million to HIH's Cotesworth syndicates at Lloyd's.

Lloyd's has house rules about significant backing for foreign insurers operating there, demanding big bank guarantees or letters of credit (LOCs) before they are allowed to accept risk.

HIH bought into Cotesworth in 1998 for about $30 million after making a spectacular mess of underwriting on its own account in the

1990s, effectively transferring all its UK business to Cotesworth. Not surprisingly given HIH's track record, Cotesworth made a bad situation worse and HIH liquidator Tony McGrath has indicated that if any one issue is going to make the $5.3 billion shortfall at HIH grow bigger, it will be Cotesworth.

After Simpson's warning Westpac hired Ernst & Young to review HIH's situation and by November 2000 Westpac got back a report from the accounting firm indicating that it did not have enough information about HIH to be able to declare whether it was insolvent. It warned, however, that there was a 'potential triggering of default clauses under various note and debt facilities'. It also said HIH was 'delicately poised'.

That is accountant-speak for *this company is probably insolvent.* There always seem to be reasons why people cannot give frank opinions about cash-strapped companies. First, a declaration of insolvent trading by an independent expert would automatically force the company to close its doors, and second, if that happened, Westpac would not see all of its money.

The Ernst & Young report was a little coy about HIH's position, but made it very clear that the Allianz deal would have disastrous effects on the company.

Aside from noting that the $200 million would not be coming, the report pointed out that the effect of the deal, which was devised in late 2000 and came into force on 1 January 2001, would be to turn HIH from a high cash flow business with significant liabilities, to a low cash flow business with almost the same liabilities. All Allianz was taking was the short-tail business that had been written by two of the three licensed insurers in the group, CIC and FAI. The third, HIH Casualty & General, would still be kept, with all the attendant long-tail risks.

A copy of the report went to APRA and Craig Thorburn, who spent sixteen weeks in 2000 outside Australia on business relating to international actuarial organisations. He took a copy with him on one of those trips to London, on 6 December 2000. Unfortunately, he only skimmed it by reading the executive summary on the Singapore–Sydney leg before passing it on to Tom Karp. His explanation to the commission was that he 'expected it was being read in Australia' by his colleagues while he was away. It wasn't. And by the time Karp had read it in turn, had become alarmed and passed it on to his boss, Graeme Thompson, chief executive of APRA, the company's collapse was only three days away.

APRA was in effect a cardboard cut-out of a regulator, all form and precious little substance.

The Palmer report noted that by the time APRA formally took over from the ISC in August 1999, 'much of the corporate memory of the chequered histories of FAI and HIH had disappeared'.

Aside from the exodus of competence and corporate knowledge, staff numbers of any sort became totally inadequate to deal with the 300-odd insurers and banks that the Diversified Institutions Divisions (DID) was meant to be overseeing. In September 2000 there were effectively only three staff members in DID when there were meant to be eight. Of those, one was on sick leave and another was 'not performing', as APRA put it. The Palmer report noted that APRA salaries were in the lowest quartile of the general employment market — never mind the better paid financial sector employment market. And although staff were often well qualified in a general sense, several with MBAs, they had almost no insurance background at all.

What happened in 1999 was that staff had to submit to a process called 'spill and fill'. There were more people coming from the eleven old regulatory bodies than the 400 slots that APRA had room for, and many chose not to bother applying, particularly as it would probably involve an unassisted move from Canberra to Sydney.

There were almost no general insurance experts in APRA. There weren't even any on the board until Rod Atfield, the former CEO of Mercantile Mutual, was made a director in August 2001, five months after HIH fell over.

APRA chief executive Graeme Thompson said his first involvement with HIH came in June of 2000 when a colleague at Treasury had been tipped off that HIH had problems. But nothing ever seemed to happen. After Mark Westfield's articles really started ringing bells in August 2000, HIH did not even come up as a topic of discussion at the next APRA board meeting.

Palmer did not pull his punches when he wrote that 'in the end, the APRA team was overwhelmed by the sheer magnitude of the issues it was encountering at HIH and had neither the manpower nor the expertise to cope with these issues'.

In fact, a regulator does not actually need a big staff to make a difference. The Motor Accident Authority of New South Wales, which was responsible for overseeing HIH's CTP (compulsory third party) insurance, significantly outperformed APRA despite only having half a dozen staff altogether.

Richard Grellman, a well-known auditor, liquidator and veteran surfer who chaired the authority, concluded that after the Allianz deal HIH might not be able to pay old claims that Allianz had not taken on when it bought the 'good' short-tail business from HIH on 1 January 2001.

Grellman told APRA in October 2000 that he proposed to appoint an inspector to HIH, as a way of helping the company to manage its way out of a dire situation without closing its doors. But he was talked out of doing so by Karp, who said APRA was considering doing the same. By the time the more powerful APRA got round to appointing an inspector of its own it was too late. The inspector, David Lombe, was due to start work on 15 March 2001, the day HIH closed its doors.

Alan Cameron, the former chairman of APRA's sister organisation, ASIC, used a telling phrase in his evidence to the commission when he said that APRA had a passive culture and 'almost a London tea and biscuits approach' to supervising the banks and insurance companies for which it was responsible. That tallied with the views of the staff at ASIC, who had spent years talking balefully about APRA's house belief that co-operation worked better than enforcement. In making his report in 1997, Stan Wallis had advocated what he called a 'less intrusive' philosophy. History proved him emphatically wrong.

Wayne Martin, QC, noted that by mid-2000 there were two significant factors which concealed the insolvency of two of the three licensed insurers in the HIH group. (HIH Casualty & General and FAI were the two insolvent companies, leaving only CIC as a solvent entity.) He identified the misleading report by HIH to APRA in late 2000 and the fact that the $300 million backing the letter of credit that allowed Cotesworth to operate should not have been counted as capital. And while their main business was unravelling, the management of HIH seemed to be off on a number of wild-goose chases of its own.

There was Brad Cooper popping in and out of the office like a cuckoo, demanding and getting money for a series of claims that went from doubtful to just plain spurious, and there was the Pacific Eagle Equities affair which began in June 2000. Ray Williams informed his directors about the Allianz deal in August, without consulting them and certainly without telling them that it would bring HIH to an effective standstill.

Wayne Martin, QC, said the main driver of that deal was the 'need to provide a transaction that would be viewed positively by the market' when HIH's much-puffed June 2000 results were released in early October.

And after all that happened, and after Ray Williams announced on 12 October that he planned to resign, there was the peculiar little deal involving a company called Business Thinking Systems, in which Ray Williams authorised a $2 million investment. This was the investment that Adler had solicited in the very same letter to Williams that challenged him for the top job at HIH.

In January 2003 Wayne Martin, QC, went on to say that Ray Williams and Rodney Adler might have committed a criminal offence in putting $2 million of HIH's money into the company, a training business in which Rodney Adler was a major shareholder and chairman. He held 35 per cent of it, and HIH 15 per cent. The judge's report agreed.

Williams authorised the $2 million investment on 5 October 2000 without reference to anyone on HIH's investment committee, two days after Adler's challenge.

As Martin put it, Adler took advantage of his 'unusual relationship' with Williams by threatening his position at the head of HIH unless he made the transaction. 'It's hard to imagine a clearer or more stark example of the breakdown in corporate governance mechanisms and the dominance of management over the board,' he added.

The following letter is a startler, from a man who was used to startling.

'I find myself in a very awkward position, I have been and continue to be inundated by institutions, and more particularly individuals, ringing me and suggesting that they place their proxy to vote at my discretion to vote at the HIH Annual General Meeting, the sole purpose of which is to assume either the Chairman or Chief Executive role,' Adler wrote on 4 October.

After telling Williams he wanted his job or the chairman's, he noted that he had only held off 'moving against' Williams, even though it would have been in HIH's best interests, 'because I cannot do something against a person that has been good to me'. But having apparently declared his hand, he then asked Williams to arrange for HIH to put $2 million into Business Thinking Systems because 'it would help grow our mutual investment'.

The company was never taken public and it reflected a statement that Adler appears to have made to journalist Ian McIlwraith of the Melbourne *Age* in August 2000. 'Anyone who has invested [in it] is patient. We know that the value of the company isn't going to go down. It's enjoyable to be private,' he said. The value of the company subsequently went down.

Once again the 'goat photograph' conspiracy theorists had a field day. What possible hold over Ray Williams did Rodney Adler have that he could ask him for his job and then turn around in the same letter and ask him for money?

With all the other financial shockers going on at HIH, $2 million does not sound like a lot. But it was $2 million wasted and even Westpac, which had been bankers to Business Thinking Systems, was amazed to discover that HIH was putting its fast-vanishing funds into a company that they expected to collapse shortly. No wonder Westpac was so keen to hire Ernst & Young to examine HIH. As one battle-scarred HIH executive put it at the time, 'It's not much of a credit reference, is it?'

Not that Williams lasted much longer. He resigned on 12 October. The price of HIH shares delivered the ultimate insult to Williams by jumping 9c after the news to close at 52c.

The shares had become little better than a 'penny dreadful' after the Allianz deal was announced in mid-September 2000. Ray Williams was an ostentatious buyer of 1 million shares but it did not stop the price from falling from 99c to 55c in one week as a reaction to the news. As one fund manager wisely put it, 'He's sold the farm.'

CHAPTER 20

THE FALLOUT

THE HIH ROYAL Commission nearly didn't happen.

An initially reluctant federal government announced it on 21 May 2001 just over two months after the HIH collapse, after Justice Owen agreed to come over from Western Australia to chair it, much to the relief of a number of judges much closer to the action.

When government ministers did change their mind, they broke the cardinal rule: never call for a commission unless you know exactly what the outcome will be. In this case, no one did. Joe Hockey, the then Minister for Financial Services and Regulation, would remember better than most because he had spent much of May doing the rounds of the media saying that there did not need to be a commission.

The federal opposition had been calling for one and so had a number of Labor State premiers, most particularly Bob Carr in New South Wales. The federal government was on the back foot and Prime Minister John Howard was pushing the line that since there was already an inquiry under way by regulator ASIC, a Royal Commission might undermine it.

That line held for a while but the tidal wave of stories of uncompleted houses, dishonoured payout cheques to quadriplegics and rumours of lavish executive lifestyles at HIH caused pressure to build rather than ease.

What broke the resolve of the government was the realisation that David Knott, who had been appointed chairman of ASIC in July 1999, had a significant conflict of interest. He was not only a board member of APRA at the time of HIH's collapse, but he had also been chief operating officer of APRA before getting the top job at ASIC. If there wasn't going to be a Royal Commission, ASIC was going to take all the running and here was the ASIC chairman towing a suitcase full of potentially very smelly APRA baggage.

The ASIC idea was 'crippled before it started', New South Wales Treasurer Michael Egan announced, and his federal overlords on the coalition side of the political fence in Canberra were forced to agree. Joe Hockey had to do a U-turn by announcing on Kerry O'Brien's '7.30 Report' on ABC television that a Royal Commission would indeed be established.

If you thought that was a government conspiracy, you would not want to stand near a cock-up.

Nearly two years later, the commission wound up after spending just short of $40 million of the taxpayers' money, interviewing 220 witnesses and filling more than 19,500 pages with transcript.

Federal Treasurer Peter Costello released it on the Wednesday before Easter, an unsatisfactory day for the press, although the report had recommended no charges against anyone involved who was close to the government, such as APRA, ASIC or the treasurer of the federal Liberal Party, Malcolm Turnbull.

It looked at first glance as though a lot of the organisations had got off pretty lightly, particularly since there was a clause in the judge's report which specifically exonerated all but the labelled few. 'Where there is no finding in this report against the person or company, the reputation of that person or company emerges entirely free of any adverse implications. It must be seen and judged accordingly,' it stated. That frustrating line, put there for legal reasons, ignored the fact that the reputations of many people and organisations have been very thoroughly sullied, whether they like it or not.

In fact, behind the 1500 pages of often diplomatic legalese there were some damning indictments, which may not have been closely read by the Madame Defarge set who have been disappointed by the modest total of heads that will roll.

The judge surprised observers by making no referrals against non-executive directors of HIH for any breach of their duties, except Rodney Adler and Charles Abbott for obtaining personal benefit. But he noted of

Ray Williams that as far as management went, there was a culture that was 'unduly deferential' to a man whose business judgment started failing him in the mid-1990s and which placed 'blind faith in a leadership that was ill-equipped for the task'. Meanwhile, the checks and balances that might have been provided by advisers and the key regulator were often not there, the judge added.

He made it clear the public had lost confidence in APRA. 'If it is to engender in the public confidence that it is well placed to rectify the shortcomings that were identified during the inquiry, APRA will have to demonstrate the requisite change has occurred in its operations structures, its understanding of its powers under the legislation, and its basic approach to prudential supervision,' he said. The subtext of the bit about understanding its powers was a reference to the fact that APRA had well-defined powers to search company offices, but never actually used them.

The judge said the APRA board should be abolished and that the management of the organisation should be left with a small group of full-time executives. That recommendation was instantly accepted by the government; it was among an impressive total of sixty-one that the Commissioner put forward, no fewer than twenty-three of them relating to improving APRA's ability to do the job it was set up to do five years previously.

The judge might only have been giving a minor caning to APRA, but APRA had been doling out its version of justice with an old and damp piece of lettuce.

ASIC got off very lightly, but with a telling query about what it thought its job might be. ASIC had only started an investigation of HIH on 26 February 2001, way too late to make any difference at all to the shareholders. 'In regulating HIH, ASIC did what might have been reasonably expected of it given the view it took of its regulator role,' he wrote. But 'I am not sure I agree with this view of the allocation of functions between ASIC and APRA,' he added. As with many confrontations during the commission, such as between Rodney Adler and Brad Cooper, he left them to it. That is not much of a spectator sport, but time was pressing.

Auditors Andersen got no specific referrals but it was made clear that the careless and often sympathetic auditing habits that its US colleagues had got into at companies such as Enron were as prevalent in their dealings with HIH. The report noted that Andersen had been 'insufficiently rigorous' in auditing HIH in 1999 and 2000 and that the auditors had relied on the numbers provided by HIH's consulting actuary, David Slee, without checking them, because Andersen had no actuaries of its own. This was one of the biggest audit firms in the world, which had been auditing HIH since 1972.

The judge stopped short of concluding that Andersen's independence was compromised by having no less than three former partners on the HIH board, but said there was a perception that it might have been.

The tenor of the report was that more often than not carelessness rather than criminality had been involved. There had been a huge number of instances where auditors had come to the wrong conclusions or had been helped to them by not getting enough information or by getting information that was just plain wrong. In one case, where Andersen partner John Buttle suggested backdating the issue of preference shares by HIH to FAI in October 2000, the judge noted that he and his colleagues 'got it badly wrong'. But he did not see evidence of malfeasance by Andersen staff. His real frustration was Australia's accounting standards and his reaction was to include no fewer than eleven recommendations about how auditing could be made more accurate. His heaviest emphasis was on Australian Accounting Standard 1023, which deals with general insurance. He noted that as it stands at the moment, it does not carry a definition of 'material transfer of risk'. Without that, it is impossible to tell whether a reinsurance policy really is reinsurance, or is one of the more rapacious and illusory forms of financial reinsurance.

The global reinsurance industry is likely to see significant ripples flow from the commission even though only one reinsurer, General Cologne Re, had any referrals made by the judge. 'Reinsurance is a legitimate and, when properly used, effective mechanism for insurers to augment their capital base,' he wrote. 'There is … a place for financial reinsurance, properly used, as well as for traditional reinsurance.'

'I do, however, have real concerns about the use — or, more accurately, the abuse — of reinsurance and its susceptibility to manipulation,' he said.

If his recommendations on tightening up auditing standards are taken up, as they are likely to be, a small but highly lucrative subset of the worldwide reinsurance industry will have to have a very major assessment of where it can legitimately go from here. If auditing demands that reinsurance should be shown for what it is, there will not be much of a market for pretend reinsurance.

The judge was clearly annoyed to find a culture at FAI and HIH where huge amounts of management time were spent looking for schemes that might satisfy the letter but not the spirit of the law. 'From time to time as I listened to the evidence about specific transactions or decisions, I found myself asking rhetorically: did anyone stand back and ask themselves the simple question — is this right?' he wrote.

That should have been the first question, he said. Clearly the reality was that, in many cases, it was never asked at all.

The emphasis on getting round the law was one of many reasons why there were only fifty-six referrals to ASIC, only eighteen people were adversely named and only seven of them are facing charges that will stand any chance of putting them behind bars. Many executives of HIH such as George Sturesteps, Terry Cassidy and Fred Lo face civil action from ASIC from which the greatest penalty, if proved, would be a fine and a disqualification from acting as a director.

The judge had long ago given a veiled warning by saying that the resources of ASIC were 'finite', thus making it clear he would only be making recommendations in cases where there should be a serious chance of the Director of Public Prosecutions (DPP) achieving a successful prosecution.

He also dropped everything not relevant to the central issue: what caused HIH to collapse. He left alone, for instance, the fact that Brad Cooper procured the removal of $1.12 million from Home Security International (HSI) only days after obtaining control of the company from HIH in December 2000, for only $1.25 million altogether. (And it was a hire purchase deal, anyway.) The judge noted that Cooper owed a duty to HSI and a related company but by the time the deal happened, HSI was no longer part of the HIH group.

That contrasted sharply with how he viewed one of the most potentially dire breaches of the New South Wales Crimes Act, where in early 2001 Cooper ordered a $118,000 BMW for the man who controlled the finances at HIH, Bill Howard. The judge concluded that there was an agreement between the two whereby Cooper would arrange the purchase of the car and Howard would make sure Cooper's various claims against HIH were settled. That cost HIH more than $11 million.

The judge knew, however, that he would never jump the gulf between what he saw as his job and the desire of many people who had suffered because of HIH to see some very public scalps. He expressed reluctance to pursue what he called 'finger pointing and the apportionment of blame'.

'I did this without enthusiasm,' he wrote. 'It is not for me to judge whether this commission has faithfully served the public interest and whether it has fulfilled the expectations the public had of it.' Unlike many people he said his view would 'not be influenced in the slightest by the number of prosecutions (if any) that flow, and the severity of the penalties that are imposed'.

He made no apology for leaving most of his focus on the 'meat and potatoes' issues such as provisioning, reinsurance and the company's offshore operations. 'Matters of blame flow from those findings; they do not precede them,' he noted.

Even in those areas there were some clear gaps: while Tony Boulden of FAI is facing a possible gaol sentence relating to information he passed to FAI's consulting actuaries in late 1997, Michael Payne, the man who started the UK operation which ended up losing a possible $1.7 billion, gets no referral and thus emerges with his reputation untarnished.

That is a distinction which some people have found hard to take, but that is the same gap as the age-old difference between conspiracy and cock-up. Corporate failure does not of itself get you sent down, and HIH's UK operations were a failure of herculean proportions. Payne as much as admitted it, saying he had 'lost the plot' before the illness that had him kicked upstairs.

As with politics, it was the cover-ups rather than the initial follies that brought the most serious allegations and referrals. Misleading and deceptive conduct, concealment, backdating and failure to pass on information were the main offences, and it was not Payne who committed them.

The judge had a downbeat but realistic message for scalp hunters: 'In a collapse of this type it would not be unnatural for an outside observer to suspect that the central players must have been fraudsters,' the judge wrote. 'They might also suspect that large sums of money must have been spirited away to the dungeons of financial institutions, in so-called safe havens. HIH is not a case where wholesale fraud and embezzlement abounded.'

'Where did the money go?' the judge asked of HIH in general.

'Some of it was wasted by extravagance, largesse, paying too much for businesses acquired, and questionable transactions. There were some trading losses. But in the main the money was never there.'

He said that HIH had got itself into a spiral that saw it paying old, under-reserved claims out of present income. 'This, in my view, is the primary reason for HIH failing — and not only failing but doing so in such an egregious way.'

'Most of the instances of possible malfeasance were born of a misconceived desire to paper over the ever-widening cracks that were appearing in the edifice that was HIH,' he said.

Where to now? The federal government has made the right noises by promising 2003 budget funding for a Special Prosecutor to help the cash-poor ASIC run the cases that are emerging from the commission. ASIC is the first port of call for almost all the referrals, and will have to do the investigation before handing files to the Director of Public Prosecution.

ASIC, meanwhile, has been getting on with investigations of its own. One of the first was to arrange a criminal re-run of the Pacific Eagle Equities case, charging Rodney Adler with misleading and deceptive conduct in relation to his alleged claim that he was using his own money to buy HIH shares in mid-2000. That is something of a legal precedent since, although the original charge levied was a breach of directors' duties, the facts of the case will have more than somewhat of an overlap. At the time of writing the case was in the committal stages.

ASIC has also laid three charges against people involved in the commission but until they appear in court, the people charged can not be identified. ASIC has adopted that tactic as a way of limiting any allegations of prejudicial behaviour against defendants, but it keeps the press on their toes. Unless the defendants choose to 'out' themselves before appearing in court, as Rene Rivkin did in late 2002 with an unrelated charge for insider trading in Qantas shares, the first most people know about the charges is when the defendants first appear in court. Adler's appearance at the Downing Centre in Sydney was only reported because someone tipped journalists off at the last minute.

The ramifications of the commission will continue for years. In Australia the liquidator of HIH, Tony McGrath of KPMG, will almost certainly press further civil actions against any people or organisation against whom he believes he has a good chance of obtaining damages on behalf of HIH's creditors. Sydney solicitor Bruce Dennis is running a class action on behalf of more than a thousand HIH shareholders who laid out some $70 million on HIH shares and who he is alleging were 'seriously misled' about the value of the shares. The named defendants are the directors of HIH, auditors Andersen and, interestingly, Hannover Reinsurance.

Insurance in Australia will never be quite the same again. The public impact of HIH was all the greater because the company had been undercharging for public liability insurance for years. Experts now say that the premiums currently being charged, which are often more than double what they were under HIH, are really only realigning themselves with the old climbing graph of what they should have been before. There are other issues such as excessive payouts for personal injury in often dubious circumstances that have served to push premiums up, and there are moves to cap those payouts and thus limit insurers' liability for whopper claims.

There won't be any new small insurers, for the simple reason that the barriers to entry are too high now that an insurer must have a 70 per cent level of confidence that it can pay out on all claims, before it even begins. That will conspire to drive premiums higher until cash-rich financial services companies do the arithmetic and conclude that rising premiums may justify expansion into that area. That is how capitalism is supposed to work, although the vagaries of the global insurance market may well keep them scared away until the window of opportunity has passed.

Builders' warranty insurance remains a nightmare, as any builder will tell you. In New South Wales it used to be government run and worked well, but became one of the delinquent children of privatisation. HIH had total dominance of that market and its collapse left a huge number of builders uninsured, although broker Dexta (run incidentally by Ashraf Kamha, of FAI fame) filled some of the hole by offering cover that was reinsured by the Allianz group. Allianz, however, withdrew from that arrangement, and the issue remains one of the biggest single headaches for builders and renovators in Australia.

But the builders are not alone in having lost confidence. Private investors are seeing episodes like HIH as good reasons to stay away from the share market, having noticed that the company spent its latter years spinning a story that had less and less to do with reality, but without censure from anybody in authority who was meant to be watching.

HIH has been central to the whole corporate governance debate as a glaring example of what can go wrong when a company makes it look as though it has good governance, when in fact it has almost none.

There is also some risk of quality candidates being reluctant to take seats on corporate boards because of the twin worries of reduced fees and increased responsibilities, particularly since the HIH, Ansett and One.Tel collapses have seen directors pilloried in the press and in public as lazy, overpaid fat cats.

Perhaps there are flaws in the model which requires a majority of independent non-executive directors on a board which is also responsible for the overview of company's strategy. Corporate knowledge and independence are not easy to find in the same candidate for a directorship. One suggestion has been to 'professionalise' directors by paying them more and also asking them to spend more time at companies than the one day a month that custom says they do.

If the HIH collapse has caused directors to realise that they have a really important role to play by asking questions of management, then perhaps the whole disaster has not been completely in vain. As with political blunders and the aftermath of wars, there is a lot of smoke and dust still flying around. It will take a few years before the really valuable lessons start to sink in. Let's hope corporate memory lasts long enough thereafter for thinking managers and directors to start acting on them.

GLOSSARY

ALAC: Accountants' Liability Assurance Company

ALAS: American Legal Attorneys' Society; Attorneys' Liability Assurance Society

ALP: Australian Labor Party

AM: member of the Order of Australia

APRA: Australian Prudential Regulation Authority (formerly ISC)

arbitrage: buying and selling of assets to exploit discrepancies between markets to make riskless profit

ASA: Australian Shareholders' Association

ASC: Australian Securities Commission

ASIC: Australian Securities and Investments Commission

ASX: Australian Stock Exchange

bordereaux: detailed listings of risks insured, premiums and losses prepared by insurance brokers for submission to clients and insurers involved. In reinsurance, a schedule listing items reinsured

BZW Australia: broker owned by Barclays in London; became ABN Amro Australia in early 1998 when Barclays sold out.

CE Heath: original parent company of HIH, named after founder Cuthbert Eden Heath

CEO: chief executive officer

CIC Insurance: formed by the merger in the 1980s of the Co-Operative Insurance Company, Carlingford Australia Insurance, and the National Insurance Company of New Zealand

CLERP: Corporate Law Economic Reform Program

CPID: Commercial and Professional Indemnity Division
CSFB: Credit Suisse First Boston
CTP: compulsory third party
DID: Diversified Institutions Division
DPP: Director of Public Prosecutions
DTI: Department of Trade and Industry (UK)
E&Y: Ernst & Young
FAI: Fire and All Risks Insurance
FBI: Federal Bureau of Investigation
FEC: Far East Capital Ltd
FFC: FAI Finance Corp
FITB: future income tax benefits
FSA: Financial Services Authority (UK)
FSAC: Financial Sector Advisory Council
GCR: General Cologne Reinsurance
GCRA: General Cologne Reinsurance Australia
goodwill: the value of future benefits expressed to be derived from
    unidentifiable assets
greenmail: buying shares in companies that may be takeover targets and holding
    them until the purchaser gets the price wanted from the bidder
GSA: Goldman Sachs Australia
GST: goods and services tax
HIH: Heath International Holdings
HSI: Home Security International
ICA: Insurance Council of Australia
INBR: incurred but not reported, i.e. claims arising from accidents or occurrence
    which have taken place prior to the close of an accounting period and are
    expected to be reported in subsequent accounting periods
ISC: Insurance and Superannuation Commission (now APRA)
LMX spiral: London Market Excess spiral
LOC: Letter Of Credit, a document authorising the addressee to pay a specified
    sum to a party specified in the letter
long-tail: applies to insurance business where the financial outcome of some claims
    may be delayed or not known for more than twelve months
M&R: Milliman & Robertson (LA-based actuaries)
MIPI: Minet International Professional Indemnity (UK-based reinsurance broker)
Ness: New Electronic Security Systems
PBL: Publishing and Broadcasting Ltd
PEE: Pacific Eagle Equities

PI: Professional indemnity insurance, a policy providing indemnity to professionals against claims made against them resulting from legal liability to others for loss or damage arising out of professional negligence on the part of the professional

PIA: Principal Investment Arm

PL: public liability

PLA: Payne Liability Agencies

prudential margin: an additional provision above the actuary's estimate for the liability for outstanding claims, to increase the probability of the provision being adequate

PwC: PricewaterhouseCoopers

QBE: Queensland-based insurer

reinsurance: a process by which an insurer (the first party), in consideration of a premium, agrees to indemnify the reinsured (the second party) against a risk insured by the reinsured under a policy in favour of the insured (the third party)

reserves (or provisions): accounting expression for liability accounts established to provide for future outgoings

reserving: the process of calculating and setting up reserves

S&P: US ratings agency Standard & Poor

SEATS: Stock Exchange Automated Trading System, the computer trading system linking all Australia share traders

SEC: Securities and Exchange Commission

short-tail: insurance business where claims are typically settled within one year of the events giving rise to the claims, e.g. fire and comprehensive motor

side letter: used in the negotiating process between reinsurer and insurer to minimise the former's risk even further by promising not to make a claim

UAS: Underwriting and Agency Services

underwriter: person or institution that agrees to take up a proportion of the risk of something, in exchange for a commission

WGMI: World Marine & General Insurances Ltd

Winterthur: Swiss insurance group, shareholder in CE Heath 1995–98

CORPORATE CHART

The HIH group comprised over 250 companies at the time of liquidation. This chart shows the most significant companies in the group. (From Background Paper No.1, 'Introduction and Corporate Chart', prepared by officers of the HIH Royal Commission, November 2001.)

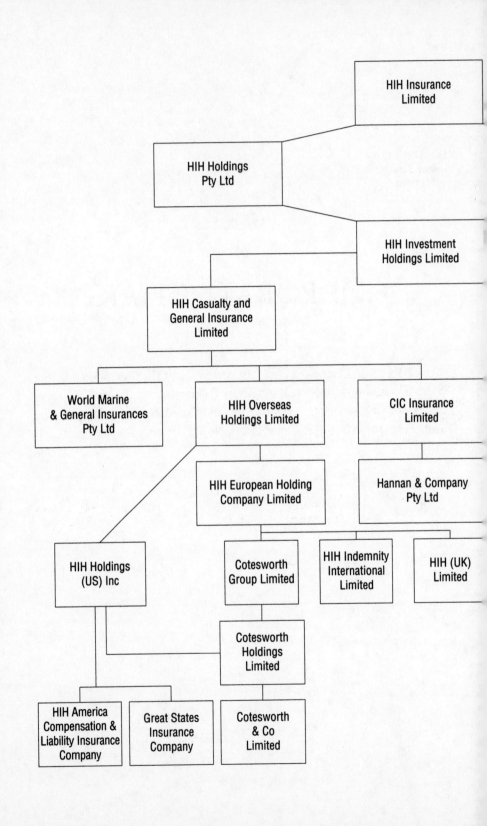

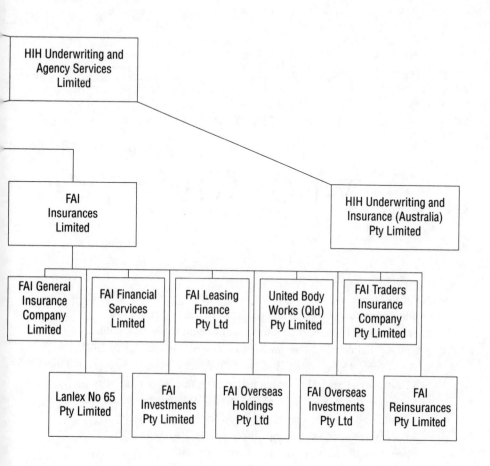

WHO'S WHO

ABBOTT, Charles — HIH: non-executive director from 30 August 1995; member Audit Committee 1999 to 2000; chairman of Steering and Board Committees in 1999. Former partner and current consultant to Blake Dawson Waldron. CIC: director from 15 August 1989 to 13 July 1995.

ADLER, Larry (died 13 December 1988) — FAI: director from 19 August 1968 to 13 December 1988; FAI General: director to 13 December 1988; FAI Traders: director to 13 December 1988; FAI Reinsurances: director 21 April 1958 to 13 December 1988; FAI Investments: director to 13 December 1988; FAI Leasing: director to 13 December 1988; United Body Works: director to 13 December 1988.

ADLER, Rodney — HIH: non-executive director from 16 April 1999 to 26 February 2001; FAI: director from 11 January 1988 to 8 December 2000, chief executive officer 1988 to 1999, member of Asset Allocation and Investment and Nomination Committees 1996 to 1998; FAI General: director from 1 February 1988 to 31 March 1999; FAI Traders: director from 1 February 1988 to 26 March 1999; FAI Reinsurances: director from 1 February 1988 to 26 March 1999; FAI Investments: director from 1 February 1988 to 16 July 1990; FAI Leasing: director from 1 February 1988 to 16 July 1990 and from 17 July 1995 to 26 March 1999; FAI Overseas: director from 14 September 1989 to 16 July 1990 and from 10 January 1997 to 26 March 1999.

ATANASKOVIC, John — Sydney corporate lawyer.

ATKINSON, Thomas Eric (Eric) — FAI: director from 10 February 1974 to
    30 November 1993; FAI General: director from 1 February 1974 to
    23 November 1993; FAI Traders: director from 29 June 1984
    to 23 November 1993; FAI Reinsurances: director from 13 April 1978 to
    23 November 1993; FAI Investments: director (dates unknown);
    FAI Leasing: director to 9 June 1989.

BALLHAUSEN, William John (John) — HIH: general manager (Investments)
    1995 to 2001; HIH Underwriting: secretary from 11 November 1986 to
    7 April 2000; HIH Casualty: secretary from 13 March 1989 to 7 April 2000.

BARNUM, Geoff — chief executive of General Cologne Reinsurance in Australia.

BONNAR, Mark — FAI International: underwriting manager in 1995, manager of
    London Representative Office in 1996.

BOULDEN, Tony — FAI: financial controller, Commercial and Professional
    Indemnity Division, made redundant in March 1999 after HIH took over FAI.

BROMLEY, Geoff — reinsurance broker, Carpenter Bowring, London.

BROWN, Leigh — Minter Ellison legal partner.

BROWN, Paul — attended Cranbrook school with Rodney Adler, investor in
    Ness, now lives in Monaco.

BURROUGHS, Stephen — FAI Group: reinsurance manager in 1998.

BUTTLE, John — Arthur Andersen: auditor of HIH and FAI General for the year
    ended 30 June 2000.

CASSIDY, Terry — HIH: executive director from 2 December 1988 to 12 October
    2000, managing director, Australia 1995 to 2001, member Investment and
    Reinsurance Committees 1996 to 1999. HIH Underwriting: director from
    1 January 1997; HIH Casualty: director from 21 October 1977; HIH U&A:
    director from 1 January 1977; CIC: director from 13 July 1995; WMGI:
    director from 17 December 1999 to 15 March 2001; FAI: director from
    25 February 1999; FAI Finance: director from 31 March 1999 to 12 January
    2000 and from 10 May 2000 to 15 March 2001; FAI General, FAI Traders,
    FAI Reinsurances, FAI Investments, FAI Leasing, FAI Overseas: director
    from March 1999. Professional accountant prior to joining HIH in 1972.

COHEN, Geoff — HIH: non-executive director and chairman from 20 January
    1992, chairman of Human Resources and Investment Committees 1995 to
    2000, member of Audit Committee 1995 to 1997 and chairman 1999 to
    2000, chairman of Due Diligence Committee 1996 to 1999, member Steering
    and Board Committee in 1999. Former senior partner of Arthur Andersen.

COOPER, Brad — director, Collingwood Football Club 1998 to 2002, FAI
    Finance Corporation 1991 to 2000, FAI Home Security Holdings 1989 to
    1997, National Kindness Day 2001 onwards, Ness Security Products August
    1995 to September 1995, Speak Easy 1994 onwards, The Goodwill Group
    1992 onwards, and Vision Publishing 1996 to 1999.

CROWLEY, Michael — stockbroker, ABN Amro.

CUBBIN, Doug — HIH: group management accountant in 1999, financial controller Accounting Operations in 2000.

DAVIES, Alan — Arthur Andersen: auditor of HIH and FAI to 30 June 1999.

DIMOS, Effy — HIH: senior manager, Reinsurance in 2000.

FODERA, Dominic — HIH: executive director from 9 May 1997 to 12 October 2000, finance director/chief financial officer 1995 to 2001, chief operating officer in 2001, member Investment and Reinsurances Committees, 1997 to 1999, member Due Diligence Committee in 1999. Former partner of Arthur Andersen. HIH Underwriting: director from 7 April 1997; HIH Casualty: director from 31 January 1996; HIH U&A: director from 31 January 1996; CIC: director from 27 May 1996; WMGI: director from 17 December 1999 to 15 March 2001; FAI: director from 25 February 1999; FAI Finance: director from 31 March 1999 to 15 March 2001; FAI General, FAI Traders, FAI Reinsurances, FAI Investments, FAI Leasing, FAI Overseas, Lanlex: director from March 1999; United Body Works: director from 26 March 1999 to 15 March 2001 and from 27 March 2001.

GARDENER, Justin — HIH: non-executive director from 2 December 1998, member Audit and Human Resource Committees 1999 to 2000. Former partner of Arthur Andersen from April 1972 to June 1998.

GORRIE, Alex — HIH: non-executive director from 30 August 1995 to November 1999, member Human Resources Committee 1997 to 1999; CIC: director from 16 June 1988 to 13 July 1995.

GOSLING, Ray — HIH: group reinsurance manager 1999 to 2001.

HAMMERSCHLAG, David, SC — Adler's counsel for the PEE Trust affair.

HARRIS, Ted — FAI: director from 20 February 1990 to 22 February 1999, member of Audit, Remuneration, Asset Allocation and Investment and Nomination Committees 1996 to 1998.

HEAD, Neville — HIH: non-executive director from 20 January 1992 to 5 August 1999, chairman of Audit Committee and member of Human Resources Committee in 1996, 1997. Solicitor and former partner of Clayton Utz.

HEPPELL, Ian — FAI: insurance research manager in 1998.

HERI, Irwin Werner (Werner) — HIH: non-executive director from 13 July 1995 to 15 October 1998.

HILL, Geoff — FAI: director from 20 September 1996 to 22 February 1999, chairman of Audit Committee 1996 to 1998.

HOLLAND, Fred — former chairman CE Heath UK.

HOSKINSON, Rodney — FAI: actuary in research department.

HOWARD, Bill — HIH general manager Financial Services 1999 to 2001; added title of general manager Investments January 2001. FAI Finance: director from 31 January 2001.

KAMHA, Ashraf — FAI: general manager, Corporate & Professional Insurance 1995 to 1997; FAI General: director from 21 February 1997 to 4 September 1998.

KEYS, Sir William (died May 2000) — FAI: director from 11 September 1984 to 18 November 1998, member of Audit Committee 1996 to 1998, FAI General: director from 11 September 1984 to 18 November 1988; FAI Traders: director from 11 September 1984 to 22 July 1997; FAI Finance: director from 15 October 1991 to 19 January 1998. Former RSL Federal President.

KING, Graeme — FAI: managing director (Hong Kong) in 1995, operations underwriting manager, Asia, in 1996, managing director, Asian operations in 1997, 1998; FAI General: director from 21 February 1997 to 31 March 1999.

KORCHINSKI, Stuart — HIH: general manager (Technical Operations) in 1995, 1996, managing director (Financial Institutions and FAI Direct) in 1997 to 2001, managing director (FAI Direct) 1999 to 2001; Hannan: director from 29 June 2000 to 8 February 2001.

LANDERER, John — FAI: director from 15 December 1988 to 25 February 1999, chairman of Remuneration, Asset Allocation and Investment and Nomination Committees 1996 to 1998; FAI General: director from 15 December 1988 to 18 April 1991; FAI Traders: director from 15 December 1988 to 18 April 1991; FAI Reinsurances: director from 15 December 1988 to 5 April 1991; FAI Investments: director from 9 June 1989 to 5 April 1991; FAI Leasing: director from 17 May 1989 to 5 April 1991; FAI Overseas: director from 14 September 1989 to 5 April 1991.

LATHAM, Chris — PricewaterhouseCooper actuary.

LEE, Anita — Arthur Andersen: member of audit group.

LO, Fred — HIH: secretary from 4 November 1991; HIH Underwriting: secretary from 2 December 1991; HIH Casualty: secretary from 9 December 1988; HIH U&A: secretary from 9 November 1988; CIC: secretary from 13 July 1995 to 15 March 2001; WMGI: secretary from 17 December 1999; FAI: secretary from 30 April 1999; FAI General: secretary from 30 April 1999 to 15 March 2001; FAI Traders: secretary from 30 April 1999 to 15 March 2001; FAI Reinsurances: secretary from 30 April 1999 to 15 March 2001; FAI Finance: secretary from 30 April 1999; FAI Investments: secretary from 30 April 1999 to 15 March 2001; FAI Leasing: secretary from 30 April 1999 to 15 March 2001; FAI Overseas: secretary from 30 April 1999 to 15 March 2001; Hannan: director from 29 June 2000 to 11 July 2000, secretary from 29 June 2000; Lanlex: secretary from 30 April 1999 to 15 March 2001; United Body Works: secretary from 30 April 1999 to 15 March 2001 and from 27 March 2001.

MACADIE, Jock — HIH: head of Financial Control & Strategy in 2001.
MACIVER, Angus — FAI: director from 5 April 1991 to 10 January 1997,
    executive director, Corporate and Professional Insurance in 1995, 1996;
    FAI General: director from 5 April 1991 to 10 January 1997; FAI Traders:
    director from 5 April 1991 to 10 January 1997; FAI Reinsurances:
    director from 5 April 1991 to 10 January 1997; FAI Finance: director
    from 22 October 1993 to 29 March 1995; FAI Overseas: director from
    22 September 1993 to 10 January 1997.
MAINPRIZE, Tim — FAI: director from 9 February 1993 to 30 November 1993
    and from 17 December 1993 to 14 January 1999, finance director 1995 to
    1998, member of Asset Allocation & Investment Committee 1996 to 1998;
    FAI General: director from 16 July 1990 to 14 January 1999; FAI Traders:
    director from 16 July 1990 to 14 January 1999; FAI Reinsurances: director
    from 16 July 1990 to 14 January 1999; FAI Finance: director from
    29 March 1995 to 31 March 1999; FAI Investments: director from 16 July
    1990 to 14 January 1999; FAI Leasing: director from 16 July 1990 to
    14 January 1999; FAI Overseas: director from 16 July 1990 to 14 January
    1999; Lanlex: director from 16 July 1990 to 14 January 1999; United Body
    Works: director from 16 July 1990 to 14 January 1999.
MCCARTHY, Peter — FAI: CTP manager in 1995, 1996, general manager,
    General Insurance Underwriting/Personal Lines Underwriting in
    1997,1998, research manager 1995 to 1997; HIH: managing director
    Statutory Classes Underwriting in 1999.
MCCARTHY, Peter V — HIH America: president.
MCGRATH, Tony — KPMG: provisional liquidator / liquidator of 19 HIH
    companies.
MCGUIRE, Eddie — Collingwood Football Club president, media personality.
MCINTOSH, Alex — KPMG: joint liquidator.
MARTIN, Wayne, QC — counsel assisting the HIH Royal Commission.
MORAN, Peter — FAI: actuary from mid-1996.
O'BRYAN, Norman, SC — counsel assisting the HIH Royal Commission.
O'CONNELL, Peter — FAI: director from 20 September 1996 to 22 February
    1999.
OWEN, Justice Neville — HIH Royal Commissioner.
PALMER, John — former head of the Canadian prudential regulation authority,
    hired in late 2001 by APRA to review APRA's role in the HIH collapse.
PAYNE, Michael — HIH: executive director from 3 September 1992 to 30 June
    1998 and non-executive director from 9 July 1998 to 12 September 2000,
    managing director, UK, 1995 to 1998, chairman Reinsurance Committee
    1995 to 1999. HIH Casualty: director from 10 July 1993 to 16 July 1999.
    Co-founder of HIH with Ray Williams.

PEIRIS, Niranjan (Niran) — FAI: group financial controller 1995 to 1998; FAI Finance: director from 19 January 1998 to 31 March 1999; FAI Investments: director from 14 January to 2 March 1999; Lanlex: director from 14 January to 26 March 1999.

PILLEMER, Russel — junior executive at Goldman Sachs Australia.

POKROSS, Jeffrey — New York based mafia informant and investment banker.

PYE, Jonathan — Arthur Andersen auditor.

RICHARDSON, Colin — HIH's corporate adviser. Worked at SG Hambros until 2000, then Deutsche Bank.

RIVKIN, Rene — stockbroker, investor and tipsheet publisher.

SCHÜRPF, Willi — HIH: non-executive director from 13 July 1995 to 15 April 1998; CIC: director from 20 November 1991 to 15 April 1998.

SCRIVENS, Martyn — Arthur Anderson auditor.

SELVARATNAM, Nick — BZW Australia: insurance analyst. Later moved to CSFB.

SIMPSON, Jeff — former HIH deputy general manager finance, resigned in 1999.

SLEE, David — HIH U&A: previous director (dates unknown). David Slee Consulting Pty Ltd: provider of actuarial services to the HIH Group 1995 to 2001.

SMALL, Ian — HIH: managing director (Contingency Risks) 1995 to 1997.

SPRATT, Robert — FAI: claims manager 1995 to 1997, group liability claims manager in 1998.

STITT QC, Robert — HIH: director from 20 January 1992 to 15 March 2001, member Audit and Human Resources Committee 1995 to 2000, member Due Diligence Committee 1997 to 1999. Barrister since 1968 and Queen's Counsel since 1983. HIH legal adviser since the company started in Australia.

STURESTEPS, George — HIH: executive director from 2 December 1988 to 12 September 2000, deputy chief executive and managing director, International 1995 to 2001, member Reinsurance Committee 1995 to 1999; HIH Underwriting: director from 24 September 1971 to 12 September 2000; HIH Casualty: director from 24 April 1989 to 12 September 2000; HIH U&A: director from 13 December 1988 to 12 September 2000; CIC: director from 13 July 1995 to 12 September 2000; WMGI: director from 21 January 2000 to 27 February 2001.

THOMPSON, Peter — HIH: general manager (International Operations) in 1995, general manager (Special Projects) in 1996, 1997, deputy managing director, UK, in 1997, 1998, managing director (Risk Management /Reinsurance) 1999 to 2001.

TILLEY, Ben — Cranbrook schoolmate of James Packer, regular card and golf partner of James' father, Kerry, and business partner of Brad Cooper.

TRAHAIR, Geoff — HIH: managing director (Research) in 1999, 2000.

TRUDE, David — CSFB: chief executive.

TUCKFIELD, John — reinsurance broker, Carpenter Bowring.

TURNBULL, Malcolm — chairman, Goldman Sachs Australia.

VANDERKEMP, Daniel — junior auditor with Arthur Andersen.

WATERS, Greg — HIH: general manager (Internal Audit) 1995 to 2001.

WEIN, Hermann Franz Randolph (Randolph) — HIH: executive director from 13 July 1995, chief executive (Asia) in 1999, chief executive in 2001, member Audit and Human Resources Committee 1995 to 1997, member Reinsurance Committee 1995 to 2000. HIH Casualty: director from 15 March 2001; HIH U&A: director from 15 March 2001; CIC: director from 21 February 1995 to 30 May 2000 and from 15 March 2001; FAI: director from 15 March 2001; FAI General: director from 15 March 2001; FAI Traders: director from 15 March 2001; FAI Finance: director from 13 July 2001. Attorney-at-law.

WESTFIELD, Mark — journalist with *The Australian* newspaper.

WHITE, Richard, SC — counsel assisting the HIH Royal Commission.

WHITE, Simon — counsel assisting the HIH Royal Commission.

WILKIE, Daniel — FAI: managing director, General Insurance 1995 to 1997, chief operating officer, Insurance in 1998; FAI General: director from 21 February 1997 to 31 March 1999.

WILLIAMS, Ray, AM — HIH: director from 2 December 1988 to 15 December 2000, chief executive from 1988 to 2000, member Steering and Board Committees 1999; HIH Underwriting: director from 24 September 1971; HIH Casualty: director from 21 October 1977 to 15 March 2001; HIH U&A: director from 10 April 1970 to 15 March 2001, principal executive officer from 10 April 1970 to 8 December 1995; CIC: director from 13 July 1995 to 15 March 2001; WMGI: director from 17 December 1999 to 15 March 2001; FAI: director from 25 February 1999 to 15 March 2001; FAI General: director from 31 March 1999 to 15 March 2001; FAI Traders: director from 26 March 1999 to 15 March 2001; FAI Reinsurances: director from 26 March 1999; FAI Finance: director from 11 January 2000 to 27 February 2001; FAI Investments: director from 26 March 1999; FAI Leasing: director from 26 March 1999; FAI Overseas: director from 26 March 1999; Lanlex: director from 26 March 1999; United Body Works: director from 26 March 1999 to 27 February 2001.

WILSON, Kent — CSFB: head of research.

WOLF, Frank — FAI: general manager, Strategic Planning 1995 to 1998.

ACKNOWLEDGMENTS

This book would not have been possible without help from the legion of experts, many of them former senior employees of FAI and HIH, who provided me with a great deal of background and inside information.

Contrary to the public view which has tarred everyone who is ex-FAI and ex-HIH with the same brush, most were diligent and ethical. They were either left out of the loop or were prevented by direct orders and counterproductive rules from taking matters further. Many gave helpful evidence to the Royal Commission but have asked to remain anonymous. Their contribution to the cause of truth and transparency has been invaluable.

Thanks to Shona Martyn of HarperCollins, who took a chance by saying yes in July 2002 to my proposal for a book, and to Sally Collings, Helen Littleton, Belinda Yuille and Helen Johnson; and to editor Neil Thomas, who helped turn it into one. Also my agent, Lyn Tranter, who has been a major positive factor in the process. Thanks also to Fairfax colleagues Trevor Sykes, Colleen Ryan and Liz Sexton for sharing some of their diligent research into some of the *arcana* of accounting and reinsurance, and for making it comprehensible. Thanks also to fellow reporters Belinda Tasker, Kylie Walker, Margot Saville, Jayne-Maree Sedgman, Andrew White, David Brearley and the late Brian 'Once Were Waratahs' Woodley for lightening some of the long days of detailed evidence.

Thanks of course to the staff of the HIH Royal Commission, who were not remotely the witch-hunting zealots they were sometimes made out to be. Press officer John Dickie and his legal team did much to explain the facts of the Commission, but they took care not to exceed their remit in any help they provided to me over this book. It is mine, not theirs, which is how it should be.

Thanks lastly to my wife, Anna, who made my book proposal look so good that Shona Martyn rang to utter the immortal phrase 'don't talk to anyone else'. Since then Anna has been a constructive critic of immense value quite apart from, with our daughters, Iona and Laura, keeping family life going through all the ups and downs. Thanks to all of them.

Andrew Main
Sydney, June 2003

INDEX